The
Language
of
Judges

Language and Legal Discourse
A series edited by
William M. O'Barr and John M. Conley

The Bilingual Courtroom:
Court Interpreters in the Judicial Process
Susan Berk-Seligson

Rules versus Relationships:
The Ethnography of Legal Discourse
John M. Conley and William M. O'Barr

Getting Justice and Getting Even:
Legal Consciousness among Working-Class Americans
Sally Engle Merry

The Language of Judges
Lawrence M. Solan

The
Language
of
Judges

Lawrence M. Solan

The University
of Chicago Press
Chicago and London

Lawrence Solan is a partner in the law firm of Orans, Elsen, and Lupert. He received his Ph.D. in linguistics from the University of Massachusetts, Amherst, and has written extensively on linguistics and the psychology of language.

THE UNIVERSITY OF CHICAGO PRESS, CHICAGO 60637
THE UNIVERSITY OF CHICAGO PRESS, LTD., LONDON
© 1993 by The University of Chicago
All rights reserved. Published 1993
Printed in the United States of America
02 01 00 99 98 97 96 95 94 93   1 2 3 4 5

ISBN: 0-226-76790-6 (cloth)
       0-226-76791-4 (paper)

Library of Congress Cataloging-in-Publication Data

Solan, Lawrence, 1952–
    The language of judges / Lawrence M. Solan.
       p.   cm. — (Language and legal discourse)
    Includes bibliographical references and index.
    1. Judicial opinions—United States—Language.   2. Judges—United
States—Language.   3. Law—United States—Language.   4. Judicial
process—United States.   5. Semantics (Law).   6. Analysis
(Philosophy).   I. Title.   II. Series.
    KF8775.S65   1993
    349.73′014—dc20
    [347.30014]   92-28628
                                                               CIP

Some of the material in chapter 2, "The Judge as Linguist," is incorporated from the *Proceedings of the Third Eastern States Conference on Linguistics.* © 1987 by Ohio State University.

For Renata and David

Contents

Preface   xi
Introduction: Judging Language   1

1   Chomsky and Cardozo: Linguistics and
the Law   10
    Cardozo's Hope: Keeping the Law Flexible   12
    Chomsky and the Nature of Linguistic Knowledge   15
    Chomsky, Cardozo, and Mrs. Palsgraf   22

2   The Judge as Linguist   28
    The Last Antecedent Rule   29
        Mrs. Anderson's Case   29
        Processing Strategies and the Last
        Antecedent Rule   31
        The Across the Board Rule: Mr. Judge   34
        Drugs and the Last Antecedent Rule   36
        Last Antecedents and Legal Canons   37
    Empty Words: The Interpretation of Pronouns   38
        Mr. Bass   40
        Pronouns and Taxation   41
    The *And/Or* Rule   45
        Problems of Scope—*And* Means *Or*   46
        Support of Delinquent Children—The Problem
        with *And/Or*   53
        Mr. Caine—*Or* Means *And*   54
    Adjectives and the Linguistics of
    Capital Punishment   55
    Why Judges Do Not Make Good Linguists   59

3   Stacking the Deck   64
        The Rule of Lenity   66
            Yermian: Lenity and the Scope of Adverbs   67
            What about *Brown*?   75
            RICO—Lenity and the Meaning of Words   77
        The Linguistics of Insurance Policies   81
            The Jacober Accident   81
            Ignoring Language—*Partridge*   85
        Understanding Ambiguous Contracts   87

4   When the Language Is Clear   93
        How Plain Can Language Be?   94
        The "Plain Language" of RICO   99
            When the Language and Its Opposite
            Are Both Plain   99
            Understanding Patterns: RICO as an
            Unclear Statute   104
            Turkette and *Russello* Revisited: Some More
            Fuzzy Concepts   106
        When Is Plain Language Enough?   108

5   Too Much Precision   118
        The Quest for Precision   119
            Pronouns, Precision, and the Law   121
                Pronouns and the Fifth Amendment   122
                Devices to Limit Ambiguity of Reference
                in Legal Language   125
                    Party of the First Part   125
                    Replacing Pronouns with Names   127
                    Said and Same   128
                Using Special Words   130
            The War against Legal Language   133
            How Much Better Can We Do?   137

6   Some Problems with Words: Trying to Understand
    the Constitution   139
        People, Corporations, and Other Creatures   140
            What Is a Corporation   140
            Corporations, the Lexicon, and the
            Fifth Amendment   143

Testimony and the Act of Speech   148
The Current State of the Fifth Amendment   149
Speech Acts: Linguistics and the
Fifth Amendment   154
Admissions   155
Admitting by Bleeding   157
What Is a Search   163
The Word "Search"   164
The Fourth Amendment and the Lexicon   166
Some Easy Cases and Some Hard Ones   170

7   Why It Hasn't Gotten Any Better   172
Anderson and the Status Quo   173
Expanding Legal Doctrine   178
Getting Tough   182
The Language of Judges   185

Notes   189
Table of Cases   211
Index   215

Preface

I FIRST NOTICED some time ago that judges periodically present in their opinions a linguistic analysis of the legal documents that they have been asked to interpret. I had earlier been trained in linguistics, and found this phenomenon both surprising and interesting. It quickly became clear to me that judges were not at all consistent in their application of linguistic analysis to the documents on which they were ruling. Over time, I realized that this happens on more than an occasional basis, and that we can learn something about the judicial system by studying instances in which judges act as linguists. I have attempted to do so, and this book is the result of my investigation.

The book has taken a long time to write. During its preparation, I have discussed it with many people, some of whom have been good enough to read portions of the manuscript and to comment on it. I wish to thank all of these people here. If I leave anyone out, it is inadvertent.

First, I would like to thank colleagues at my law firm, Orans, Elsen and Lupert. There is an unpleasant rumor that intellectually exciting work ends when a legal career begins. I have not had that experience. To the contrary, my firm has always been very supportive of my pursuing this work, with people pointing out to me important examples and discussing the issues with me. Of course, the arguments presented in this book, shortcomings and all, are my responsibility.

As always, I have had many discussions with friends and colleagues in the academic community. I am especially grateful to Mark Baltin, Bob Freidin, and Helen Goodluck for their valuable discussions and opinions over the years. Sally Thomason and Barbara Partee were very helpful to me, especially early in this project. I appreciate both their input and their support. I wish also to mention the late Warren Lehman, whose recent death continues to sadden me, and Ron Butters, Mack O'Barr, and John Conley, who also read various drafts of the manuscript.

A number of other people have looked at portions of the manuscript and have commented on them. Among them are Noam Chomsky, Gil Harman, Donna Jo Napoli, Barry Furrow, Lisa Feiner, and Gordon Hutner. My thanks to Gary Sunshine and Elizabeth Rader for their helpful editorial suggestions and discussion.

Justice Stewart Pollock not only discussed some important issues with me, but gave me a great deal of encouragement during this entire project. My gratitude to him for this and for his overall support cannot be measured.

I was very fortunate to have had Judge Richard Posner and Professor Jack Chambers review an earlier draft of the manuscript for the University of Chicago Press. Their comments were extremely helpful, and have been incorporated into the book. They also have my thanks. In addition, Geoffrey Huck, from the very beginning, has shown himself to be an exceptionally good editor, providing me with excellent advice mixed always with good humor.

Finally, my wife, Anita Solan, a fine editor in her own right, has helped me not only by her review of portions of the manuscript, but, more important, by her support and her shared enthusiasm as I completed this project. In light of her already enormous obligations in her own career and as a mother, her help and support are all that more special to me. Our children, Renata and David, to whom this book is dedicated, have been growing up assuming that my working on this book is just a normal part of family life. They do not know how much they deserve my thanks.

Introduction:
Judging Language

As FAR AS I can tell, judges usually care deeply about making the best decision they can, and about conveying their decision in a manner that makes the decision appear as fair as possible to the parties, and often to the public. If I were a judge, I would certainly care about these things, as would just about anyone with even a minimal sense of responsibility to others. My first job after law school was as law clerk to an extraordinarily talented judge, Stewart G. Pollock, an associate justice of the Supreme Court of New Jersey. No doubt the sympathy that I have with a judge's burden has grown out of that very special experience. But the point is more general and very basic: Any judge who takes himself and his position seriously struggles with these dual tasks—decision making and presentation.

This book is about how and why judges write about the structure and meaning of language to justify their decisions. Judges are frequently called upon to interpret statutes and other legal documents. Often the parties disagree about what the document says they are obliged to do or to refrain from doing. When that happens, and one party sues, or the government prosecutes, a judge must decide what the document means. To do this, judges frequently present a sort of linguistic analysis of the document in dispute. As we will see throughout this book, their use of linguistic argument as justification is by no means consistent, and is frequently incoherent and idiosyncratic. We will explore and speculate about why this is so, and try to learn something about the legal system in the process.

The decisions that judges make have enormous consequences in people's lives. Most often, there are two sides to the conflict that the judge has to resolve, with legitimate reasons for either side to win, both as a matter of law, and as a matter of the judge's personal system of values. (I do not mean to imply that these two systems are always distinct.) All practicing lawyers have seen judges struggle with cases that are difficult to decide. But when

1

the end comes, in most instances one side must win and the other lose. By the time a judge has to rule, either at a trial or in deciding an appeal, the time for compromise has generally expired.

In the abstract, one might expect that the presentation of a decision should be no more difficult than the decision making itself, since the judge need only say what led him to decide as he did. That is, it is natural to assume that presentation merely records the decision-making process and mirrors it.

At times, this hypothesis indeed seems to reflect reality, especially in easy cases. If a statute of limitations prevents a patient from suing a doctor more than three years after the alleged malpractice was committed, then a judge dismissing a case based on the statute of limitations has only to say what he is doing. Or if someone is given a traffic ticket for driving without a valid driver's license, having forgotten to renew his license when the notice came in the mail, a judge finding him guilty and fining him should not have much difficulty saying why. A huge body of cases falls into this realm, in which there is little interesting to say about the problem of presentation apart from the decision-making process itself, except for commentary on the quality and clarity of each judge's prose.

What about more difficult decisions? Here, problems arise. First, because judges wield such enormous power, there is pressure on them to speak decisively. It would be very difficult for an appellate judge to say, "I hereby affirm your death sentence, although this was a very close question, and I understand that I could just as easily have interpreted the law as requiring me to reverse your death sentence and save your life," even if such a statement is an entirely accurate reflection of what is on the judge's mind, and even if the judge has lost many nights of sleep anguishing over the awesome decision that his job requires him to make. Instead, the appellate judge is likely to focus his opinion on the reasons for affirming the death sentence, and brush aside the arguments to the contrary. Any lawyer who has been on the losing side of a close question will recall the shock of reading how easily the judge rejects the losing arguments out of hand, as if they could not have been made by a thinking person.[1] The pressure to speak with a definitive voice works as a wedge, driving apart decision making on the one hand and presentation on the other. Rarely do judges, in their written opinions, discuss the degree of difficulty of the decision.

A second force separating decision making and presentation is the requirement that judges rely upon a received corpus of law and neutral principles to decide cases.[2] Judicial opinions regularly refer to earlier decisions of courts, and to statutes, regulations, and the like. Opinions do not as often rely on statements like "I think that those sentenced to death get too many appeals, so I routinely vote to affirm death sentences in order to increase the number of executions per year." Any judge who is an adamant supporter of the death penalty may feel this way, and these feelings may be a driving force behind his decisions, but he will almost never say this in an opinion. Similarly, a judge who has hostility toward insurance companies, and who routinely does what he can to help individuals collect from insurers regardless of the merits of the claim, will rarely say so in an opinion, relying instead on cases, statutes, and various statements about the law.

These two considerations—power and neutrality—inevitably exert a force on judges that increases the temptation to report the reasons behind their decisions less than fully and openly. Moreover, these factors, coercion and legitimate process, are core concepts that define the law, a conclusion reached by legal writers with otherwise diverse views.[3] In fact, judicial decisions invariably involve the exercise of state power, which includes not only the incarceration and sometimes the killing of those convicted of having committed crimes, but also the compulsion to pay money to a plaintiff or the directive that a plaintiff cannot collect from a defendant and must himself absorb whatever loss or harm he has suffered.

These pressures do not operate consistently or uniformly. An opinion by Justice Morris Pashman, a former justice on the Supreme Court of New Jersey, serves to illustrate. In *Mahoney v. Mahoney*,[4] a 1982 case, a man who had just earned his M.B.A. degree sought a divorce. While the husband was in school, his wife had supported both of them. Because the wife was working and making a good living, she did not qualify to receive alimony, which is based on need. To explain why the Court required the husband to reimburse the wife for her expenditures for his education, Justice Pashman had this to say:

> One spouse ought not to receive a divorce complaint when the other receives a diploma. Those spouses supported through professional school should recognize that they may be called upon to reimburse the supporting spouses for the financial contributions they received in pursuit of their professional training *And they cannot deny the basic fairness of this result*.[5] (Emphasis added)

Pashman here states only that he is doing what he believes is the decent thing to do, and that it is so decent that even Mr. Mahoney should recognize its fairness, and pay with a smile. The passage has the flavor of an old gangster movie, in which the criminal gladly goes off to prison, knowing that he must pay his debt to society before returning to the glamorous, but lawful existence that will be waiting for him (or her, in the case of *The Maltese Falcon*). That the justices on the Supreme Court of New Jersey voted seven to zero in favor of this decision bolsters the opinion as one absorbing popular morality into the law. We will see much more of this philosophy when we look in chapter 1 at some of the writings of Benjamin Cardozo.

Not all judicial opinions, however, openly express such pleasure at the use of state power to achieve a particular distribution of responsibility. Linguistics enters the scene as one of a number of crutches on which judges can rely to help make their decisions appear both definitive and neutral when candor is more difficult or risky.[6] To see how, let us first look at a second case decided by the Supreme Court of New Jersey, this one both older and far less direct than Justice Pashman's opinion in the *Mahoney* case.

In *State v. Cohen,*[7] Corey Cohen had been arrested for possession of marijuana while driving his van across the George Washington Bridge from New York to New Jersey. The van was impounded, and brought to a garage in Fort Lee, New Jersey. A few months later, Cohen wanted to pick up his van, and called the garage to make arrangements. The garage owner promptly called the arresting police officer, who was a member of the Port Authority Police, a special police force that patrols the George Washington Bridge and other facilities run by the Port Authority of New York and New Jersey.[8]

The officer mistakenly thought that there was an existing warrant for Cohen's arrest for his failure to appear in court, so the officer went to the garage to arrest Cohen once again, which he did. Cohen had arrived with two friends in a van driven by one of the friends. The judge hearing the defendants' application to dismiss the case found that the following then occurred:

> [W]hen Cohen entered the office, he was placed under arrest and when one of the officers walked over to the van, a door was open; marijuana was smelled and a quantity of marijuana was found concealed in the van. The officer testified that upon smelling the marijuana he placed the other two defendants under arrest and made a search incident to such arrest.[9]

The judge held that the arrest and the search of the friend's van were illegal, since the Port Authority Police did not have jurisdiction to conduct their police work in New Jersey communities ordinarily serviced by their own police forces. The judge therefore ruled that the seized drugs could not be used at trial. When the decision was upheld on appeal, the prosecutor appealed once again, this time to the Supreme Court of New Jersey.

The Supreme Court held that the Port Authority Police did have jurisdiction to make the arrests. However, the Court affirmed the dismissal of the prosecutions, ruling on a combination of linguistic and constitutional grounds.

Since the search of the van occurred without a warrant, it is permissible under the Fourth and Fourteenth Amendments to the Constitution only under exceptional circumstances, for instance, if the door to the van were already open and the police could smell the marijuana without intruding into the private space of the automobile. With this in mind, the Court ruled:

> The motion judge, in considering the whole factual context of the search, stated in his opinion . . . that "when one of the officers walked over to the van, the door was *open;* marijuana was smelled" and the search ensued (emphasis added). If this was meant to imply that the vehicle door was casually or coincidentally "open," so that the perception or smell of the odor of marijuana might justify the search, we believe an error in dictation or transcription must have occurred making necessary a correction of the record. Our careful examination of the motion testimony discloses that all witnesses agreed that the door was affirmatively "opened" rather than casually "open." . . .
>
> It is apparent that we should amend the motion judge's opinion to concord with the undisputed proofs before him. We therefore conclude that the door was "opened" either by the police or by [the garage owner] at their command. The legal result is the same.[10]

Thus, the Court relied on the difference in meaning between *open,* an adjective, and *opened,* a participle, to decide the case. The former describes only the position of the door, the latter the action of rendering it open. (In fact, *opened* is ambiguous in that it can mean "had been opened," which would not help Mr. Cohen and his friends at all.) The decision of the motion judge, who seemed to object to the Port Authority Police's treatment of these three young men, was upheld by the Supreme Court's correction of a hypothesized "error in dictation or transcription."

This result is very unusual. Ordinarily, when an appellate court has any doubts about the factual findings of a trial court (or motion court in this case), the appellate court will send the case back to the lower court for new proceedings to clarify the findings. We can only guess why the Supreme

Court of New Jersey went so far as to "correct" the record, but the most likely answer is that both the Supreme Court and the trial court understood that additional proceedings would show that there was no error in dictation or transcription. After all, if the motion judge had real reason to believe that the police had opened the door to the car, he would certainly have accepted that as an additional reason for dismissing the case. As the case now stands, the Port Authority Police maintain their jurisdiction, but their heavy-handedness in Cohen's case went unrewarded.

A disturbing question now comes to mind. What if another case with similar facts concerning the conduct of a search makes its way to court? The rationale behind the decision in *State v. Cohen* has become a precedent, available as subsequent justification of other judicial decisions. Is it now the law in New Jersey that the word "open" can be changed to "opened" whenever a court decides that an error in dictation or transcription could be of some help? This has not happened. For the most part, "open" still means "open" in New Jersey. But this kind of phenomenon—the rigidification of linguistic argument into actual principles of law—does indeed occur throughout the judicial system, and is the subject of much of this book.

When linguistic analysis becomes the rule of law, problems immediately ensue.[11] At the root of the difficulty is the fact that there is no real relationship between these linguistic principles, on the one hand, and notions of justice, on the other. After all, how can we tell in advance just when our sense of fairness will urge us to say again that "open" really should be "opened"? Maybe in the next case, we will want to say that "opened" really should have been "open." When a court relies on a linguistic argument to justify a decision in case one, application of that same linguistic argument may lead to an unfair result in case two, which in turn leads the judge in the second case either to avoid the linguistic argument entirely or to find a linguistic argument that yields the desired result. Thus, frequently we find linguistic principles of law existing side by side with their related counter-principles, with no theory telling us when to apply the original principle or when to get the opposite result by applying the counterprinciple.[12]

This sequence of events leaves legal doctrine in a fragile state. The linguistic principles whose use was questionable in the first place have now generated their opposites. And judges, under pressure to write decisively and within the range of acceptable argumentation, frequently succumb to the temptation of using some of these linguistic principles to justify their decisions, without any explanation of why one principle was chosen instead of another, creating the appearance that it could never have been otherwise.

Moreover, this state of affairs has grown not from a pervasive infection of corruption, or from the habitual appointment of untalented judges to high positions in the courts, but rather from the well-intended efforts of judges to do a good job. And many of these judges are as good at their jobs as anyone could be expected to be.

As we shall see, judges regularly find themselves in a double or triple bind. Assume for the sake of argument that the Supreme Court of New Jersey in *State v. Cohen,* had as its goal allowing Cohen and his friends to go free because of the excessively aggressive (albeit legal) behavior of the Port Authority Police, without doing serious damage to the ability of the police to function generally. To do this, the Court had two options. First, it could have simply announced what it was trying to do. But this would have necessarily compromised the notion that a rule of law controls the decision-making process. For if a court can decide that legal arrests are sometimes better disallowed, then the distinction between what is legal and what is illegal disappears. Thus, by being entirely forthright about the reasons for its decision, the court risks robbing from the legal system some of its legitimacy.[13]

But the second option, the one that the Supreme Court of New Jersey chose, leads to the same loss of legitimacy because of the Court's having been caught at a perceived lack of candor. Of course, I cannot say for sure that the Court was not being honest, but I can say that the Court does not appear to me to have been completely up front about its reasons. When a court lacks candor, and the readers know it, the result can only be that the readers have less reason to trust that what the court says corresponds to what it means, and this results in a decrease in the legitimacy of the decision-making process. Thus, both options, candor and non-candor, in certain difficult cases, lead to the same result: a decrease in the legitimacy of the process.

As the reader may have noticed, there existed a third option in *State v. Cohen.* The Court could have been hard-nosed for the sake of the system, and have upheld the arrests, even if the members of the Court thought that this would not be fair. I have presented portions of the work described in this book at many college campuses over the past several years, and invariably a bright, disgusted student suggests that all of this talk is too soft. If courts would only apply the law as it is written, without any hocus-pocus, there would be a little more cruelty, but at least we would have a system with integrity.

This approach, whatever its merits, only works some of the time. It works when the stated principles of law would seem to yield with some clarity a particular result in a given case, even though that result strikes the judge as wrong in the case before him. But the approach does not work at all in instances in which it is not particularly clear what result the stated principles of law demand in a given case. In those cases, being meanspirited to preserve clean lines between the legal and the illegal is not possible since there are no such clean lines.

From the above, the reader can see that the system provides enormous opportunities for criticism but very few for improvement. This is why the problems of judging explained so well by Cardozo, as we will see directly in chapter 1, still exist today with just as much force.

In chapter 1, we will look more closely at the temptation facing judges to write judicial opinions with less than complete candor, and we will see more clearly how linguistic analysis enters the picture. To do this, we will look at some writings of Benjamin Cardozo, a great judge, and of Noam Chomsky, who has for the past thirty or so years been the most influential intellectual force behind contemporary linguistics. I hope to show that the very nature of our knowledge of language makes linguistic analysis especially tempting for judges to use as justification for their decisions, even in cases where the judge is motivated by a very different agenda.

Chapter 2 focuses on cases in which linguistic principles form the basis of judicial decisions. The chapter begins by looking at a legal principle called "the last antecedent rule," which tells us how to interpret ambiguous phrases, with the rule applying differently from case to case. We will also examine a death penalty case whose outcome depended on the scope of adjectives, decisions based on the interpretation of pronouns, and a series of cases interpreting the words "and" and "or."

In chapter 3 we turn to a particular set of substantive legal principles: rules that dictate that a particular party should win when the outcome of a case depends on the meaning of an ambiguous document. Chapter 4 continues the presentation by focusing on the plain language rule, which in essence is the other side of the principles discussed in chapter 3. The plain language rule dictates that when the language of a statute or contract is clear, courts should assume that the language itself reflects the intention of the drafters, and that the courts should do no more than apply the statute or contract to the facts before the court.

Chapter 5 takes a slight turn in focus. Aware that language has generated so much litigation, lawyers have, over the centuries, developed peculiar syntactic devices, intended to make legal language more "precise" than ordinary language. Among these efforts are expressions like "party of the first part," "said defendant," and the like. Chapter 5 is an examination of these sorts of antiquated syntactic devices and the reaction to them, which has been sharply critical, sometimes resulting in the enactment of statutes requiring that certain legal documents be written in plain English.

Chapter 6 expands on another question first raised in chapter 1: the extent to which the rules of grammar that we use in speaking and understanding language are definitive and the extent to which they leave open the possibility of numerous interpretations. I will address the issue by looking at two provisions in the Constitution: the Fourth Amendment's prohibition against unreasonable searches and seizures, and the Fifth Amendment's prohibition against compelled self-incrimination.

Chapter 7, the final chapter, returns us to the questions that I raised at the beginning of this introduction. By the time that the reader gets to chapter 7, I hope to have shown that the pressures that operate on judges to write decisively and to limit what they say to certain acceptable argumentation have led to an incoherent body of legal principles based on linguistic analysis. In this chapter, I explore some of the consequences of these practices, and propose, in a very general way, some directions for improvement that seem to me to be promising.

Finally, I would like to comment on the scope of this book. By coincidence and as a result of my personal history, I happen to be among the few people that have studied both linguistics and law formally. I know for certain that almost none of the readers of this book will have this same training, and in any event I would not recommend it. Consequently, I have the task, if I am to be understood, of explaining the law to those who have not studied the law, and of explaining linguistics to those who have not studied linguistics, and of doing all of this in a way that keeps what I have to say interesting. In working toward this goal, I have not attempted to compile an encyclopedia of linguistically oriented legal cases. Rather, I have limited myself to what I hope are instructive examples of more general phenomena, whose study can teach us something about the legal system.

1 | Chomsky and Cardozo:
Linguistics and the Law

WHEN I WAS making my decision to go to law school in the late 1970s, I consulted a number of practicing lawyers that I knew at that time. Several of them gave me the same advice: so much of the law is simply a matter of linguistics that the transition from thinking about linguistic theory to thinking about legal matters should be a natural one. Furthermore, they encouraged, my background in linguistics should give me an advantage as a lawyer over those colleagues who have never studied linguistics.

This book is an inquiry into how ideas about our understanding of language have made their way into the legal process, and what can be learned about the law from looking at what judges themselves say in their writings about our knowledge of language. By virtue of our having been exposed to language during early childhood, we all know our native language. That is, we know how to speak it and understand it, with great rapidity and with little effort, and we learned to do this with no real training. We know that some strings of words are sentences ("The lawyer became enraged when the judge so curtly overruled his objection"), and that others are not ("The lawyer became enraged when the so judge curtly his overruled objection"). We can process the words that we hear, based in large part on the syntactic structure of the sentences that contain them, to come up with meanings for them. And when more than one meaning is possible for a particular sentence, we know that too. We routinely put our knowledge of language to use without any awareness of what processes are operating in our heads, just as we perceive color without consciously analyzing wavelengths.

Judges, of course, use language in just this way when they write opinions setting forth the reasoning behind their decisions. They can only write using language, and they use language the way the rest of us do.

But knowledge of language plays a more interesting role in judicial decision making. Judges are frequently confronted with disputes about the meaning of a particular document or statement, whether a statute, a contract, an insurance policy, or the proper wording of the judge's instructions to the jury. In these cases, the judge's chore is to decide what the disputed language means, or whether the statement is ambiguous and the words of the statement underdetermine its meaning. To make this decision, the judge must not only use his knowledge of language to read and write, but he must think somewhat abstractly about the use of language in the document or statement in dispute, and opine about this language. The arguments presented in the judge's opinion will therefore be linguistic arguments, arguments about why the language in dispute should result in one side winning instead of the other. Most of this book is a study of what happens when judges take on the role of linguist as they decide cases based on their application of linguistic principles to some disputed language. We will see that the best judges are not always the best linguists.

Returning for a moment to my friends who advised me to go to law school because "the law is simply a matter of linguistics," I am still not sure what they meant. If they meant that lawyers spend all their time using language, that is, writing, speaking, and reading, their remarks are true but uninteresting. In fact, the sheer volume of words that lawyers use is a matter of public ridicule, and an embarrassment to the profession. More and more, courts have been imposing page limits on lawyers' submissions, in an effort to control the situation by fiat.

If, on the other hand, my friends meant that lawyers must think linguistically when the issue in a case is the meaning of a document, and that they should think this way when writing documents in an effort to avoid future disputes, then their advice is very interesting, if overstated. Legal issues about language arise from time to time, although they are by no means a singular preoccupation for lawyers or judges. But studying them can, in my opinion, teach us a great deal about the legal system, not all of it positive, I am afraid. Throughout this book, we will see how judges resort to linguistic argumentation in what appears to be an effort to find a seemingly scientific and neutral justification for difficult decisions. In many instances, the linguistic argumentation either falls hopelessly flat, collapsing into incoherence, or can best be seen as window dressing, part of an effort to mask some other agenda that is at the root of the judge's opinion. To see how and why this happens, let us begin by looking at some work of two important thinkers of this century: Benjamin Cardozo and Noam Chomsky.

Cardozo's Hope: Keeping the Law Flexible

Benjamin Cardozo sat as a justice on the Supreme Court of the United States from 1932 until his death in 1938. But his greatest achievements came during the fifteen years or so before his appointment to the Supreme Court, during which time he sat on the highest court of the state of New York, the New York Court of Appeals. For much of this time, he sat as Chief Judge.

To American law students, Cardozo is most famous for deciding the fate of Mrs. Palsgraf,[1] to which we return later. But what makes Cardozo especially interesting is that he wrote extensively about how to judge and about the problems of judging while he was on the bench.[2] Few judges, even the great ones, have had the will or the courage to write seriously about the difficulties of their profession, setting a standard against which their own judicial decisions can later be judged.

The overriding theme of Cardozo's extrajudicial writings is the tension between the need for the law to be both sufficiently flexible to accommodate new cases as they arise and sufficiently rigid to maintain its predictive power. If the law is not flexible enough, then it is doomed to irrelevance and to becoming the source of injustice. If the law is too flexible, then it becomes so unstable that it fails to define with any reliability people's rights and obligations, even in seemingly simple situations. This results in decay of the rule of law.

For example, the Fourth Amendment to the Constitution, which prohibits the government from engaging in unreasonable searches and seizures, was written some two hundred years ago, not long after Benjamin Franklin's experimentation with electric currents. How should this provision be interpreted in our twentieth century world in which government has access to sophisticated electronic eavesdropping and surveillance devices? In chapter 6 we will see how some linguistic features of the word "search" can help answer this question. For now, however, the question serves to illustrate Cardozo's problem: How can a judge be responsive to novel situations in a changing world without forsaking entirely the foundations of the legal tradition?[3] Cardozo likens this difficulty to the tension between rest and motion, between stability and progress.[4]

In his best-known book, *The Nature of the Judicial Process,* written in 1921 while he sat on the New York Court of Appeals, Cardozo fantasizes about an ideal world in which the dual goals—progress and stability—are in harmony:

No doubt the ideal system, if it were attainable, would be a code at once so flexible and so minute, as to supply in advance for every conceivable situation the just and fitting rule. But life is too complex to bring the attainment of this ideal within the compass of human powers.[5]

As we shall see, Cardozo is correct only about the unattainability of this ideal as to *some* human powers. With respect to others, the ability to speak and understand language in particular, Cardozo's fantasy describes the reality. Within the domain of language, people indeed know "a code at once so flexible and so minute, as to supply in advance for every conceivable situation the . . . fitting rule." (Justice plays no role in our ability to speak and understand sentences.) That "code" is what linguists call a generative grammar, the set of internalized rules and principles that permit us, unselfconsciously, to speak and understand language with ease and with great rapidity.

If Cardozo has understated "the compass of human powers," he certainly has not missed the boat completely. The human power on which Cardozo focuses, the power to make rules governing human interaction, does not even approach the ideal. Yet judges, in their judicial opinions, regularly write to create the impression that their decision is "the only possible decision," one derived by applying readily ascertainable neutral principles to the set of novel events that is the subject of the dispute being adjudicated. And they do this even when the arguments in favor of the contrary result are forceful. Cardozo comments on this tendency:

> Our survey of judicial methods teaches us, I think, the lesson that the whole subject-matter of jurisprudence is more plastic, more malleable, the moulds less definitely cast, the bounds of right and wrong less preordained and constant, than most of us, without the aid of some such analysis, have been accustomed to believe. We like to picture to ourselves the field of the law as accurately mapped and plotted. We draw our little lines, and they are hardly down before we blur them. As in time and space, so here. Divisions are working hypotheses, adopted for convenience. We are tending more and more toward an appreciation of the truth that, after all, there are few rules; there are chiefly standards and degrees.[6]

The temptation for judges to issue pronouncements as though there were no alternative—as though Cardozo's ideal were the reality—must be enormous. The consequences of a judicial decision for the parties before the court can literally be a matter of life and death. Moreover, ordinarily, one party wins and the other loses. Either a death sentence is reversed or it is not; either a decision awarding damages to one party is affirmed, or it is not. Litigating is by and large a zero sum game, with the power of the state insuring that the winner really wins. Under this sort of pressure, when a judge decides a case, and has to justify his decision in a written opinion, he may well feel obliged to argue forcefully for his position, making it clear that after careful research and study, he had no choice but to decide in favor of one side and against the other. I know that if I were a judge, I would be tempted to present a decision in just that way, as judges frequently do.

But to ignore the "malleability" of the law, as Cardozo puts it, carries a price, which Cardozo recognizes. In response to those who would like to view the law as able to give clear and certain answers as novel situations are presented, Cardozo responds: "The curse of this fluidity, of an ever shifting approximation, is one that law must bear, or other curses yet more dreadful will be invited in exchange."[7] The curse that Cardozo had in mind was the curse of injustice that results from the blind application of a "mechanical jurisprudence," to use the words of Roscoe Pound.[8] We may laugh at the looseness of the legal maxim that statutes are to be interpreted to avoid absurd results,[9] but when we read in the newspaper that some "legal technicality" has led to what we perceive as an obvious miscarriage of justice, the matter is no longer funny.

There is another harm that occurs when judges succumb to the fantasy that their decisions are somehow logically necessary, or could not have been otherwise. The harm is the loss of legitimacy of the entire judicial process that comes as a by-product of the lack of candor. The loss is ironic, in that it results precisely from the effort to increase the legitimacy of the judicial process by perpetrating the fiction that the outcome of each case is fixed by independent principles. This puts the judge in a very difficult position. He can only sustain the legitimacy of the process by admitting that the process is imperfect, an admission that tends to reduce legitimacy. Cardozo wrote of this irony:

> There has been a certain lack of candor in much of the discussion of the theme, or rather perhaps in the refusal to discuss it, as if judges must lose respect and confidence by the reminder that they are subject to human limitations. I do not doubt the grandeur of the conception which lifts them into the realm of pure reason, above and beyond the sweep of perturbing and deflecting forces. None the less, if there is anything of reality in my

analysis of the judicial process, they do not stand aloof on these
chill and distant heights; and we shall not help the cause of truth
by acting and speaking as if they do. The great tides and currents
which engulf the rest of men, do not turn aside in their course,
and pass the judges by.[10]

How do judges advance their efforts to create the impression that they are
not "subject to the human limitations" that Cardozo claims must be acknowledged? As Ronald Dworkin points out,[11] judicial decision making involves the exercise of state power subject to legitimate political process. And
"legitimate political process" can be interpreted broadly, although perhaps
not broadly enough to give judges the latitude to state all of the motivations
behind some of their decisions, as we shall see. Courts are free to rely on
statutes, earlier decisions of courts, and at times, on what a judge takes to be
independent neutral principles.

It is at this point that the judge's use of linguistic argumentation comes
into play. As I said earlier, the limitations of "human powers" that Cardozo
spends so much energy integrating into the job of judging simply do not
apply to the human power to speak and understand language. This is not to
say that spoken language and written language are always so clear that no
question can ever exist as to what meaning a speaker or writer intended to
convey. The core of our linguistic knowledge, the part that linguists call a
"generative grammar," is, however, indeed the type of "code" for which Cardozo yearns. Therefore, to the extent that a judge can decide a case by resort
to this special human power, he can avoid the difficulties of having to rely,
for example, on one set of precedents when he and the parties know full well
that a different body of precedents could have been invoked to justify the
opposite result. In fact, appellate decisions are not rendered until both parties have submitted in briefs the authorities on which they hope the court
will rely.

Let us look a little more closely at what the human power of language is all
about before we return to Cardozo and problems of the judicial process.

Chomsky and the Nature of Linguistic Knowledge

I have alluded to the human power to speak and understand language, con-
trasting it with the human inability to create laws that definitively set forth
the consequences of human behavior. The tone of my remarks, extolling this
human capacity, may seem at odds with the lawyer's typical view of language, which is a boobytrapped code full of potential for vagueness, im-

precision, ambiguity, and other sources of misunderstanding—a medium in which disputes foment. Both perspectives have merit, once we sort out the various aspects of our linguistic knowledge.

To do this, we turn to the work of Noam Chomsky, whose writings begin-ning in the 1950s have changed the nature of linguistic inquiry into a field focusing its investigations on knowledge of language as a human cognitive faculty.[12] The aspect of this power to which the field directs most of its atten-tion is the power to know and use what linguists call a "generative gram-mar," that is, the set of rules and principles that lie at the core of our ability to decode the structure and meaning of sentences as we hear them. Chomsky describes the nature of the inquiry in his 1975 book, *Reflections on Language:*

> The theory of language is simply that part of human psychology that is concerned with one particular "mental organ," human language. Stimulated by appropriate and continuing experi-ence, the language faculty creates a grammar that generates sen-tences with formal and semantic properties. We say that a person knows the language generated by this grammar.[13]

What makes the linguist's task of forming a precise characterization of this language faculty especially challenging is that the resultant theory must be at once sufficiently well defined to account for the fact that members of the same community speak and understand each other with ease, using and hearing scores of novel utterances daily without ever giving the matter a thought, and at the same time sufficiently flexible to permit the rapid acqui-sition of this same ability with any possible human language. After all, chil-dren do not know at birth which language they will be learning. The language faculty must permit the rapid acquisition of any possible human language, based on the experience of hearing only a minute number of the infinitely many sentences that each language can generate. As Chomsky notes:

> Thus, it is clear that the language each person acquires is a rich and complex construction hopelessly underdetermined by the fragmentary evidence available.
>
> . . . .
>
> Nevertheless, individuals in a speech community have devel-oped essentially the same language. This fact can be explained only on the assumption that these individuals employ highly re-strictive principles that guide the construction of grammar. Fur-thermore, humans are, obviously, not designed to learn one

human language rather than another; the system of principles must be a species property. Powerful constraints must be operative restricting the variety of languages. It is natural that in our daily life we should concern ourselves only with differences among people, ignoring uniformities of structure. But different intellectual demands arise when we seek to understand what kind of organism a human really is.[14]

Because of this essential tension—the tension that derives from the need for a theory that is at once so flexible and so minute as to supply a detailed set of rules for each possible human language, to paraphrase Cardozo—investigation into the nature of linguistic knowledge is a complicated task, as Chomsky points out. The key to the inquiry is the hypothesis that humans are born with a highly developed language faculty, which upon exposure to language at an appropriate level of maturity can quickly develop an internalization of the principles governing that language being acquired. Much of linguistic research consists of efforts to integrate into the theory generalizations, sometimes very abstract ones, which apply across languages, and thus may be seen as part of this human faculty. In his 1988 *Managua Lectures,* Chomsky describes this innate endowment:

> It seems that the child approaches the task of acquiring a language with a rich conceptual framework already in place and also with a rich system of assumptions about sound structure and the structure of more complex utterances. These constitute the parts of our knowledge that come "from the original hand of nature," in Hume's phrase. They constitute one part of the human biological endowment, to be awakened by experience and to be sharpened and enriched in the course of the child's interactions with the human and material world.[15]

The fact that much of our knowledge of language can be attributed to our biological endowment is significant, for it accounts for the relative ease and speed with which we acquire this knowledge. At the same time, the biological nature of our linguistic capacity endows our knowledge of language with a special status in everyday human interactions. Each time we meet a native speaker of our language, we assume that we will be mutually understood, much the same way that we assume that we each have virtually identical physical organs, such as lungs and kidneys, that we each perceive color and depth, etc. As we will see later, the universal nature of our knowledge of language makes it especially tempting for courts to use language in justifying decisions outside the realm, say, of a selection of precedents from a large set of conflicting ones.

Let us consider a few illustrations of this knowledge. First, to take an example from the early linguistic literature, all speakers of English know[16] that English has a set of auxiliary or helping verbs, such as *may, can, be, have,* etc., and that to form a yes-no question from a sentence containing an auxiliary verb, one inverts the auxiliary and the subject of the sentence. The sentences in (1) illustrate this phenomenon:

(1)   a. Fred was trying to convince the jury that the victim misidentified the defendant as the perpetrator of the crime.

b. Was Fred trying to convince the jury that the victim misidentified the defendant . . . ?

Along these same lines, we also know that (2) is not a sentence of English:

(2)   Was trying to convince the jury Fred that the victim misidentified the defendant . . . ?

We also know, in this same sense, that when there is no auxiliary verb, some form of the word "do" appears,

(3)   Did Fred try to convince the jury . . . ?

and that when there is more than one auxiliary verb, the subject of the sentence inverts with only the first auxiliary verb to form a question. Thus, we know that (4) is not a sentence of English:

(4)   Will be Fred trying to convince the jury . . . ?

Finally, we know in this sense that the inversion rule applies only to the main clause of the sentence, even when auxiliary verbs contained in a subordinate clause intervene.[17] Compare (5), which is grammatical,

(5)   Did [the juror who was sitting on the left] listen to the summation?

with (6), which is not:

(6)   Was the juror who sitting on the left listen to the summation?

My picture of the English auxiliary system is not complete. Nor does it reflect the latest views on the relationships among all of these sentences.[18] But the examples discussed thus far should suffice to illustrate the nature of linguistic knowledge at our ready disposal. It operates on linguistic structures, is precise, and at times, complicated. Of course, it is not the case that the human language faculty demands that all languages permit questions to be formed by inverting the subject with an auxiliary verb. Many languages do not. But our language faculty must be sufficiently restrictive ("minute" to use Cardozo's term) to define the sort of rule systems that are possible when a language does permit this sort of question to be formed. This accounts for why it is that children do not have to undergo years of training before they can operate quickly and easily within this system. To the contrary, it all seems to happen automatically.

For the reasons just discussed, linguists have concerned themselves over the past twenty or so years largely with those aspects of linguistic knowledge that limit the ways in which sentences can be formed or understood. Interestingly, the ungrammatical sentences discussed above teach us as much as do the grammatical ones. For together, they define our knowledge of this small portion of English.

Let us look at a second example. As we will see in more detail in chapters 2 and 5, pronouns can refer to almost anyone. Consider (7):

(7)   Fred thought he had convinced the jury.

In (7), *he* can refer to *Fred,* or to any other male. Our knowledge of language tells us nothing else about to whom *he* refers. But in (8), on the other hand,

(8)   He thought Fred had convinced the jury

our knowledge of English tells us that *he* cannot refer to *Fred.* No one hearing (8) would even pause to consider whether *he* and *Fred* refer to the same individual. In this way, our internal generative grammar limits, but does not reduce to one, the range of possible interpretations of pronouns.[19] Apart from *Fred, he* can still refer to any male.

Of course, in our ability to understand (7) and (8), we know much more than the possible antecedents of *he.* For example, we know that in (8) *he* is the subject of the main clause of the sentence, whose verb is *thought.* We also know that the sentence contains a subordinate clause, *Fred had convinced the jury,* and that the subordinate clause does not make the sentence ungrammatical. However, if the verb of the main clause had been, say, *wanted,* the sentence would be ungrammatical, unless the subordinate clause were altered to *to convince the jury,* or some similar structure containing an infinitive. We know these facts, because as children we unconsciously absorbed the properties of the verbs *think* and *want,* and because we know the forms that subordinate clauses can and cannot take in English. Continuing with (8), we recognize *the jury* as the direct object of *convinced.* And we know that *convince* requires a direct object, in that a sentence like *He thought Fred had convinced except the third juror* is ungrammatical, although understandable. There is much more. But even from this brief discussion it should be apparent that our knowledge of language is very sophisticated, and understanding language in the ordinary course of human interaction requires us to apply a host of principles and to decode complicated structural relationships of which we are not consciously aware unless we give the matter special study.

Returning to the apparent tension between the linguist's view of language as a highly regular and formalizable system of knowledge, and the lawyer's notion of language as a breeding ground for incoherence, (7) and (8) cast some light on this matter as well. As these examples show, the application of the principles of generative grammar does not definitively answer all questions about meaning, despite the many that it does answer. In this case, the interpretation of pronouns is left open to inferences based on context, worldly knowledge, and other bits of essentially nonlinguistic information.

Our knowledge of language, again in the sense of generative grammar, leaves open many other aspects of interpretation, a few of which we will see later in this book. For example, when certain phrases appear at the end of a sentence, our generative grammars permit them to be interpreted as modifying one of a number of earlier phrases, as (9) illustrates:

(9)   The witness saw a man and a woman running down the street.

This sentence is ambiguous with respect to who was running down the street. The witness could have seen both a man and a woman running, or he could have seen a man who was not running and a woman who was. For that matter, the witness himself may have been the only runner. ("Running down the street, the witness saw a man and a woman.") When this type of syntactic structure appears in a legal document, and a dispute arises over its interpretation, judges are sometimes forced to decide which of these possible interpretations will determine the outcome of a case. As we will see in chapter 2, judges are not consistent in resolution of these cases.

To take an example that we will examine more closely in chapter 6, many verbs imply the existence of certain objects (called "arguments") even when these objects are not explicitly stated. For instance, the word *search* ordinarily takes as its direct object the place being searched, and as the object of a prepositional phrase the goal of the search:

(10) The police searched the room for the heroin.

But at times, the objects of the word *search* remain unspecified, as in "the police continued to search all night." Nonetheless, we continue to understand the sentence as meaning that the police were searching some place for something. Exactly what is being searched and what is being sought are left for us to infer from context or to guess. In chapter 6, we will see that much of the debate over the Fourth Amendment to the Constitution can be seen as a fight over which x's and which y's are protected from unreasonable government searches in the expression "the police searched x for y."

As one last example of meaning left open in part by our internal generative grammars, consider the scope of adverbs. In chapter 3 we will see cases decided by the Supreme Court of the United States in which the scope of "knowingly" was at issue in a statute whose structure (simplified here) is reflected in (11).

(11) Whoever knowingly sells food stamps in an illegal manner shall
      be punished.

(11) is ambiguous. "Knowingly" can be understood as modifying "sells food stamps" or as modifying the entire phrase, "sells food stamps in an illegal manner." That is, our knowledge of English permits us to interpret (11) in one of two ways. What should a court do when a defendant claims that he knowingly sold the food stamps, but did not know that the sale was illegal since he had not read the statute books?

Our knowledge of language, then, has several components. At the core is a generative grammar that specifies in detail how to put together well-formed sentences, and tells us a good deal about how they may and may not be interpreted. But our knowledge of language, in this sense, underdetermines certain aspects of meaning, which must be inferred from context, or simply be left open. Even in these few pages, we have seen that the scope of modifiers, the antecedents of pronouns, and inferences about the objects of verbs are all subject to additional interpretation based on context and knowledge about the world. Many more examples exist, the most obvious being which meaning of a word is intended when a speaker uses a word with more than one possible meaning, or even subtly different senses of the same meaning. All of this must be inferred, and is a potential source of dispute, since neither our innate language faculty nor the specific rules of English can reduce to one the possible meanings of all expressions.

In a sense, then, linguists concern themselves with what our generative grammars prescribe about form and meaning, while lawyers bemoan the fact that there is a residue of underdetermination over which people may fight.

Chomsky, Cardozo, and Mrs. Palsgraf

Let us now return to Cardozo's assessment of the legal process. Earlier, I focused on three of Cardozo's observations: First, the ideal legal system, which supplies in advance answers to novel disputes, is unattainable; second, the law is more malleable than we would like to think; and third, judges are not always entirely candid about the first two points.

At a metaphorical level, not too far removed from reality to be meaningful, I believe, Cardozo is forthrightly acknowledging that legal doctrine is not able to define a generative grammar for human interaction, whose rules specify which behavior is acceptable, which behavior is unacceptable, and the consequences of unacceptable behavior.[20] With such high stakes and with the requirement that judges justify their decisions in written opinions, judges are tempted, however, to give the impression that the law does have such generative power, and they sometimes yield to that temptation.

In his statement "there are few rules; there are chiefly standards and degrees,"[21] Cardozo highlights the difference between knowledge of language on the one hand, and knowledge of legal principles on the other. As I showed earlier, and as we will see much more throughout this book, neither system of knowledge is entirely predictive. Just as legal rules do not fully define what behavior is permissible, some aspects of sentence meaning and word meaning are not fully determined by our internalized generative grammars.

But the limitations on our capacities in these two domains are qualitatively different. With respect to language, we not only unconsciously know and follow rules of grammar without any real training, but we also unconsciously know where the rules stop short of providing a single interpretation for an utterance. Language meaning is largely predictable, and we can define with some certainty the situations in which it is not predictable. We know that a single word can have different senses, that pronouns can refer to a variety of potential antecedents, and so on. Moreover, as the word "generative" implies, we apply our internalized knowledge of language routinely to the infinitely many new sentences that we hear and speak each day.

As Cardozo points out, in contrast, it is impossible to define with any precision to what extent legal rules apply, or should apply, to a new situation. Of course there are easy cases. But for novel cases, should we extend a legal concept to include new, unforeseen events, should we apply the old concept mechanically, or should we switch to a different concept that now appears to encompass both the rationale for the old rule and new considerations? Cardozo correctly states that we are reduced to "standards and degrees" in answering this question.

The situation is akin to the everyday difficulties we experience in deciding which of several possible words to use. The problem is a conceptual one: our decision depends on which concept we wish to express, and we are not always sure. In this limited domain, legal and linguistic indeterminacy join forces to produce uncertainty.

Cardozo's record of following his own advice on these issues is admirable, but not perfect. In his most famous opinion, *Palsgraf v. Long Island R. Co.,* Cardozo speaks with the greatest certainty about a matter that was and still is controversial, and for which precedents would have supported the opposite result. Mrs. Palsgraf had been hurt while standing on a platform at a train station waiting for her train. As another train began to pull out of the station, a passenger holding a package tried to catch that train. One guard on the train tried to help him by pulling him aboard, while another guard, standing on the platform, tried to help by pushing him onto the train from behind. In the process, the passenger's package was dislodged and fell onto the tracks. Unbeknown to the guards, the package contained fireworks, which exploded, causing some scales to fall on Mrs. Palsgraf, who was standing at the other end of the platform, many feet away.[22] Mrs. Palsgraf sued the railroad.

Should the railroad be held liable to Mrs. Palsgraf for her injuries? Chief Judge Cardozo and three others prevailed, saying no. Cardozo reasoned that while the guards may have acted negligently toward the passenger they were trying to help, they breached no duty to Mrs. Palsgraf, since they could not conceivably have known in advance what would happen if the package were to fall on the tracks. Judge Andrews, writing in dissent for a minority of three, disagreed, observing that the guards acted negligently and that their negligence caused injury, which should be enough to hold the railroad liable. According to Andrews, it should not matter that the particular injury that occurred was unforeseen, since it was foreseeable that *some* injury would occur.

Both the majority and the dissent argued forcefully, relying on judicial precedent and on projections of how each rule of law would apply in other situations. Neither side admitted that the precedents cited by the other could conceivably form the basis of a persuasive argument. In effect, Cardozo and Andrews each wrote as if trying to appear that he and only he had discovered the law.

This is not to say that Cardozo suffered from a chronic lack of candor in his judicial writings. Even in *Palsgraf,* Cardozo presented arguments, independent of the judicial precedents cited, that demonstrate his efforts to fashion a rule that would reflect the norm, in his view, of what duty people owed one another in the mainstream of the society of his time. Cardozo repeatedly espoused this view of the law, essentially governmental confirmation of the normative, in *The Nature of the Judicial Process* and in other writings.

In another famous opinion, *MacPherson v. Buick Motor Co.,*[23] written in 1916 (twelve years before *Palsgraf*), Cardozo expressly recognized the changing, contingent nature of legal decision making as societal norms develop. *MacPherson* is studied in law schools as a case that sets the foundation of contemporary products liability law. The plaintiff was injured when a wheel on his car made of defective wood broke. The "general rule" at the time was that the seller of a product was liable only to the buyer if the product proved defective. MacPherson, however, did not buy his car directly from Buick Motors. Like most people, he bought his car from a dealer, although he wanted Buick Motors to be held liable for his injuries.

In arguing against the application of the general rule, Cardozo wrote:

> The dealer was indeed the one person of whom it might be said with some approach to certainty that by him the car would not be used. Yet the defendant would have us say that he was the one person whom it was under a legal duty to protect. The law does not lead us to so inconsequent a conclusion. Precedents drawn from the days of travel by stagecoach do not fit the conditions of travel to-day. The principle that the danger must be imminent does not change, but the things subject to the principle do change. They are whatever the needs of life in a developing civilization require them to be.[24]

Cardozo cited precedents to show that the general rule had its exceptions, namely, manufacturers of inherently dangerous products had been found in the past to be liable for injuries caused to nondirect purchasers ultimately injured by the product. But even here Cardozo used the precedent not to create the false impression that there could be no contrary authority, but rather to illustrate contemporary values:

We are not required at this time either to approve or to disapprove the application of the rule that was made in these cases. It is enough that they help to characterize the trend of judicial thought.[25]

We find similar language in *Allegheny College v. National Chautauqua County Bank*,[26] a case in which it was decided that a donor's pledge to have his estate give money to a college upon his death was enforceable as a contract. At issue was the fact that the college had not actually paid for the gift. Ordinarily, promises are enforceable as contracts only when they are paid for with some type of "consideration." On the doctrine of consideration, Cardozo commented:

> The half truths of one generation tend at times to perpetuate themselves in the law as the whole truth of another, when constant repetition brings it about that qualifications, taken once for granted, are disregarded or forgotten. The doctrine of consideration has not escaped the common lot.[27]

In ruling that the pledge may be enforced, Cardozo stretched the doctrine of consideration to the limit, and almost certainly past the limit.[28] However, remarking on certain judicially recognized exceptions to the consideration requirement, he noted:

> The result speaks for itself irrespective of the motive. Decisions which have stood so long, and which are supported by so many considerations of public policy and reason, will not be overruled to save the symmetry of a concept which itself came into our law, not so much from any reasoned conviction of its justice, as from historical accidents of practice and procedure. . . . The concept survives as one of the distinctive features of our legal system. We have no thought to suggest that it is obsolete or on the way to be abandoned. As in the case of other concepts, however, the pressure of exceptions has led to irregularities of form.[29]

While I have not attempted here a systematic review of all of Cardozo's opinions, these few highlights suggest that he not only wrote outside the courthouse about the contingent nature of judicial decision making, but he acknowledged it in many of his opinions, including some of the controversial ones. Portions of *Palsgraf* and other opinions show that Cardozo was not entirely immune from the temptation to write opinions in an effort to create the impression that the result reached was the only one possible, given the then current state of legal doctrine. Nonetheless, Cardozo generally incorporated in his opinions the philosophy he espoused elsewhere.[30]

When the judge is asked to resolve a dispute over the meaning of language, linguistic theory provides more than a metaphor for a court's effort to preserve legitimacy by confusing the ideal for reality. Frequently, for example, the issue in a case is whether the language in question is subject to a single interpretation or whether it is ambiguous. Put somewhat differently, the question is whether the meaning of the disputed language is determined fully by our generative grammars, or whether disputed aspects of the meaning are left open as part of the residue of meaning that our internal grammars do not fully determine. We will see courts ignoring multiple interpretations in some instances and apparently fabricating them in others.

These difficulties can be seen as the judge's succumbing to the temptation about which Cardozo warns, and to which I alluded in the Introduction. To justify difficult and sometimes obviously painful decisions, judges sometimes write as authoritatively about language as they do about judicial precedents. When it comes to our knowledge of language, this confidence comes quite easily. Unlike judicial precedents, which always require inferences and which sometimes require selection of a subset of seemingly conflicting authority, our knowledge of language, in the Chomskian sense, is contingent only on our biology and on our having had adequate experience in childhood to acquire the language. When a judge says that one party wins and the other loses because the language of the governing statute clearly favors the winner, he is relying on a neutral and universal body of knowledge—our internalized knowledge of the English language.

Reliance on linguistic knowledge is very much like reliance on other generally known, fixed facts about the world and about ourselves, such as the fact that objects fall when they are dropped, and the fact that our eyes permit us to see colors. Thus a judge reducing a dispute to one that can be resolved by reference to our knowledge of language has taken the dispute out of the realm of the contingent and the uncertain, and has placed it in the realm of biological necessity. To take a simple, but by no means trivial example, no one would interpret defendant John's statement "Bill killed himself" as a confession that John killed Bill. This is because we, as speakers of English, know that the antecedent of a reflexive pronoun must be contained in the clause containing the reflexive.[31] When the language becomes more complicated disputes sometimes do arise, and judges frequently try to resolve them in the same way that we would resolve a dispute about "Bill killed himself": by straightforward reference to what we know about English.

Throughout this book we will see many well-reasoned opinions. But the appeal of neutral linguistic principles as justification for a decision will loom especially large when the judge's "real reasons" for the decision are not ones that are properly articulated in a judicial opinion. Such reasons may include helping someone wronged collect from an insurance company because the company can better stand the loss, or perhaps removing the legal obstacles that seem to stand in the way of executing those convicted of capital crimes. The more difficult it is for a judge to state in the opinion what drove him to the decision the more tempting independent noncontroversial argumentation becomes, such as arguments based on our knowledge of language. Ironically, as I said earlier, this quest for legitimacy results in its diminution, since the erosion of integrity itself causes the decay of respect for the judiciary. No one, knowing the difficult issues facing a court, feels satisfied when a decision announced is based on what seems to be a legal technicality instead of on the real issues.

Contemporary legal theorists have focused a great deal of attention on the fact that legal doctrine permits a narrower range of justificatory argumentation than does, say, ordinary political discourse. On the left, the critical legal studies movement, echoing but expanding to some extent the voices of the legal realists who wrote principally in the second quarter of this century, call for the expansion of legal doctrine to permit the courts to engage in open discussion of the deeper considerations of distributive justice which now must go unspoken. On the other side of the coin, the law and economics movement has, with considerable success already, asked courts to expand legal doctrine to include considerations of free market economics. We will return to all of this briefly in chapter 7, after seeing the various ways in which linguistics has infiltrated legal doctrine.

Cardozo expressed his concern almost seventy years ago, but it seems no less relevant now. In what follows, we will see both examples of the flaws in the system that Cardozo described, and instances of how linguistic insights can help to organize judicial thought in an effort to reduce the magnitude of the gap between what appears to drive judges to decide as they do and what they are confined to say to justify their decisions.

2| The Judge as Linguist

FROM TIME to time, judges rely on what appear to be subtle principles of linguistic theory to determine the outcome of cases before them. Decisions based on linguistic argumentation determine such seemingly unrelated matters as whether a convicted murderer will be put to death, whether an individual was properly convicted of a drug felony, and whether the company that insures a driver involved in a serious automobile accident will have to pay to compensate others for injuries and property damage that the driver caused. As anyone who has ever been involved in a lawsuit already knows, and as anyone who has been a defendant in a criminal prosecution knows even better, participants in the legal system regularly play for high stakes.

The linguistic issues arise when lawyers for opposing parties attempt to convince a court that a statute or insurance policy or contract or some other legal document should be interpreted to favor their own clients' interests with respect to a dispute whose resolution depends crucially on the proper construal of the particular document. Assuming no disagreement about the events that occurred, it is for the court to decide what should follow from applying the language of the document to the events. In so doing, the judge, urged in different directions by the opposing lawyers, will often resort to legally recognized principles of interpretation, such as attempting to divine the intention of the drafters of the document. On occasion, these principles are linguistic, and it is upon these that I will focus.

This chapter will explore several examples of linguistic principles used by judges to justify their decisions as to the proper resolution of lawsuits and criminal prosecutions. Included among the examples are a linguistic-legal principle called the last antecedent rule, principles governing the interpretation of conjunction and disjunction (*and* and *or*), rules for the interpretation of pronouns, and a debate about the proper scope of adjectives.

28   An examination of what judges say about linguistics and of their own

roles as linguists casts some light on the judicial process for the reasons discussed in chapter 1. From the discussion that follows, it should become clear that the linguistic principles frequently do not operate as the courts claim they do. Moreover, disputes exist even among judges in the same court about both the proper characterization of the linguistic rules and their relevance to the decision-making process. Consequently, as legal scholars have noted for decades,[1] principles of interpretation sometimes exist side by side with their opposites, creating a body of mutually inconsistent legal rules, available to any lawyer or judge who wishes to use them to support almost any position whatsoever. Under pressure to write decisively, judges do indeed take advantage of this loose set of interpretive principles.

The Last Antecedent Rule

Let us begin by examining a principle of law called the "last antecedent rule." The rule is widely applied both by the federal courts and by the courts of various states. Here, I will focus on the rule as applied by the courts of California. I have limited the discussion to a single jurisdiction in order to permit historical analysis of the rule's application, and in order to reduce the likelihood of mistaking as a general phenomenon a few sporadic cases from around the country decided over long periods of time. Legal scholars regularly draw conclusions about which judicial decisions should be regarded as "leading cases" based almost exclusively on their judgment about which decisions are substantively significant. While these judgments cannot be avoided, at the very least some care should be taken to insure that deep consideration of a few aberrant events is not misunderstood for "discovering the law."

MRS. ANDERSON'S CASE

The last antecedent rule has been a part of California law since the late nineteenth century. It is stated below, quoted from a 1969 California appellate court decision, *Anderson v. State Farm Mutual Automobile Insurance Co.*[2]

> A limiting clause is to be confined to the last antecedent, unless the context or evident meaning requires a different construction.

The *Anderson* case involved a car owner's lawsuit against her insurance company. In an entertaining fashion, the appellate court explained that Mrs. Anderson had left a California county fair, and had driven off with a Mr. Larson in Mr. Larson's car. The newly met couple arrived at a restaurant where they spent several hours, after which time Mr. Larson excused himself to go to the restroom, never to return. Mrs. Anderson, who had consumed only part of a single drink during this period, testified that she left the restaurant and drove off in what she thought was Mr. Larson's car. It was not. Rather, it was Mr. Yocum's Cadillac. While driving Mr. Yocum's car, Mrs. Anderson was involved in an accident, which damaged Mr. Yocum's car. Mr. Yocum sued Mrs. Anderson and won a judgment of about thirteen thousand dollars. Mrs. Anderson tried to collect from State Farm, her own insurer, but the insurance company denied coverage. She then sued State Farm.

In deciding the case, the court relied on the following portion of Mrs. Anderson's automobile insurance policy:

> Such insurance as is afforded by this policy . . . with respect to the owned automobile applies to the use of a non-owned automobile by the named insured . . . *and* any other person or organization legally responsible for use by the named insured . . . of an automobile not owned or hired by such other person or organization *provided such use is with the permission of the owner or person in lawful possession of such automobile*. (Emphasis added)[3]

The policy covers two distinct classes of drivers in the event that an accident occurs involving a car not owned by the insured. The first is "the named insured." The second is a class of people or organizations "legally responsible for use by the named insured" of a non-owned automobile, whatever that means. In this instance, the named insured (Mrs. Anderson) caused the accident. Is she covered by her policy even though she lacked the permission of the owner of the car that she was driving? Applying the last antecedent rule, the court said yes. The court reasoned that the second of the two classes of potential drivers is the last antecedent, and therefore the owner's permission is not needed when the car is driven by the named insured herself. Had the car been driven by someone legally responsible for use by Mrs. Anderson, and not Mrs. Anderson herself, then the owner's permission would have been required. The court also took into account the fact that no comma separates the second class of drivers and the *provided* clause. The absence of any punctuation, the court reasoned, may be taken as evidence of the intended linkage between the *provided* clause and the second of the two classes of drivers. Presumably, Mr. Yocum eventually got his thirteen thousand from Mrs. Anderson's insurance company.

Processing Strategies and the Last Antecedent Rule

The application of the last antecedent rule to permit Mrs. Anderson to collect from her insurance company seems strained at best. I suspect that most readers share my intuition that the relevant language in Mrs. Anderson's policy is more naturally interpreted as preventing her from collecting when she is driving someone else's car without permission. In this subsection we shall explore why that is the case.

First, note that the *Anderson* court's statement of the last antecedent rule requires that a limiting clause be confined to the last antecedent *"unless the context or evident meaning requires a different construction."* In this sense, the rule is best viewed as a strategy for interpreting modifying clauses as opposed to an absolute prohibition against certain interpretations. This distinction is significant, because, as native speakers of English (or other languages), our knowledge of the language contains both types of devices: interpretive strategies that function to ease the rapid processing of language as it is heard or read, but which can be overridden if their application leads to nonsensical or ungrammatical interpretations of sentences, and rules of grammar, which make certain interpretations impossible, such as those discussed in chapter 1. The relationship between the grammar and the interpretive strategies is currently a topic of investigation by linguists and psychologists of language.[4] Below we will see that this relationship is at the heart of Mrs. Anderson's victory and its seeming peculiarity.

Even without the "unless" caveat quoted in the preceding paragraph, the last antecedent rule resembles a strategy that has been discussed in the linguistic literature: the late closure strategy, a strategy for sentence processing first proposed by Lyn Frazier.[5]

Late closure is defined by Frazier as follows:

> The Late Closure strategy specifies that incoming items are preferentially analyzed as a constituent of the phrase or clause currently being processed.[6]

The strategy assumes, as does much work in theoretical psycholinguistics, that in order to understand language as rapidly as it is spoken, our brains build syntactic structures on an ongoing basis as we hear the words of a sentence. The late closure strategy is postulated as an initial hypothesis that reduces the number of decisions that have to be made in assigning syntactic structure to the words we hear, and thus makes the rapid processing of sentences easier. It simply says that whenever possible, new items are considered to be part of the phrase currently being processed, as opposed to part of a new phrase that needs to be constructed.

At times, the late closure strategy misdirects us, so that we initially attempt to assign the wrong structure to a sentence, forcing us to go back and reanalyze the words that we have already processed. This is exactly what happens when we take "the garden path" in interpreting (1):

(1)   After he cross-examined the witness was in tears.

In trying to understand (1), we initially attempt to incorporate *the witness* into the phrase being processed: the verb phrase of the clause beginning "he cross-examined." Only after continuing to process the sentence do we discover that *the witness* is actually the subject of the main clause of the sentence—not the direct object of the initial subordinate clause, *after he cross-examined*. The fact that we take these garden paths constitutes evidence that we really do employ the late closure principle, or something like it.

Returning to the last antecedent rule and Mrs. Anderson, we can begin to explain what is so unnatural about the court's construal of the insurance policy. The syntactic structure of the policy, in relevant part, is presented in the following tree diagram. The symbols S, NP, VP, and PP stand for sentence, noun phrase, verb phrase, and prepositional phrase, respectively.

provided . . .

Note that NP_1 is a compound noun phrase consisting of NP_2 and NP_3. In *Anderson,* the insurance company argued in effect that the *provided* clause at the end of the sentence is attached directly to NP_1, and thus modifies the entire noun phrase and thereby both of its conjuncts: NP_2 and NP_3. Recall that NP_2 corresponds to "the named insured" and NP_3 corresponds to "any other person . . . legally responsible for use by the named insured . . . " Mrs. Anderson, who won, argued that the *provided* clause is in effect attached to NP_3, and therefore modifies only the last (in this case second) conjunct. Put somewhat differently, the dispute between the parties was whether, in using the late closure strategy, the processor regards NP_1 or NP_3 as the phrase currently being processed.

In general, grammatical operations do not disrupt a coordinate structure, that is, a structure consisting of elements joined by *and*. They look at the larger phrase, rather than at the conjuncts within the larger construct. John Ross first formalized this principle in his 1967 doctoral dissertation, calling it the "coordinate structure constraint."[7] Compare the grammaticalness of (2) and (3).

(2)   Which testimony and documents did she introduce into evidence?

(3)   Which testimony did she introduce documents and into evidence?

Although no one ever told us as children to avoid asking questions in the form of (3), we know not to do so, because our internalized generative grammars, of the sort discussed in chapter 1, do not even give us the opportunity to consider using such structures. While a speaker may have an entirely legitimate reason for wanting to know the answer to (3), the question cannot be asked in that form because it is not English. For example, one may wish to ask either (2) or (3) in response to someone's having uttered (4).

(4)   Sara introduced a lot of testimony and documents into evidence.

Because of the coordinate structure constraint, however, only (2) is a possible question in English. (3) violates the coordinate structure constraint because it attempts to question only part of the coordinate phrase, "testimony and documents."

Looking again at the last antecedent rule and Mrs. Anderson, we need to determine whether our internal processor's application of the late closure strategy is subject to the coordinate structure constraint. If it is, then our brains consider the "phrase currently being processed" to be the larger phrase, which is the opposite of what the *Anderson* Court decided. Consider (5):

(5)   John saw a woman and a man with a young child.

In (5), my preference is for a reading in which the young child is with both the woman and the man rather than a reading in which the child is only with the man, suggesting the application of something like the coordinate structure constraint.[8] Note that, consistent with late closure, the grammatically possible reading in which John is with the child at the time he saw the other two adults is an unlikely interpretation.

Again, application of the coordinate structure constraint is at odds with the ruling in the *Anderson* case, in which a clause was held, as a matter of law, to modify only the second of two conjuncts. At least for those readers who share my intuitions about the preferred reading of sentences like (5), this account explains our initial intuition that the ruling was strained.

THE ACROSS THE BOARD RULE: MR. JUDGE

The intuitions of some judges match my own. In 1975, a different panel of judges in the same court that decided *Anderson* on the basis of the last antecedent rule decided *Board of Trustees of the Santa Maria Joint Union High School District v. Judge*.[9] In *Judge,* however, the Court applied a legal principle just the opposite of the last antecedent rule. Citing a 1938 case as authority, the court rejected the last antecedent rule in favor of the rule set forth below:

> [W]hen a clause follows several words in a statute and is applicable as much to the first word as to the others in the list, the clause should be applied to all of the words which preceded it.[10]

Let us refer to this legal principle as the "across the board rule." Of course, as we have just seen, the across the board rule is not really an alternative to the last antecedent rule. Rather, it is a particular application of the last antecedent rule to instances in which the last antecedent could be either a compound phrase taken as a whole or the last conjunct of the compound phrase.

In the *Judge* case, Theodor Judge, a school teacher, had been discharged as a result of his felony conviction for cultivating a single marijuana plant at his home. When the school board attempted to fire him, he requested a hearing, and the matter ended up in court. The trial court held that the board could not discharge Mr. Judge. The appellate court agreed, applying the across the board rule to the California statute governing the discharge of teachers. The relevant statutory language is presented below:

> No permanent employee shall be dismissed except for one or more of the following causes: . . . (h) Conviction of a felony or of any crime involving moral turpitude.[11]

The court held that "involving moral turpitude" modifies both disjuncts of subdivision (h). It further held that cultivating a marijuana plant, though a felony, is not a crime of moral turpitude. Mr. Judge kept his job.

In comparing the plights of Mrs. Anderson and Mr. Judge, an interesting linguistic question arises. The application of the last antecedent rule to Mrs. Anderson's insurance policy seemed unnatural. Why is it, then, that the *Judge* court, apparently more sensitive to these linguistic nuances than the *Anderson* court, also rendered an interpretation that seems to strain our understanding of English? That is, why do we sense that "involving moral turpitude" applies only to "any crime" in the phrase "conviction of a felony or of any crime involving moral turpitude?"

The answer to these questions lies in two domains. The first is pragmatic. A felony is a type of crime. That is, an act cannot be a felony without being a crime. Similarly, crimes involving moral turpitude constitute a type of crime, albeit one that lacks the formal definition of a felony. Therefore, when one hears or reads "of a felony or of any crime involving moral turpitude," one's first inclination is to guess that the speaker or writer intended to single out two types of crime: felonies and those crimes (felonies or otherwise) that involve moral turpitude. The alternative interpretation juxtaposes conviction of a felony on the one hand with conviction of a crime on the other. This makes little sense since felonies are necessarily crimes, and felonies involving moral turpitude by definition are crimes involving moral turpitude. As a strategy, the across the board rule, actually only a special case of the last antecedent rule, can be overruled when "the context or evident meaning requires a different construction." Here, the context and evident meaning create just such an environment.

A second factor makes the interpretation of the statute in *Judge* seem unnatural: the second occurrence of the word "of" in the relevant subsection of the statute. This creates an additional layer of structure, as illustrated in the diagram below:

Consider what the phrase "involving moral turpitude" can modify. The choices are PP_1 and NP_2. Construing the phrase as modifying PP_3 is equivalent to construing it as modifying NP_2. The extra structure makes application of the across the board rule more difficult, as (6) illustrates:

(6)   Perry eats lunch in his office or in the park with a friend.

The more likely interpretation of (6) is the one in which the friend joins Perry for lunch only in the park. Had the statute not included the second occurrence of the word "of," there would be only one prepositional phrase with two NP's, and the choice would have been between NP_1 and NP_2, making the structure similar to that of Mrs. Anderson's insurance policy. At least according to my intuitions, the across the board interpretation is more likely when the second "of" is deleted.

The last antecedent and across the board rules have lived side by side in California for decades. In 1978, the Supreme Court of California[12] described the across the board rule as an exception to the last antecedent rule, an analysis that is difficult if not impossible to understand since the court supplied no theory of when to apply the general rule and when to apply the exception. In defining the principles, courts almost always state them as subject to common sense, limiting their application to ambiguous constructions in which the context does not demand that the principle be abandoned. Many additional cases exist in which one or the other of these principles is presented as argumentation for a particular outcome, sometimes as the basis for interpreting criminal statutes. It is frequently referred to as a rule of grammar, and is never regarded as an arbitrary legal convention, like the colors of traffic signals. Most often it is listed as one of a number of principles of statutory interpretation.

DRUGS AND THE LAST ANTECEDENT RULE

The last antecedent rule is not limited to instances in which there are compound phrases. In *People v. Hardin,*[13] the court upheld a narcotics conviction based in part on the application of the last antecedent rule to the following statutory provision:

> [E]very person who . . . sells any controlled substance which is
> . . . specified in subdivision (d), of Section 11055, unless upon
> the prescription of a physician [etc.] . . . shall be punished.
>
> . . . .
>
>   (d) Any material, compound, mixture, or preparation which
>   contains any quantity of the following substances *having a po-*

tential for abuse associated with a stimulant effect on the central nervous system [emphasis added]:

 (1) Amphetamine . . .
 (2) . . . .
 (3) . . . methamphetamine[14]

Hardin had been convicted for selling a quantity of methamphetamine sufficiently small that it is not clear that the amount he sold had in and of itself a potential for abuse. The court's description of the facts implies that Mr. Hardin was planning to "rip off" the purchaser of the drugs (a government agent, unbeknownst to Hardin), by selling an envelope containing a non-narcotic powder. However, chemical analysis revealed small traces of methamphetamine in the envelope. His attorneys argued to the court that the emphasized portion of the statute modifies the entire quantifier phrase "any quantity of the following substances," while the government argued that the underlined portion modifies only the noun phrase "the following substances." The court, applying the last antecedent rule, opted for the shorter noun phrase. Of course, since the statute that Mr. Hardin was convicted of violating does not contain conjoined noun phrases, Mr. Hardin was not afforded the possibility of the across the board rule instead of the last antecedent rule. Thanks to the last antecedent rule, Mr. Hardin's conviction for selling methamphetamine was affirmed.

LAST ANTECEDENTS AND LEGAL CANONS

The last antecedent rule is one of a large set of interpretive principles generally called the "canons of construction" in the legal literature. Other examples are: a more specific statute will be given precedence over the more general one; the expression of one thing signifies the exclusion of others (often stated in Latin: *expressio unius est exclusio alterius*); general terms in a list take their meaning from specific ones (*ejusdem generis*); when the language is plain, the plain meaning shall govern; and many others. The canons are generally discussed in connection with the interpretation of statutes.

For at least the past forty years, these canons have been in disrepute among legal scholars, particularly since Karl Llewellyn's work showing how they most frequently have their opposite counterparts, in much the same way that the last antecedent rule and across the board rules coexist.[15] As Llewellyn shows, the canons have no predictive power, in that one or another maxim can be drawn from the lot to support any result. Despite this critical literature, judges continue to use these maxims as justification for their decisions, and there is no reason to believe that they will stop doing so any time soon.

Recently, however, legal theorists have been rethinking the role of these maxims. For example, in an interesting paper, Geoffrey Miller[16] has related the canons to the pragmatic rules of conversation proposed by the philosopher Paul Grice.[17] The maxim *ejusdem generis,* for example, relates to a Gricean conversational convention that tells us to interpret utterances that we hear as not providing more information than is called for.

If Miller is correct, then the canons are more or less a set of strategies for attempting to pull the most appropriate meaning out of a text when more than one interpretation is possible. Since, in both the conversational and legal worlds, the notion "most appropriate" tells us very little about how to interpret what we hear in all kinds of novel situations, we should expect to find numerous and sometimes conflicting strategies developing, which is exactly what we do find. Warren Lehman has called the canons "rough-and-ready empirical statements, which, however, can be properly used only by those of practical wisdom."[18] Judge Posner likens them to proverbs such as "haste makes waste," and comments that "they no more enable difficult questions of interpretation to be answered than the maxims of everyday life enable the difficult problems of everyday living to be solved."[19]

This perspective on the canons of interpretation is consistent with my presentation of cases employing the last antecedent rule, in that the last antecedent rule more accurately reflects an interpretive strategy than a rule of grammar. The problem with the cases that I have discussed, then, is not the last antecedent rule itself. Rather, it is the courts' presentation of the last antecedent rule as a hard and fast rule of law, instead of as a preliminary strategy for helping a judge to interpret a statute (or insurance policy) appropriately in the context of the dispute that he must resolve. The same holds true for the other canons, although with respect to many of them, as Miller points out, the preliminary strategies involve pragmatics rather than aspects of sentence processing.

Empty Words: The Interpretation of Pronouns

Pronouns are semantically degenerate. That is, while they contain some information, they do not contain enough on their own to name the individual to which they are intended to refer. Thus, pronouns are a natural source of uncertainty in interpretation. In chapter 5, I will show some ways in which legal writers attempt to avoid using pronouns in order to create the impression (which is actually false) that they have eliminated the ambiguity inherent in the use of natural language. Here, I will limit myself to instances in which the interpretation of pronouns forms the basis for a judicial decision, and what judges say about the linguistics of pronominal interpretation. Before doing so, however, a brief introduction to the linguistic issues surrounding the interpretation of pronouns is necessary.

Three distinct types of information contribute to our understanding a pronoun when we hear one: the syntactic structure in which the pronoun occurs; the case, number, and gender of the particular pronoun used; and the context in which the pronoun is used. For reasons that will be made clear in chapter 5, legal writers have concerned themselves with the second and third of these, but not with the first. In fact, information about the syntactic structure in which the pronoun occurs constitutes tacit knowledge shared by all native speakers of English and is not necessarily part of conscious knowledge at all, an observation to which we will return. Here, let us focus on the second type of information: information specific to the particular pronominal form being used. The linguistic issue arises when a decision must be made as to the rights or obligations of a particular individual based on the interpretation of a legal document. The document contains a pronoun, and our ability to construe the pronoun as referring to the person or entity whose rights are in dispute turns out to be the subject of the judicial decision.

As illustrated in (7), pronouns agree in number and gender with their antecedents.

(7)   Perry told Della that he should be relying on Paul Drake.
                                    she

In (7), when the pronoun is *he*, it can refer either to *Perry* or to a male not mentioned at all in the sentence. When, on the other hand, the pronoun is *she*, it can refer to *Della* or to some unnamed female. In either case, any unmentioned referent must agree in number and gender with the pronoun. Below are presented four examples of cases in which the gender of the pronoun was an important issue in the resolution of legal disputes by federal courts of appeals. The first case involves a reversal of a criminal conviction for acquiring a controlled substance (Demerol) by fraud. The others are all cases involving taxation—a criminal prosecution and two disputes about the tax liability of trusts, in which the notion of personhood plays a crucial role.

MR. BASS

In *United States v. Bass*,[20] a 1974 case, the United States Court of Appeals for the Fifth Circuit reversed a conviction for five counts of acquiring a controlled substance by misrepresentation, fraud, forgery, deception, or subterfuge, in contravention of federal law. Bruce L. Bass had been suffering from an intestinal disorder, regional or terminal enteritis, an extremely painful disease. Having been hospitalized and treated with the painkiller Demerol, Mr. Bass became involuntarily addicted to that drug. He was accused of having forged prescriptions for Demerol, of having altered the number of refills available on otherwise legitimate prescriptions, and of having obtained the drug by subterfuge, seeing two doctors within a day but failing to tell the second doctor that he had already received a prescription for the painkiller from the first doctor. At his trial, Mr. Bass pleaded temporary insanity, calling to the witness stand doctors who testified that "on or about the dates charged in the indictment, Bass had been subject to severe attacks, and that during such attacks he suffered extremely high temperatures, lapsed into delirium and unconsciousness, exhibited substantial anxiety, and on one occasion discussed suicide."[21] One of the doctors testified that Mr. Bass had suffered temporary brain damage as a result of the high temperatures. Mr. Bass was convicted and sentenced to eight years in prison.

While federal law requires that a defendant raise the issue of his or her insanity, once this issue is presented, the burden in a criminal case shifts to the government to prove beyond a reasonable doubt that the defendant was sane at the time that the crime was committed. (Compare this to the California rule discussed in the next section in connection with *People v. Skinner*.) The government called one expert witness on this matter who acknowledged that Mr. Bass's doctors were in a better position to judge his sanity. Nonetheless, Mr. Bass was convicted on all counts. The instruction that the judge gave to the jury is, in part, as follows:

> Of course, the Government has the burden of proof, or proving, or proving the guilt of the defendant beyond a reasonable doubt, and in a case of this kind, where the, where the Defendant raises the issue of insanity, then the question of insanity is also the burden, the burden is on the Government as to the insanity of the Defendant. And that must be established beyond a reasonable doubt, and in other words, if you have a reasonable doubt as to the insanity, then, of course, you would find for the Defendant. But it is, it is your decision to make, but the burden

of establishing both the sanity and the, and the acts alleged is on
the Government, and they must establish *it* beyond a reasonable
doubt.[22] (Emphasis added)

The appellate court found this instruction sufficiently confusing to reverse Mr. Bass's conviction. First, the court held, while it is the government's
burden to prove the defendant's sanity, the instruction speaks of insanity as
something that the government must establish, an error that may well have
caused confusion in the minds of at least some of the jurors. Second, the
court focused on the use of the word *it* at the end of the instruction, emphasized above. Because *it* is a singular pronoun, the court reasoned, a juror
may well have chosen as the antecedent for *it* the second of the two conjuncts, "the acts alleged." A juror who did this would of necessity miss the
fact that the government must establish beyond a reasonable doubt the sanity of the defendant as well as the acts alleged. This possible confusion in
pronominal reference formed part of the basis for the court's reversal of the
conviction.

I doubt that any jury would be confused by the error in number agreement committed by the judge issuing the instruction. Moreover, it is clear
from the opinion that even without the pronominal issue the court would
have reversed Mr. Bass's conviction. But the court was able to establish a
textual justification for its holding in this case, and took advantage of that
opportunity.

PRONOUNS AND TAXATION

Corporations are sometimes referred to as "legal persons" under the
law in that corporations frequently have the same rights and obligations as
real people.[23] On occasion, however, it makes a difference whether a document or statement was intended to refer to people or to purely legal entities,
such as corporations or banks. Below is a discussion of three cases in which
this issue has arisen and has been decided based on pronominal gender and
number. The first involves a criminal prosecution for tax evasion, and the
other two the taxability of certain trusts under federal law.

In *United States v. Sourapas,*[24] decided in 1975 by the United States Court
of Appeals for the Ninth Circuit, the court considered the interpretation of
pronouns used in an Internal Revenue Service press release. The proper assignment of antecedents to the pronouns was the determinative issue in the
case. The dispute involved a regulation promulgated through the release
which required the IRS to advise taxpayers under investigation of their constitutional rights. A portion of the release is printed below:

One function of a Special Agent is to investigate possible criminal violations of Internal Revenue laws. At the initial meeting
with a taxpayer, a Special Agent is now required to identify himself, describe his function, and advise the taxpayer that anything
he says may be used against *him*. The Special Agent will also tell
the taxpayer that *he* cannot be compelled to incriminate *himself*
by answering any questions or producing any documents, and
that *he* has the right to seek the assistance of an attorney before
responding.[25] (Emphasis added)

As a matter of law, both people and corporations are subject to income
taxation, but only people are protected by the provision of the Fifth Amendment of the Constitution that prohibits government from compelling self-
incriminating testimony. Consequently, when government is investigating
both a corporation and an individual for criminal wrongdoing, the individual can refuse to cooperate, even if a subpoena is issued. A corporation lacks
this right, and the custodian of a corporation's records must turn over documents to a government official who properly subpoenas them even if these
documents incriminate the corporation or an individual associated with it.
In *Sourapas,* the government was investigating both Mr. Sourapas and his
corporation, Crest Beverage Company, for tax evasion. As part of that investigation, the government obtained various records, but did not follow the
procedures outlined in the release quoted above. The result of the investigation was an indictment, naming both Mr. Sourapas and the corporation.
The two defendants moved to suppress as illegally seized the documents
that the government had obtained. The United States District Court
granted this motion, and the government appealed.

On appeal, the court held that the corporate documents that had been
seized were within the protection of neither the Constitution nor the IRS
press release. Relying crucially on the release's use of the personal pronouns
he, him, and *himself,* the court reasoned that the regulation was not intended
to apply to corporations, and that the corporate taxpayer's rights had not
been violated when corporate records were taken without the requisite
warning. Had the release used the word *it,* the result presumably would
have been different. At least for purposes of prosecuting the corporation,
the government was free to use the documents at trial.

Two interesting cases with opposite results illustrate that courts are not always so concerned with the application of the agreement rules. In affirming
the lower court's holding in favor of the government, the United States

Court of Appeals for the Third Circuit was not impressed in *Mathey v. United States*,[26] with the appellant's argument based on number agreement.

Before her death in 1965, Mrs. Mathey had established a series of trusts for the benefit of her grandchildren. At the time she died, the trusts contained assets of over $800,000. The trust instruments permitted Mrs. Mathey to change the trustee at any time, an option that she did not exercise. Until her death, a bank served as trustee. Under the Internal Revenue Code then in effect, the assets of a trust were subject to estate tax if the individual who contributed the funds to the trust (the grantor) reserved for himself or herself in the trust instrument the right to "alter, amend, revoke or terminate" the trust.[27] This has been interpreted to mean that trust assets are taxable as part of a decedent's estate when the trust instrument reserves for the grantor (later to be the decedent) the right to name himself or herself as successor trustee. The issue before the court was whether Mrs. Mathey had reserved for herself the power to remove the bank as trustee and substitute herself as trustee, whether or not she actually exercised this power. A portion of the trust instrument is presented below:

> Upon *its* removal as above provided, any Corporate Trustee, shall be entitled to reimbursement from the trusts hereunder for all loans and advances, if any, theretofore made by *it* and all expenses, including expenses incurred by *it* in connection with the settlement of *its* accounts as Trustee. Likewise in the case of the change or removal of any corporate Trustee, *it* shall be entitled to all fees to which *it* would be entitled if the trust were fully administered or if the trusts for which *it* is Trustee were then to terminate.[28] (Emphasis added)

Mrs. Mathey's estate lost. Its argument that the use of the word "it" in the trust instrument signified Mrs. Mathey's intention that only corporations act as trustee fell on deaf ears. As pointed out by the government's expert witness (it is not clear what expertise this expert had), the word "it" in the trust instrument is associated not with the new, successor trustee, but with the old trustee. Thus, one cannot conclude from the presence of the word "it" that Mrs. Mathey intended that only corporations serve as successor trustee. The court of appeals summarized:

> The district court found that use of the neuter pronoun did not signify an intent on Mrs. Mathey's part to allow a corporation only to be named as a successor trustee, and that therefore an individual could be substituted for the original trustee. We can-

not say that the district court's finding as to the meaning of the word "it" in the trust agreements was clearly erroneous.[29]

Citing *Mathey,* a federal court of appeals more recently decided a case in which the issue also was the interpretation of "it." In *First National Bank of Denver v. United States,*[30] the court of appeals specifically rejected the linguistic arguments accepted by the trial court:

> The district court relied in part on the fact that the trustee was consistently referred to in the trust instrument by means of the neuter pronoun "it", thus implying that the trustee must be a corporation rather than a natural person.[31]

The district court had distinguished this case from *Mathey,* claiming that in the earlier case the pronoun in the trust instrument could be construed as referring only to the present trustee, while in this case *it* is used to refer both to the current trustee and to any potential future trustee. The trust agreement in *First National Bank* is excerpted below:

> The Trustee may, at its election, resign, and the Grantor may at any time during her lifetime change the Trustee and, after her death either the Grantor's brother, John W. Morey, or her son, Barry Morey Sullivan, may at any time during their lifetimes change the Trustee. Should the Trustee or any successor as trustee merge or consolidate with any other corporation, then the corporation with which the Trustee has merged or consolidated shall act in its place and stead. Should the Trustee resign and elect to appoint a successor, then such other bank or trust company in the City and County of Denver having a capital and surplus of at least $1,000,000 as the retiring Trustee nominates shall act in its place and stead.[32]

In my own reading of the excerpts from the trust instruments provided in the opinions, I find no such distinction. Unimpressed with the entire argument based on possible antecedents for the pronoun, the appellate court affirmed the lower court's judgment in favor of the taxpayer based on other considerations.

As these examples illustrate, courts are not consistent in taking linguistic argumentation seriously. This suggests that judges have some misgivings about relying on the language of documents being construed. Courts sometimes use the rules of number and gender agreement as evidence even where this probably is not warranted, and refuse to take advantage of rules governing pronominal reference at times when the evidence is clearly available. Considering these facts in the context of the other examples discussed in this chapter, it appears that this is actually a special case of a more general phenomenon: the selective use of interpretive principles to bolster the appearance that the judge had little or no choice in the matter.

The *And/Or* Rule

Let us now look at a third linguistic-legal phenomenon: the set of rules governing the interpretation of *and* and *or*. This time, we will focus our attention primarily on federal and state courts of New York, although I will also discuss a California case of particular interest.

The difficulty in interpreting *and* and *or* is so well recognized in the law that a special hand-waving canon of construction exists in both federal law and the law of many states, neutralizing the difference between the two terms. Below is New York's version:

> Generally, the words "or" and "and" in a statute may be construed as interchangeable when necessary to effectuate legislative intent.[33]

The commentator on the statute explains the rationale for the rule as follows:

> A common mistake made by the drafters of statutes is the use of the word "and" when "or" is intended or vice versa. The popular use of "or" and "and" is notoriously loose and inaccurate, and this use is reflected in the wording of statutes. When it is apparent that the Legislature has erroneously used the wrong word, the courts will make the necessary change in the statute in order that it shall conform to the legislative intent.[34]

The authors of treatises[35] and the judges of many courts recognize similar principles.

Despite the presence of this principle (let us call it the "and/or rule"), when it comes to the interpretation of legal documents, *and* generally means *and* and *or* generally is construed disjunctively, as meaning "either/or." While a substantial enough case literature applying the and/or rule exists, the frequency of the application of the principle is minuscule compared to the number of times that statutes and other legal documents use conjunction and disjunction. Therefore, it makes sense to ask whether courts limit the rule's application to particular circumstances or whether judges apply the rule randomly for idiosyncratic purposes.

Interestingly, as the examples discussed below illustrate, there really does appear to be confusion in the use of *and* and *or*. As far as I can tell, the and/or rule is generally applied in three sets of circumstances, two of which are linguistic. First, when the connector (*and* or *or*) is within the scope of some logical operator, such as a negative, some difficulty in interpreting the connector's meaning may occur because of problems in sorting out the scope of the various terms. Second, the word *or* presents some problems. While logicians use the word to mean "and/or," in natural language it frequently is used to mean one but not both of two items. Finally, some cases seem to involve no linguistic problem at all. It is the presence of this final group of cases that renders the application of the and/or rule incoherent from any doctrinal point of view.

Problems of Scope—*And* Means *Or*

New York has a statute that protects people from false advertising by permitting them to sue a business that falsely advertises a product. Generally, damages are the difference between the purchase price and the advertised price of a product or service. The court has the discretion to assess treble damages against a false advertiser. The statute reads in relevant part as follows:

> Any person who has been injured by reason of any violation of [the section that proscribes false advertising] . . . may bring an action in his own name to enjoin such unlawful act or practice *and* to recover his actual damages or fifty dollars, whichever is greater. The court may, in its discretion, increase the award of damages to an amount not to exceed three times the actual damages up to one thousand dollars, if the court finds the defendant willfully or knowingly violated this section. The court may award reasonable attorney's fees to a prevailing plaintiff.[36] (Emphasis added)

In *Beslity v. Manhattan Honda*,[37] a consumer, the victim of false advertising, sued for the difference between the price he paid for his Honda and what he alleged was the advertised price. While the dealer argued that the advertisement applied to a model other than the one that Mr. Beslity purchased, Mr. Beslity was able to convince the court that the features in the advertised car were contained only in the model that he wished to purchase.

Nonetheless, Mr. Beslity lost. The trial court held that the statute quoted above requires that an aggrieved person sue both to enjoin the unlawful act and for damages. Since the advertisement was no longer being printed, and since Mr. Beslity had already purchased his car, he had no reason to sue for an injunction. His failure to do so, the court reasoned, resulted in his inability to take advantage of the statute.

Applying the and/or rule, the appellate court reversed. The court held that the intent of the legislature in enacting the statute was to allow consumers to elect their remedy. It was not to allow lawsuits only in those instances in which the consumer had elected both remedies.[38] The appellate court awarded Mr. Beslity fifty dollars in damages.

For ease of discussion, let us abbreviate the relevant statutory language as follows:

> Any person who has been injured may bring an action to enjoin
> and to recover damages.

The key words are *to* and *may*. Ordinarily, when *may* is applied to a group of conjuncts, its meaning is distributed over the list of conjuncts.[39] Consider (8):

(8)   You may take depositions and request documents.

To me, (8) grants permission to engage in two activities: taking depositions and requesting documents. It does not require that both activities occur. That is, a judge uttering (8) would not regard a lawyer's requesting documents but failing to take depositions as a violation of a judicial directive. We can capture this fact as follows:

(9)   may(x and y) = may x and may y

Section 350-d(3) of the General Business Law contains an occurrence of the word *may* that does not obey principle (9). Permission is not distributed among the conjuncts. The problem appears to be that the statute permits only a single activity—bringing an action. That action, it is later explained, may be for two purposes—an injunction or damages. The relationship among these elements of the statute is illustrated by (10).

(10) may (bring an action (to enjoin and to recover damages))

May cannot be distributed between the conjuncts. Note, however, that the form of (10) differs from that of (9) in that *may* does not modify conjoined verbs directly. Rather, it modifies a single verb which itself has a complement containing a clause with conjoined verb phrases. Thus, we should not expect (9) to apply, and it does not. Consequently, the words of the statute actually do mean that only an action that requests both an injunction and damages is permitted. Changing "and" to "or" would permit an action to be brought for either purpose, without being brought for both purposes. Because the rules of construal are difficult to apply here, the application of the and/or rule makes sense in this case. It may well be that the statute contains a drafting error resulting from difficulty with the scope of *may.*

A similar application of the and/or rule led to an acquittal for reason of insanity in a California case, *People v. Skinner,*[40] a case decided by the Supreme Court of California. In response to what had been perceived as a judicial loosening of the requirements for pleading insanity, the California voters adopted into law in 1982 a change in the criminal law known as Proposition 8, which essentially reinstated into California law the traditional requirements for proving insanity. It is stated below:

> In any criminal proceeding, including any juvenile court proceeding, in which a plea of not guilty by reason of insanity is entered, this defense shall be found by the trier of fact only when the accused person proves by a preponderance of the evidence that he or she was *incapable* of knowing or understanding the nature and quality of his or her act *and* of distinguishing right from wrong at the time of the commission of the offense.[41] (Emphasis added)

Mr. Skinner admitted to having strangled his wife while he was home on a day pass from a mental hospital where he was being treated for paranoic schizophrenia. The trial court found that he was unable to distinguish right from wrong but that he was not incapable of knowing or understanding the nature of his act. The insanity defense was rejected, and Mr. Skinner was convicted of second degree murder.

On appeal, Mr. Skinner's attorneys argued that the emphasized "and" in the statute should be read "or," and that based on this adjustment, Mr. Skinner should be acquitted. The court agreed, holding that to do otherwise would make it far more difficult to prove insanity than under the traditional requirements. (Note, incidentally, that the burden of proving insanity under Proposition 8 is on the defendant, which differs from the federal rule discussed in the last section in the context of *United States v. Bass.*) Since the history of Proposition 8 indicates that it was not intended to contract the insanity defense to such a degree, and since substitution of "or" would make Proposition 8 consistent with the traditional insanity defense, application of the and/or rule was considered appropriate.

Historically, as pointed out by a California court in *People v. Horn*,[42], California courts regularly used *and* and *or* interchangeably in restating the traditional rule. As the court in *Horn* suggests, part of the difficulty may lie in the relationship between conjunction and negation. Consider the following rule of logic, which is also relevant to the capital punishment case discussed later on (*California v. Brown*):

(11) a. not (a and b) = not a or not b
      b. not (a or b) = not a and not b

Together, these principles are known as "De Morgan's Rules," or "De Morgan's Law."[43]

The California jury instruction pertaining to the insanity defense applied De Morgan's Rule accurately. A person is to be found sane if he is capable of knowing *and* understanding the nature of his acts *and* can distinguish right from wrong. He is to be found insane if he is not capable of knowing *or* understanding the nature of his acts *or* if he is incapable of distinguishing right from wrong. Like the relationship between conjunction and the scope of *may*, the relationship between conjunction and negation is a potential source of confusion. Thus the and/or rule.[44]

RECENTLY, the and/or rule and De Morgan's Law have made their way to the forefront of a debate about the scope of one of the most powerful and aggressive crime-fighting weapons in the federal government's statutory arsenal: forfeiture of property used to perpetrate certain drug-related crimes.[45]

The forfeiture provisions of the Comprehensive Crime Control Act of 1984 permit the United States government to seize property that the government can prove is being used to commit crimes related to narcotics sales. It is used more and more by government agencies to justify the seizure of houses, boats, and cars that are the locations of drug trade. To seize the property the government brings a lawsuit against the property itself, alleging that it is being used for criminal drug activity. The owner of the property must be notified, and can raise as a defense lack of knowledge of or consent in the crimes. The statute reads as follows:

§881. Forfeitures

(a) Property subject
The following shall be subject to forfeiture to the United States and no property right shall exist in them: . . .

(7) All real property, including any right, title, and interest (including any leasehold interest) in the whole of any lot or tract of land and any appurtenances or improvements, which is used, or intended to be used, in any manner or part, to commit, or to facilitate the commission of, a violation of this title punishable by more than one year's imprisonment, except that no property shall be forfeited under this paragraph, to the extent of an interest of an owner, by reason of any act or omission established by that owner to have been committed or omitted *without the knowledge or consent of that owner.*[46] (Emphasis added)

At issue in recent court cases is the proper interpretation of the phrase, "without the knowledge or consent of that owner." The situation arises when the owner of property that the government wishes to seize (and keep) claims that he knew that crimes were being committed there, but that he did not consent to them. Under these circumstances, two federal judges in New York had come to opposite conclusions.

In *United States v. Certain Real Property and Premises Known as 171–02 Liberty Avenue ("172–02 Liberty Avenue")*,[47] the government attempted to seize a building that was well known as a place where drug deals were made. In fact, drug dealers using the building had erected special fences on the second floor to make police raids more difficult.

The building was owned by Redino Greco, and was essentially abandoned, although Mr. Greco was in the process of repairing it for resale. The police were in close touch with Mr. Greco, who cooperated with them by allowing the police to tear down the fences, by pressing charges against trespassers, and in other ways. The police, however, became dissatisfied with the level of Mr. Greco's cooperation after his failure to help implement a system for distinguishing between legitimate construction contractors and individuals reconstructing the fences to keep out the police. Eventually, the federal government brought a forfeiture action to seize the house.

Mr. Greco argued that while he obviously had knowledge that his property was being used for illegal activities (after all, he had been cooperating with the police), he did not consent to the drug trafficking that was taking place in his building. Thus, the crimes were "without the knowledge *or* consent of the owner."

The court agreed:

> [T]he court interprets the statute as creating an affirmative defense where the illegal acts giving rise to the forfeiture occurred without the knowledge *or without the consent* of the owner. If Congress had meant to require a showing of lack of knowledge in all cases, as suggested by the Government, it could have done so by replacing "or" with "and."[48]

While I agree with this result in *172–02 Liberty Avenue* for reasons discussed below, the matter is not as simple as all that. The word *without* certainly has a negative connotation. If *without* triggers De Morgan's Rules (principle (11)), then "without knowledge or consent" is properly interpreted as "without knowledge and without consent." But it is beyond dispute that Greco did have knowledge. Under the statutory language, should the government have won?

This alternative interpretation was adopted in 1990 by a different judge from the same federal court in *United States v. Certain Real Property and Premises Known as 890 Noyac Road* ("*890 Noyac Road*").[49] Recognizing a tension between a legal principle that says that "or" is ordinarily read disjunctively as "either/or," and De Morgan's Rules, which say that within the scope of negation "or" is read as "and," the court rejected the use of any interpretive principles, holding instead that a disjunctive reading of "or" would lead to an absurd result. Thus, the court read the statute to require that the owner neither know nor consent, and thereby validated the seizure of property.

But there is nothing absurd about a rule that an owner without knowledge, or with knowledge but without consent, be immune from having his property seized by the government. To the contrary, the government may wish to commend those who know that their property is being abused and who do something about it. Apparently, it did just that for Mr. Greco at an earlier stage in the investigation.

The court in *890 Noyac Road* likened the disjunctive interpretation of "knowledge or consent" to a purely disjunctive reading of an insurance policy provision requiring the insurer to pay benefits for "loss of life, limb, sight or time." Such a reading would lead to an absurd result if the insurer could disclaim coverage because an insured lost both limb and sight, but not life or time. But this argues only for an "and/or" interpretation of the insurance policy, which is just what the court rejected in *890 Noyac Road*.

Thus we are again left with competing and linguistically inadequate analyses of the same construction. In fact, this construction is a difficult one. As (12) shows, De Morgan's Law does seem to apply to it:

(12) She drove the car without the knowledge *or* consent of the
      owner. The owner knew but did not consent.

(12) sounds odd since we most naturally interpret "without knowledge or consent" as "without knowledge and without consent." To the extent that we are able to make sense of (12) at all it is because we attempt to interpret "knowledge or consent" as a single semantic unit, meaning something like "knowing consent." In fact, we have no way of telling whether the drafters of the statute intended that De Morgan's Rules apply or not, and whether they intended that "knowledge or consent" be treated as a single concept. Because of all this confusion, the forfeiture statute seems to be a perfect candidate for application of the "and/or" rule.

Moreover, like the California statute discussed earlier that distinguished between felonies on the one hand and crimes on the other,[50] the forfeiture statute deals with two classes that are not exclusive of each other. In order to consent to an activity, one must have knowledge of it. For this reason, a court requiring that an owner neither know nor consent, such as the *890 Noyac Road* court, essentially renders the consent requirement in the statute as meaningless, since proof that the owner knows makes it unnecessary to reach the issue of consent. But a court requiring that an owner either not know or not consent, such as the *171–02 Liberty Avenue* court, essentially renders superfluous the knowledge requirement in the statute, since proof of a lack of consent will always suffice to defeat forfeiture. This problem adds to the difficulty of interpreting the statute.

It strikes me as extraordinarily harsh for a court to construe a complex and confusing statute as permitting the government to seize the property of an owner who objects to the misuse of his property. Despite the seeming inadequacy of the linguistic analysis, this is no doubt what motivated the court in Mr. Greco's case. The opposite result would permit the government to take the property of even the most vehement opponent of drug use simply because he found out that his property was being abused, even if he did everything he could to stop it.

The United States Court of Appeals for the Second Circuit has since resolved the issue, in *United States v. 141st Street Corp.*[51] In that case, the owner again claimed that he was aware of drug activity on his property, but did not consent to it. Concluding that "[t]he plain language of section 881(a)(7) is, at best, confusing,"[52] the court took two steps. First, it adopted the position of the District Court in *171–02 Liberty Avenue* that an innocent owner must prove either that he did not know or that he did not consent. The court reasoned: "Requiring a claimant to disprove both knowledge and consent ignores Congress' desire to preserve the property of innocent owners and, as indicated, renders the phrase 'or consent' superfluous, a result that should be avoided."[53] Second, the court defined "consent" as "the failure to take all reasonable steps to prevent illicit use of the premises once one acquires knowledge of that use."[54]

This result does reasonable justice to the purpose of the statute and to our everyday sense of fairness, but pays little attention to the statutory language as written. Of course, that is exactly what the and/or rule tells courts to do to avoid injustice or anomoly.

SUPPORT OF DELINQUENT CHILDREN—THE PROBLEM WITH *And/Or*

After Joseph Siebel was committed to a school for delinquent children in 1957, the Department of Welfare of the City of New York attempted to coerce both the child's father and his stepmother to contribute to the child's support. The child's father was ordered to contribute something, but not enough to support him. The stepmother, Margaret J. Siebel, was also ordered to contribute (twenty dollars per month) following a hearing concerned with her ability to support the child. Mrs. Siebel appealed and won. The Department of Welfare then appealed to the Court of Appeals, New York's highest court, and won a reversal of the earlier appeal, accomplishing a reinstatement of the original order that Mrs. Siebel contribute twenty dollars per month, in *Department of Welfare of City of New York v. Siebel*.[55]

At issue was the interpretation of the statute that requires certain relatives to contribute to the support of children. The statute is presented below in relevant part:

> 2. If in the opinion of the department of welfare such parent or legal custodian is able to contribute in whole or in part the commissioner of welfare shall thereupon institute a proceeding . . . to compel such parent *or* other person legally chargeable to contribute such portion of such expense on account of the maintenance of such child as shall be proper and just . . .[56] (Emphasis added)

Other provisions in the law make it clear that stepparents at times bear legal responsibility for the support of their stepchildren. The issue here was the interpretation of *or*. If *or* in the statute is interpreted to mean either one or the other but not both, then the fact that the Department had already compelled the father to contribute would be sufficient to let Mrs. Siebel off the hook. If, on the other hand, *or* is construed to mean either one or the other or both, then Mrs. Siebel must pay. The court took the second of these two options, and compelled Mrs. Siebel's payments. Interestingly, the court did this using the and/or rule.

At the beginning of this section I mentioned that logicians interpret *or* to mean and/or while in common usage *or* generally is thought to mean either, but not both. In essence, the court in *Siebel* held that *or* is to be construed as *and* whenever possible, and as *or* otherwise, an interpretation somewhat different from both the logical and everyday meanings of *or*. That is, there need not be more than one person responsible for support, but when there is, both must pay.

Other applications of the and/or rule actually transform *or* into *and*. These cases hold that only if the conditions set by both of two conjuncts are met has an individual actually violated the law or met his or her obligations under the law. Consider the case of Mr. Caine.

MR. CAINE—*Or* Means *And*

In *People v. Caine*,[57] Mr. Paul Caine was arrested on charges of harassment, a crime in New York that is defined as follows:

> A person is guilty of harassment when, with intent to harass, annoy or alarm another person . . .
> (5) He engages in a course of conduct *or* repeatedly commits acts which alarm or seriously annoy such other person and which serve no legitimate purpose.[58] (Emphasis added)

The facts of the case, as described by the court, are presented below:

> On February 20, 1972 the complaining police officer stopped the defendant for a traffic infraction and while writing the tickets the defendant approached and argued with the officer. He was advised by the officer to go back to his car but returned again. At this time the defendant stated that the officer could shove the summons up his F—— a——. In response to the officer's questioning "what did you say?" the invective was repeated. At this point the officer alighted from his car and again directed the de-

fendant to return to his vehicle. Again the defendant is alleged to
have stated, "Go f—— yourself" and in response to the officer's
inquiry repeated the words.[59]

The issue in *Caine* was whether the defendant's behavior violated the statute. The court held that it did not, making crucial use of the and/or rule.

The statute requires that the defendant engage in a course of conduct or
repeatedly commit certain acts. Apparently concerned that the obscenities
uttered by Mr. Caine sufficed to establish a course of conduct, the court applied the and/or rule, holding that both a course of conduct and the repeti-
tion of these acts be proven before an individual can be convicted of
harassment.[60]

The court also found that Mr. Caine did not act with the requisite intent.
He did not have the intent to harass, annoy, or alarm another person, but
only demonstrated an "immature outburst." Considering this finding, in itself sufficient to warrant Mr. Caine's acquittal, we may ask why the and/or
rule played any role at all in the decision of this case. The answer to this
question, it seems to me, is related to the answer to the question why the last
antecedent and across the board rules exist side by side. At times, judges find
it necessary to adduce "scientific" principles to justify their decisions, especially in the light of statutory language that would seem to dictate a contrary
result. As a consequence, they sometimes turn to linguistic principles to explain the outcome of the cases that they are asked to decide. The and/or rule,
like the last antecedent rule and rules governing the interpretation of pronouns, as the few examples discussed here demonstrate, has its basis in some
very real linguistic phenomena. But its application is very difficult to explain
in terms independent of the results achieved.

Adjectives and the Linguistics of Capital Punishment

At the beginning of this chapter, I pointed out that linguistic issues often
appear in judicial opinions under circumstances in which the facts of the situation are not in dispute but the application of the law to those facts is a
matter of controversy. This point was only recently instantiated by the
United States Supreme Court in *California v. Brown*,[61] in which the Court
reinstated the death sentence of an individual convicted of murder, reversing the decision of the Supreme Court of California. At issue in *Brown* was
the validity of Brown's death sentence under the Eighth Amendment to the
Constitution, which prohibits cruel and unusual punishment. California,
whose courts had sentenced Brown to death, has a death penalty which has

been held constitutional. However, the judge's instructions to the jury, it was argued, were improper, rendering the death penalty unconstitutional as applied in this case.

Brown had been convicted by a California jury of the forcible rape and first degree murder of a fifteen-year-old girl. Under California law, consistent with the guidelines set forth by the United States Supreme Court for what constitutes a constitutionally valid death penalty statute, a second trial is held after the conviction to determine whether the death penalty is to be imposed. At the end of this second trial, the judge instructed the jury on how to apply the law to the facts that had been presented. As part of this charge, the jurors were told that they

> must not be swayed by mere sentiment, conjecture, sympathy, passion, prejudice, public opinion or public feeling.[62]

Relying on various opinions of the United States Supreme Court, the Supreme Court of California, hearing the case on appeal, disallowed the death sentence, holding that "federal constitutional law forbids an instruction which denies a capital defendant the right to have the jury consider any 'sympathy factor' raised by the evidence when determining the appropriate penalty."[63] In a 5–4 decision, the United States Supreme Court reversed again. Interestingly, all nine justices accepted the legal analysis proffered by the California court. The disagreement was a linguistic one: whether the jury instruction did adequately inform the jurors of their legal duty to consider in mitigation evidence of Mr. Brown's character and background.

Writing on behalf of four justices, Chief Justice Rehnquist, in the Court's majority opinion, held that the instruction is entirely consistent with the requirements of the Constitution. First, the Court focused on the fact that *sympathy* is part of a longer list of items that the jury was instructed not to be swayed by. Because the law clearly prohibits jurors from considering the other members of the list, the Court reasoned: "Reading the instruction as a whole, as we must, it is no more than a catalog of the kind of factors that could improperly influence a juror's decision to vote for or against the death penalty."[64]

Secondly, the Court directed its attention to the word "mere." In this regard, the Chief Justice wrote:

> By concentrating on the noun "sympathy," respondent ignores the crucial fact that the jury was instructed to avoid basing its decision on *mere* sympathy. Even a juror who insisted on focus-

ing on this one phrase in the instruction would likely interpret the phrase as an admonition to ignore emotional responses that are not rooted in the aggravating and mitigating evidence introduced during the penalty phase. While strained in the abstract, respondent's interpretation is simply untenable when viewed in light of the surrounding circumstances. This instruction was given at the end of the penalty phase, only after respondent had produced 13 witnesses in his favor. Yet respondent's interpretation would have these two words transform three days of favorable testimony into a virtual charade. . . .[65]

Writing in dissent on behalf of himself and three other justices, Justice Brennan rejected the majority's linguistic argument, concluding that the scope of "mere" cannot sensibly be construed to encompass "sympathy":

The instruction, however, counsels the jury not to be swayed by "mere sentiment, conjecture, sympathy, passion, prejudice, public opinion or public feeling." A juror could logically conclude that "mere" modified only "sentiment," so it is by no means clear that the instruction would likely be construed to preclude reliance on "mere sympathy." In order for "mere" to be regarded as modifying "sympathy," as the Court contends, "mere" must be read to modify all the other terms in the instruction as well: conjecture, passion, prejudice, public opinion, or public feeling. By the Court's own logic, since "mere" serves to distinguish "tethered" from "untethered" sympathy, it also serves to distinguish "tethered" from "untethered" versions of all the other emotions listed. Yet surely no one could maintain, for instance, that some "tethered" form of prejudice relating to the case at hand could ever be appropriate in capital sentencing deliberations.[66]

Justice Brennan further argued that the instruction gives the jury no guidance on how to distinguish between the impermissible "mere" sympathy and the permissible ordinary sympathy. "The defendant literally staked his life in this case on the prospect that a jury confronted with evidence of his psychological problems and harsh family background would react sympathetically, and any instruction that would preclude such a response cannot stand."[67]

Before examining more closely the linguistic dispute in *Brown*, we should note that the discussion thus far has accounted for the votes of only eight of the nine justices on the Supreme Court. Missing from the tally is the vote of

Justice O'Connor, who voted with the majority, but wrote a separate concurring opinion. Staying away from the debate about language, Justice
O'Connor recommended that the California Supreme Court take another
look at the jury instructions and the prosecutor's closing argument to determine whether, taken as a whole, the instructions and argument adequately
apprised the jurors of their duty to consider all mitigating factors. As a result
of this possibility of an additional review, Justice O'Connor voted with the
majority. What she believes the likely result of this review would be is left
unsaid.

Returning to the linguistic debate, the issue can be reduced to the determination of the proper scope of two words: "not" and "mere." Consider
first the scope of "not." The instruction warns the jury not to be swayed by
"mere sentiment, conjecture, sympathy, passion, prejudice, public opinion
or public feeling." It is clear that this entire list is within the scope of *not,*
implicating De Morgan's Law (11a). For example, the sentence "I didn't eat
potatoes or string beans yesterday" means that yesterday, I didn't eat potatoes *and* I didn't eat string beans. The instruction, therefore, means that
the jury is not to be swayed by each of the items on the list.

Let us now consider how *mere* fits into the interpretation. Two interpretations are possible. First, consistent with Chief Justice Rehnquist's position,
it is entirely possible that *mere* was intended to modify the entire list. We can
represent that interpretation as follows:

> be swayed (not(mere(sentiment, conjecture, sympathy, passion
> . . . or public feeling)))

The distribution of parentheses is intended to show that all of the items on
the list are within the scope of *mere.* On the other hand, it is possible that
mere was intended to modify only the first of the disjuncts: *sentiment.* That
interpretation can be represented by altering the scope of *mere:*

> be swayed (not(mere sentiment, conjecture, sympathy, passion
> . . .or public feeling))

Note that here *mere* is only part of one of the disjuncts, *mere sentiment,* and
not continues to modify the entire list. This is the interpretation that Justice
Brennan espoused.

Which interpretation is correct? Both are possible, but Justice Brennan's
is preferred. Consider the following examples:

(13) I've been suffering from a mere headache and a cold.

(14) I've merely been suffering from a headache and a cold.

In the first example, the preferred interpretation is that only the headache is mere, while in the second *merely* modifies both maladies. Structurally, it is (13) that is similar to the jury instruction in *Brown*. Of course, it is possible to interpret *mere* in (13) as modifying both conjuncts, but this is unlikely to be the intended meaning. The same is true of the majority's reading of the jury instruction in *Brown*.

Justice Brennan's interpretation makes more sense for other reasons pointed out by Justice Brennan himself and quoted above. If conjecture and prejudice should never form the basis of a juror's decision to impose the death penalty, what sense could it possibly make to warn the jury not to be swayed by *mere* conjecture or prejudice? If anything, such a warning would convey the message that a certain amount of conjecture or prejudice is good stuff as long as it is combined with other considerations.

Far more important and fundamental than the question of who wins the great adjectival debate is the question of whether Mr. Brown's life or anyone else's life should depend on its resolution. Like the incorporation of both the last antecedent rule and its opposite into the law, the debate about adjectival scope serves the function of masking a far deeper disagreement about the core of our system of justice. The disagreement concerns the circumstances, if any, under which the government should put its citizens to death. It is the relationship between these two debates—linguistic and substantive—that is the focus of the next section.

Why Judges Do Not Make Good Linguists

Let us continue with our discussion of *Brown*. I concluded that the jury instruction that Brown challenged is probably ambiguous between the interpretations proposed by the majority and dissenting opinions. I would expect that some readers agree with my preference for the reading with narrow adjectival scope (the dissenting interpretation) while others prefer the reading in which the adjective *mere* is given wide scope (the majority interpretation). These preferences are a function of the application of certain strategies, such as the minimal attachment and late closure strategies, which are routinely applied during the ordinary processing of language.[68] Given this, an interesting question arises. Is it believable that the justices on the United States Supreme Court actually prefer the readings that they support in their opinions?

Justice Brennan's dissent provides an interesting beginning to answering this question. Before engaging in the linguistic debate, he noted that he opposes imposition of the death penalty in this and every case because he believes that it constitutes cruel and unusual punishment. In fact, Brennan always voted against death sentences for this reason. Chief Justice Rehnquist, on the other hand, is an avid supporter of the death penalty, rarely voting against the imposition of death when the opportunity presents itself.

An analysis of Rehnquist's voting record (now a few years old) indicates that in thirty-three death penalty cases he had voted to overturn the death penalty only twice, both of which cases received unanimous court decisions.[69] On four occasions, his vote in favor of the death penalty constituted a lone dissent. In one such case, *Green v. Georgia,*[70] the rest of the Court took only two pages to reverse a death sentence, where the trial court had applied the hearsay rule and had refused to allow the jury to hear evidence that the defendant's friend and not the defendant himself had committed the murder for which the death sentence had been imposed.

Some of Chief Justice Rehnquist's statements from the bench are consistent with his voting history. For example, on November 3, 1981, *The New York Times* reported on the oral argument in *Eddings v. Oklahoma* as follows:

> Justice William H. Rehnquist, a strong supporter of capital punishment, was sharply questioning Mr. Eddings's lawyer, Jay C. Baker. He asked, "Why should the taxpayers have to bear the cost" of confining and treating the youth for the next 15 to 30 years.
>   The attorney's answer referred to "the expense of litigation," the tens of thousands of dollars spent to prosecute Mr. Eddings. Justice Rehnquist cited the cost to taxpayers of repeated appeals of death sentences. Then Justice Marshall, an opponent of the death penalty, interrupted, asking, "It would have been cheaper just to shoot him right after he was arrested, wouldn't it?" Justice Rehnquist did not respond.

Eddings involved the legitimacy of applying the death penalty to a boy who committed a murder at the age of sixteen.[71] The efforts of now Chief Justice Rehnquist continue, with speeches and administrative attempts addressed to limiting the rights of those sentenced to death to appeal their sentence.[72]

While the voting records of the other justices on the *Brown* court are not always as clear as those of Rehnquist and Brennan, Justices White and O'Connor generally vote in favor of capital punishment, while Justices Marshall (who, like Brennan, was on the *Brown* court but has since retired), Stevens, and Blackmun generally oppose the death penalty in the cases before them. In fact, like Justice Brennan, Justice Marshall routinely voted against the death penalty. This leads to an interesting conclusion. Taken at face value, it would appear that the cognitive preferences for adjectival scope exhibited in the various opinions in *Brown* correlate closely with the voting records of the justices on capital punishment cases. While it is not entirely clear what causes some to prefer one reading over the other, it taxes the imagination to conclude that cognitive preferences concerning the interpretation of adjectives are governed by one's views on the death penalty. Consequently, the only reasonable conclusion is that the entire discussion about adjectival scope in *Brown* was motivated by other, nonlinguistic considerations.

In fairness to Justice Brennan, his dissenting opinion not only states its author's general opposition to capital punishment, but also speaks in terms of what a juror hearing the instructions might have concluded about their meaning. The majority opinion, on the other hand, avoids any reference to the Chief Justice's voting record, and gets right to the activity of linguistic analysis, not acknowledging that the jury might have assigned the instruction an interpretation different from Rehnquist's own. It is difficult to escape the conclusion that the opinion is simply a vehicle to see to it that a convicted killer will die. To the extent that judges use linguistic analysis to add scientific credibility to a decision made on other grounds, judges lose the capacity to be good linguists, which leads to the inevitable failure of their efforts to legitimize through creating the appearance of science.

The judge as bad linguist shows itself as a theme in each of the other examples discussed earlier in this chapter. Most notable are the cases decided under the last antecedent rule. Why did Mrs. Anderson receive the benefit of the last antecedent rule instead of the cost of the across the board rule? Perhaps even more puzzling, why was the last antecedent rule applied to convict Mr. Hardin of selling methamphetamine, while the across the board rule was applied to help Mr. Judge to keep his teaching job after his conviction for growing a marijuana plant? The answers to these questions do not lie in the linguistic rules upon which the judicial decisions were based. Rather, they lie in the situations that were before the judges who had to make these decisions.

I do not know what went through the minds of the judges deciding the *Anderson, Judge,* and *Hardin* cases. However, having read the opinions written by these judges, I have a pretty good idea of what would have presented some difficult choices for me if I had been deciding these cases. For example, in Mrs. Anderson's case, the insurance company's obligation to pay probably would not affect Mrs. Anderson's life nearly as much as it would Mr. Yocum's, whose Cadillac was badly damaged through no fault of his own. The alternative to Mrs. Anderson's winning her lawsuit against her insurer is Mr. Yocum having to recover the thirteen thousand dollars owed him from Mrs. Anderson herself. As between the insurance company and Mr. Yocum, it is not unreasonable to at least hope that Mr. Yocum, a completely innocent victim, will get the thirteen thousand dollars. In fact, legal principles do exist that dictate that insurance policies are to be construed in such a way as to provide coverage in the maximum number of instances. This rule, itself incoherent in its application, will be the subject of a portion of the next chapter. The *Anderson* court relied on this principle in addition to the last antecedent rule in making its decision. In effect, the court appears to have used whatever rhetorical and doctrinal devices it had available to resolve the matter in Mrs. Anderson's favor.

My impressions of the *Judge* and *Hardin* cases lead to the same sorts of conclusions. A school teacher whose career is at stake for having a marijuana plant growing by his window would receive a lot more of my sympathy than an individual attempting to "rip off" a government agent in a drug sale. Whether linguistic analysis should be the device through which these relative sympathies are expressed in the law is an entirely different matter. The expression of good intentions through incoherent doctrinal devices serves to accomplish what appears to be substantial justice from a normative point of view at the expense of some of the law's integrity. In fact, this is the consequence of attempts to legitimize in general, a conclusion to which we will return in the last chapter of this book.

Similar questions are raised by the other two linguistic devices discussed in this chapter. The selective application of the and/or rule does not undermine the linguistic legitimacy of that rule, whose application sometimes makes perfectly good sense. Rather, it undermines the legitimacy of the institutions that apply the rule. Selective attention to the number and gender of pronouns has the same effect. Thus, judges do not make good linguists because they are using linguistic principles to accomplish an agenda distinct from the principles about which they write. For the most part we can only guess what these agendas are, although evidence sometimes exists, such as voting records on capital punishment cases. Abandonment of the linguistic (and other similar) principles would have serious consequences for the judiciary because it would expose the agendas that are hidden by these doctrinal rules. This, in turn, would leave courts with the choice between abandoning the agendas themselves in favor of a mechanical jurisprudence, or keeping the agendas but expanding the scope of the justificatory discourse. As Cardozo pointed out many years ago, both options have their risks.

Significantly, the use of these linguistic devices cuts across a variety of judicial tasks. Thus we find courts applying the last antecedent rule in the interpretation of a contract (*Anderson*) and in the interpretation of various statutes (*Judge* and *Hardin*). Issues concerning the interpretation of pronouns, as we have seen, arise in the construal of jury instructions (*Bass*), government press releases (*Sourapas*) and trust instruments (*Mathey* and *First National Bank of Denver*). Problems with *and* and *or* occur in connection with the interpretation of statutes (e.g., the federal forfeiture statute) and jury instructions (*Skinner*).

These are but a few examples of what appears to be a rather general phenomenon: judges attempting to act fairly while reacting to pressure to write decisively and within the bounds of acceptable argumentation. Guido Calabresi may well be correct in his statement that "much of the current criticism of judicial activism, and of our judicial system generally, can be traced to the rather desperate responses of our courts to a multitude of obsolete statutes in the face of the manifest incapacity of legislatures to keep those statutes up to date."[73] Concern about judicial intrusion into activities that are considered properly within the sphere of the legislature has been a matter of great debate for many years, both among legal scholars and in the courts, as we shall touch on in chapter 4. It appears to me, however, that our courts respond similarly to a wide range of challenges.[74]

Chapters 3 and 4 will discuss phenomena related to those presented above. As we shall discover, rules "stacking the deck" in favor of one party over another, and rules requiring that plain language be applied before other principles are invoked, suffer in their application from the same difficulties as do the linguistic principles we have already seen.

3 | Stacking the Deck

AMBIGUITY IN human language often has very serious ramifications for the judicial system. The enforcement of contractual rights and obligations, for example, has as its foundation the notion that once an individual agrees to do something, he should be held responsible for the consequences of not keeping his promise. But what happens when the contract containing the promise is not clear? It is very difficult to reconcile the notion of individual rights and responsibilities with the inability to determine exactly what was promised in the first place.

Ambiguity results any time that our knowledge of language, in the sense of our internalized system of rules and principles described in chapter 1, fails to limit to one the possible interpretations of a sentence. This occurs not only when our internal grammars permit us to assign more than one syntactic structure to a string of words, as in (1), an example discussed by Chomsky in his early work,[1]

(1)   Flying planes can be dangerous.

but also when our system permits multiple interpretations of particular words. The gross effect is that our knowledge of language, as sophisticated as it is, leaves unanswered all sorts of questions about how to interpret particular utterances. And litigants are not at all too shy to use the existence of ambiguity to their advantage.

Rules for the resolution of linguistic ambiguity have made their way into the law, and are the subject of many legal principles. Some courts have stated that the last antecedent rule,[2] discussed in the previous chapter, is one such principle. That is, the need to apply the last antecedent rule arises only when the sentence whose interpretation is in issue is seen as ambiguous. This is no doubt true. For example, no court, presumably, would apply the last antecedent rule to a sentence like (2), contained in a hypothetical contract for the sale of real estate.

(2)   Seller will convey the property to buyer after repairing the
         roof.

The rules of English grammar dictate that the understood subject of the embedded clause, "after repairing the roof," is the subject of the main clause, "seller." But "buyer" is the last possible antecedent before the embedded clause. Applying the last antecedent rule to (2) would, therefore, yield an incorrect interpretation of the sentence in which the buyer will repair the roof. The last antecedent rule does not overrule the grammatical principle that causes us to have only one interpretation. It thus makes sense to conclude that the last antecedent rule is applied only to resolve perceived ambiguity. Other canons of construction mentioned in chapter 2 can be seen in a similar light. They tell us where to look for help when more than one interpretation is available, although they most often refer to contextual rather than linguistic factors.

The resolution of ambiguity in legal documents is not always based on linguistic considerations, such as the determination of which antecedent is the "last" antecedent. Some rules of law that address the interpretation of documents look to the legal consequences of interpretation rather than to linguistic issues alone, and stack the deck in favor of one party and against another. Sometimes called "substantive canons of construction,"[3] these have been the subject of considerable discussion in the recent legal literature, and are the subject of this chapter.

There exist many such principles. To mention a few: ambiguities in contractual arbitration clauses are construed to require arbitration; newer statutes are not construed to imply the repeal of older ones when there is a possible inconsistency; when possible, statutes are interpreted to avoid significant constitutional problems; and statutes are interpreted consistent with a strong presumption of Native American tribal authority.[4]

Cass Sunstein, in his interesting book *After the Rights Revolution*, has proposed an entire network of these interpretive rules, and includes substantive justification for his proposals and a set of principles for resolving conflicts among them.[5] For example, expanding on the presumption of interpretation favorable to Indian tribes, Sunstein suggests an interpretive principle requiring that ambiguous statutes be generally construed in favor of disadvantaged groups, whose interests are often underrepresented in the enforcement of legal rights.[6] Considering that courts already recognize

many substantive interpretive rules, which form a haphazard array of preferences on which judges can rely, Sunstein should clearly be applauded for his
program of consciously deciding on and valuing the principles that the system should adopt. However, because courts are selective in both their use of
these principles and their determination of ambiguity, I am somewhat skep-
tical about the success of such a program. We will return to this issue later,
after looking at a few examples of courts' applying rules that stack the deck in
the case of ambiguity.

One result-oriented linguistic-legal principle was briefly discussed in
chapter 2, in the context of Mrs. Anderson's dispute with her insurance
company: the principle that requires ambiguities in insurance policies to be
resolved against the insurer and in favor of the insured. A second principle
of this sort, actually the general case of the first, requires that any contract be
construed against the party that drafted it. We will discuss both of these
principles below. In addition, we will examine a principle of criminal law
called the rule of lenity, which calls for the strict construction of criminal
statutes, resolving ambiguities in favor of the person accused of committing
a crime.

Because ambiguity triggers the application of these principles, the central
debate with respect to their application often focuses on the question of
whether a particular statute or insurance policy or contract is ambiguous at
all. Invariably, one party will benefit from the application of these principles
and the other will suffer. Defendants in criminal cases, not surprisingly, regularly find the statutes that they are accused of violating to be hopelessly
ambiguous, while prosecuting attorneys tell the court that the same language is as clear as day. Almost always, the linguistic intuitions of the litigants concerning ambiguity correspond to their personal interests. Also not
surprisingly in light of the material presented in earlier chapters, courts apply these principles in a manner that leads the careful observer to develop
serious questions about the predictability, and perhaps even the sincerity, of
their application in particular cases. We begin with the rule of lenity.

The Rule of Lenity

The foundations underlying the rule of lenity, a principle deeply embedded
in the jurisprudence of federal and state law in the United States, are twofold. First, those accused of crimes are entitled to notice of what is illegal. If
a criminal statute is ambiguous, then an individual should not be subjected
to criminal penalty without ever having been given adequate notice that the

behavior complained of constitutes a crime.[7] The second rationale is that crimes are statutorily defined. That is, courts lack the power to decide that an activity should be punished as a crime when the legislature has not enacted a statute deeming that activity a crime. Therefore, when a statute is ambiguous, ambiguity must be resolved in favor of the accused in order to avoid unwanted expansion of the judiciary's role in the political system.[8]

Restating the rule, Justice Blackmun quoted from from a line of more recent cases dating back to 1952:

> [W]hen choice has to be made between two readings of what conduct Congress has made a crime, it is appropriate, before we choose the harsher alternative, to require that Congress should have spoken in language that is clear and definite.[9] (Citations omitted)

The rule of lenity, then, requires that when a criminal statute is ambiguous, it be afforded the narrower reading, the reading in which fewer activities come within the definition of the crime. This is what is meant by "strict construction" of a criminal statute.

Heated debate often accompanies application of this rule. Sometimes, the debate focuses on whether a particular statute triggers the rule at all. For example, is a statute that calls for disciplinary action against a state employee sufficiently penal in nature to justify application of the rule? Is a civil statute allowing a plaintiff to recover three times his loss penal in nature, triggering the rule of lenity?[10]

Much of the debate centers on whether a statute in question readily lends itself to multiple readings. The determination of whether a statute is ambiguous is a linguistic issue that must be resolved as a prerequisite for deciding the applicability of the rule of lenity. The cases discussed below, decided by the Supreme Court of the United States, focus their attention on the issue of what is ambiguous.

YERMIAN: LENITY AND THE SCOPE OF ADVERBS

It is a general principle of criminal law that conviction for having committed a crime requires proof of some sort of guilty state of mind, or *mens rea*. Without such a requirement, the state would be in a position to punish people for the consequences of actions in which they did not even intend to engage. (There are exceptions, such as negligent homicide, recognized by most states, which generally requires "gross" negligence.) In two recent Supreme Court cases, the statement of the *mens rea* requirement in particular criminal statutes became the subject of controversy, leading to debate about the proper application of the rule of lenity.

Section 1001 of the United States Criminal Code,[11] a favorite of prosecutors, holds people criminally liable for making false statements to government officials. The statute says:

> Whoever, in any matter within the jurisdiction of any department or agency of the United States *knowingly and willfully* falsifies, conceals or covers up by any trick, scheme, or device a material fact, or makes any false, fictitious or fraudulent statements or representations, or makes or uses any false writing or document knowing the same to contain any false, fictitious or fraudulent statement or entry, shall be fined not more than $10,000 or imprisoned not more than five years, or both. (Emphasis added)

In *United States v. Yermian,*[12] the Supreme Court was asked to determine the scope of the emphasized portion of this statute, that is, the scope of the *mens rea* requirement.

In 1979, Esmian Yermian was an employee of Gulton Industries, a defense contractor. To be permitted to work on defense contracts in which he would be exposed to classified information, Yermian, like other employees, had to obtain security clearance from the Department of Defense. Doing so required him to answer a series of questions contained on a document entitled "Worksheet For Preparation of Personnel Security Questionnaire," presented to him by his employer. Yermian did not mention, in response to a question about whether he had been charged with any crimes in the past, that he had earlier been convicted of mail fraud, a federal felony. Another Gulton Industries employee typed Yermian's answers onto a form entitled "Department of Defense Personnel Security Questionnaire," which Yermian later signed, over a statement certifying that his answers were "true, complete, and correct . . . " and that he understood that false statements might subject him to criminal prosecution under section 1001.

Criminal prosecution under section 1001 is exactly what happened. Admitting that he had answered the questionnaire falsely, Yermian claimed at trial that he did not realize that it would actually be sent to the Department of Defense. Rather, he thought that he was lying only to his employer, an activity in which he had engaged once before when he omitted to disclose his mail fraud conviction on his employment application. His "sole defense

. . . was that he had no actual knowledge that his false statements would be transmitted to a federal agency."[13]

The potential success of Yermian's defense rested on what instructions the judge would give to the jury, a decision which itself rested on the scope of "knowingly and willfully" in the statute. Yermian requested that the judge instruct the jurors that in order to reach a guilty verdict they must find not only that he knowingly and willfully made the false statements, a fact not in dispute, but also that he knowingly and willfully made any such statements within the jurisdiction of a federal agency, an allegation that he denied. The district court judge refused to instruct the jury as Mr. Yermian requested. Instead, he issued the following instruction:

> Three essential elements are required to be proved in order to establish the offense charged in the indictment:
> FIRST: That the defendant made . . . a false writing . . . in relation to a matter within the jurisdiction of a department or agency of the United States as charged;
> SECOND: That he did such act or acts with knowledge of the accused that the writing or document was false or fictitious and fraudulent in some material particular, as alleged;
> THIRD: That the defendant knew or should have known that the information was to be submitted to a government agency;
> FOURTH: That he did such act or acts knowingly and willfully.[14]

Yermian was convicted.

The United States Court of Appeals for the Ninth Circuit reversed, holding that the trial court should have interpreted "knowingly and willfully" as modifying both the requirement that false statements be made and the requirement that the statements be made within the jurisdiction of a federal department or agency. The Supreme Court, in a 5–4 decision, reversed again, reinstating the conviction.

Writing for the majority, Justice Powell reviewed the legislative history of section 1001 and concluded that the plain language of the statute, combined with the historical record, forces one to conclude that Congress did not intend that the government had to prove a defendant's knowledge that falsehoods would be transmitted to a federal agency for a conviction to stand. The Court rejected any application of the rule of lenity, concluding that the statute was unambiguous, rendering that interpretive rule inapplicable.

The dissenting opinion, written by Justice Rehnquist, disagreed with the majority's linguistic analysis: "[T]he Court's reasoning here amounts to little more than simply pointing to the ambiguous phrases and proclaiming them clear. In my view, it is quite impossible to tell which phrases the terms 'knowingly and willfully' modify, and the magic wand of *ipse dixit* does nothing to resolve that ambiguity."[15]

The linguistic issue in the case was whether the emphasized portion of the statute, repeated below, comes within the scope of "knowingly and willfully":

> Whoever, *in any matter within the jurisdiction of any department or agency of the United States* knowingly and willfully . . . makes any false . . . statements . . .

The debate among the justices developed into an argument about the linguistic consequences of the appearance of the emphasized portion of the statute in a position preposed to the beginning of the sentence. Both sides compared the language to that of an earlier version of the statute in which the corresponding language was not preposed, but rather occurred after *knowingly and willfully*. Because, as Justice Rehnquist noted in his dissent, the legislative history of section 1001 shows that the revision from the earlier version of the statute to the current one was not intended to make substantive changes in the jurisdictional requirement of the crime, the interpretation of the earlier statute can shed some light on the intended meaning of the later one. The justices, however, also disagreed about the possible interpretations of the 1934 predecessor, presented below:

> [W]hoever shall knowingly and willfully . . . make . . . any false or fraudulent statements or representations, . . . *in any matter within the jurisdiction of any department or agency of the United States* . . . shall be fined . . . or imprisoned. (Emphasis added)

The majority believed the earlier statute to be unambiguous, consistent with its reading of the current statute, while the dissent found the earlier version just as unclear as it found the current one.

Does the position of the *in any matter within the jurisdiction* phrase affect the range of possible interpretations of the statute? It certainly seems to do so. To understand the relationship between the position of prepositional phrases and the scope of adverbs, let us examine some simpler examples. Consider (3).

(3)   Fred knowingly sold securities without a permit.

To me, at least, (3) is ambiguous. It can mean either that Fred knowingly sold securities, and that he just happened to have sold them without a permit (perhaps without any knowledge that a permit is even required), or that Fred intentionally failed to get a permit, perhaps to avoid subjecting himself to regulations that apply to permit holders.[16]

Preposing the prepositional phrase to the beginning of the sentence eliminates the scope ambiguity in (3). Compare (3) with (4).

(4)   Without a permit, Fred knowingly sold securities.

I find it very difficult to understand (4) as meaning that Fred intentionally neglected to get a permit before selling securities. Linguists have for many years recognized that the position of a prepositional phrase in sentences like (3) and (4) affects certain aspects of semantic interpretation.[17] Similarly, (5) and (6) differ in that the pronoun in (5) cannot refer to *the President*, while the pronoun in (6), on the other hand, may.

(5)   He fell asleep during the President's photo session.

(6)   During the President's photo session, he fell asleep.

These facts comprise part of the tacit knowledge that enables us to speak and understand our native language, without special training and more or less effortlessly.[18]

Returning to Yermian's plight, the example sentences presented above lead to a rather perplexing state of affairs. If we apply to section 1001 the linguistic principles reflected in the examples, then it appears that the current statute, with the preposed *in any matter* clause, means what the majority opinion says that it means: the statute is not ambiguous. I agree with the majority. I find it extremely difficult to understand section 1001, read literally, as requiring that the defendant intend that the falsehood be within the jurisdiction of a federal agency. On the other hand, it certainly seems to me that the older version of the statute, in which the *in any matter* clause is not preposed, means what the dissent says it means. Namely, the earlier statute is ambiguous.

Taking at face value the relevance of the predecessor statute, we can best conclude that in revising the statute, Congress inadvertently altered the *mens rea* requirement by preposing the *in any matter* clause to the front of the statute. As Justice Rehnquist pointed out in dissent, any other conclusion would necessarily mean that the statute required no guilty state of mind at all with respect to government involvement in the misrepresentations.

The difficulty of such a result is illustrated by the instruction that the trial court gave the jury in the prosecution of Mr. Yermian. By requiring that the government prove that Yermian knew or should have known that his false statements were within the jurisdiction of a federal agency, the Court imposed its own *mens rea* requirement.[19]

The *Yermian* case, then, resembles the interpretive dilemmas that trigger application of the and/or rule, discussed in the previous chapter. Faced with the need to find a neutral basis for a decision, all nine justices took internally incoherent positions on the language of the statute and its predecessors. We need only recall Cardozo's warnings. *Yermian,* however, is not the Supreme Court's final word on the scope of adverbs. The Court had the opportunity to revisit the issue just one year later, in a case to which we now turn.

Frank Liparota had been convicted of unlawfully acquiring and possessing food stamps. Co-owner of the Moon Sandwich Shop in Chicago, an establishment not authorized to accept food stamps, Liparota had been charged with buying food stamps from an undercover government agent for amounts less than their face value. He appealed to the United States Court of Appeals for the Seventh Circuit, and lost. Based on the arguments concerning the scope of adverbs in the relevant statute, the Supreme Court reversed in a 6–2 decision (Justice Powell did not participate).[20] The statute is presented below in relevant part:

> [W]hoever *knowingly* uses, transfers, acquires, alters, or possesses coupons or authorization cards *in any manner not authorized by this chapter or the regulations issued pursuant to this chapter* shall, if such coupons or authorization cards are of a value of $100 or more, be guilty of a felony and shall, upon the first conviction thereof, be fined not more than $10,000 or imprisoned for not more than five years, or both, and, upon the second and any subsequent conviction thereof, shall [be punished more severely].[21] (Emphasis added)

Again the case rested on the scope of the word "knowingly," and again the issue arose in the context of the judge's instruction to the jury. The crucial question was whether the phrase "in any manner not authorized by this chapter or the regulations issued pursuant to this chapter" comes within the scope of the adverb "knowingly." If it does, Liparota's conviction had to be reversed, since the government was required, but failed, to prove this element of the crime. If it does not, Liparota was presumably convicted properly.

Liparota had requested that the jury be told that the government must prove (beyond a reasonable doubt) that "the defendant knowingly did an act which the law forbids, purposely intending to violate the law." Rejecting Liparota's proposed jury charge, the trial court instead instructed the jury as follows:

> When the word "knowingly" is used in these instructions, it means that the Defendant realized what he was doing, and was aware of the nature of his conduct, and did not act through ignorance, mistake, or accident. Knowledge may be proved by defendant's conduct and by all of the facts and circumstances surrounding the case.[22]

The trial judge further instructed the jury that the government must prove that Liparota "knowingly and wilfully acquired the food stamps."[23]

Writing for the majority, Justice Brennan determined that the statute was ambiguous, and that the rule of lenity therefore should apply, which resulted in a reversal of the conviction. Justice Brennan wrote:

> Although Congress certainly intended by the use of the word "knowingly" to require *some* mental state with respect to *some* element of the crime defined in Section 2024(b), the interpretations proffered by both parties accord with congressional intent to this extent. Beyond this, the words themselves provide little guidance. Either interpretation would accord with ordinary usage. The legislative history of the statute contains nothing that would clarify the congressional purpose on this point.[24]

Significantly, the statute in *Liparota* differs from that in *Yermian* in a crucial linguistic respect: the *in any matter* clause in the *Liparota* statute does not appear at the front of the sentence, unlike the corresponding clause in the *Yermian* statute. To me, only the *Liparota* statute is ambiguous. Most of the justices in the Supreme Court agreed with this assessment. In fact, two of them who voted to affirm Yermian's conviction voted to reverse that of Liparota, which possibly reflected less political controversy about the statute under which Mr. Liparota was convicted. Note that if we create a hypothetical food stamps statute in which the *in any manner* phrase is preposed, the statute loses its ambiguity:

> [W]hoever, *in any manner not authorized by this chapter or the regulations issued pursuant to this chapter, knowingly* uses, transfers, acquires, alters, or possesses coupons or authorization cards

shall, if such coupons or authorization cards are of a value of $100 or more, be guilty of a felony and shall, upon the first conviction thereof, be fined not more than $10,000 or imprisoned for not more than five years, or both, and, upon the second and any subsequent conviction thereof, shall [be punished more severely].

Had the statute been worded as such, I doubt that Mr. Liparota would have received all the votes that he did receive.

The dissenting opinion, written by Justice White on behalf of himself and Chief Justice Burger, disagreed. Not surprisingly, Justice White returned to the *Yermian* case for support. Comparison of the two decisions raises a linguistically interesting jurisprudential issue. In *Yermian*, the majority rejected the notion that preposing reduces ambiguity, holding that the preposed and nonpreposed versions of Section 1001 were both unambiguous. Does that set a linguistic-legal precedent, defining our cognitive abilities as a matter of law? Having decided *Yermian*, the Court could conclude that it should incorporate into the law the linguistic principle that preposing a prepositional phrase does not reduce the ambiguity of the scope of an adverb, despite the fact that exactly the opposite is true. This is precisely the point that I raised in relation to another linguistic matter in the Introduction, in connection with *State v. Cohen*.

Justice White said that the *Yermian* decision is indeed the law, and that it should be followed. Although such a rule would suffer from being both linguistically counterintuitive and doctrinally unnecessary (since judges are perfectly capable of construing individually the language of each statute that they are asked to interpret), Justice White's argument makes no less sense than do arguments for the introduction of the other legal principles of statutory interpretation. In fact, it is the rigidification of the argumentation underlying linguistically based judicial decisions that is the source of such rules as the last antecedent rule and the and/or rule, discussed in chapter 2. Nonetheless, the other justices did not respond to this argument in *Liparota*.

Justice White raised some other difficulties with the statute. It is a general principle of law that ignorance of the law is not an excuse for breaking it. A bank robber cannot argue in his defense that while he had obviously engaged in an antisocial act, he had not consulted the statute books before doing so, and therefore should be exonerated. But the food stamp statute, as interpreted by the majority, seems to require just such knowledge of the law.

White suggests that this is not what was intended. Rather, the phrase *in any manner not authorized by this chapter or the regulations issued pursuant to this chapter* should be read as shorthand for the entire list of ways in which it is illegal to use food stamps. For example, as Justice White points out, it is illegal to use food stamps to purchase cigarettes or alcohol. Justice White would read the *in any manner* clause as a list, members of which include *to purchase cigarettes* and *to purchase alcohol*. Under this reading of the statute, Liparota was properly convicted even if he never read the law, as long as his actions were intentional. Of course, Justice White's interpretation, while possible, runs afoul of the rule of lenity. Since he does not know whether the statute was intended to require knowledge of the law, despite the general principle that ignorance of the law is no excuse, the rule of lenity should require that the more restrictive reading of the statute govern the outcome of the case.

WHAT ABOUT *Brown?*

In his dissent in *Yermian,* Justice Rehnquist raised an interesting point not yet discussed. Criticizing the majority for failing to admit that section 1001 is subject to multiple interpretations, he noted:

> The fact that the Court's "natural reading" has not seemed so natural to the judges of the Ninth and Fifth Circuits, nor for that matter to me, indicates that the Court's reading, though certainly a plausible one, is not at all compelled by the statutory language.[25]

Rehnquist is correct. Our ordinary sense of ambiguity includes instances in which people differ with respect to possible interpretations of the same sentence.

If Justice Rehnquist's point about the ambiguity of the statute in *Yermian* makes sense (despite the linguistic analysis presented earlier in which I attempted to demonstrate that the statute is not at all ambiguous), then an important question arises: What about Mr. Brown? Recall from chapter 2 that Brown was sentenced to death for murder, and his sentence was upheld by the narrowest of margins, based on a reading of a jury instruction upon which the justices of the Supreme Court did not agree. The instruction admonished that the jurors "must not be swayed by mere sentiment, conjecture, sympathy, passion, prejudice, public opinion or public feeling," and the issue addressed by the judges was the scope of the adjective "mere."

With the five justices in the majority offering one interpretation and the four dissenting justices another, the instruction was by definition ambiguous according to Justice Rehnquist's sense of ambiguity. Therefore, the rule of lenity should apply.

Moreover, while one may argue that the rule of lenity applies to the interpretation of statutes and that Brown's problem was an ambiguous jury instruction, such a distinction does not form a convincing basis for sending Mr. Brown to his death. The very reasons for applying the rule to statutes call for its application to jury instructions. Given the ambiguity of the jury instruction in *Brown,* the failure of the Court to apply the rule of lenity is difficult to explain on principled grounds.

Also difficult to reconcile in light of the rule of lenity is the conviction of Mr. Hardin. Recall from chapter 2 that Hardin was convicted by a California court of selling a small amount of methamphetamine to an undercover agent. Applying the last antecedent rule to the criminal statute (repeated below), the appellate court affirmed his conviction.[26]

> [E]very person who . . . sells any controlled substance which is . . . specified in subdivision (d), of Section 11055, unless upon the prescription of a physician [etc.] . . . shall be punished.
>
> . . .
>
> (d) Any material, compound, mixture, or preparation which contains any quantity of the following substances *having a potential for abuse associated with a stimulant effect on the central nervous system* [emphasis added]:
> (1) Amphetamine . . .
> (3) . . . methamphetamine

The court held that the emphasized portion of the statute modifies *substances* and not *any quantity.*

Had the court chosen the rule of lenity instead of the last antecedent rule as the basis for its decision, it would have had to reverse Hardin's conviction. While to me the court's interpretation of the statute is the more natural one, it is difficult to justify Hardin's conviction solely on those grounds. After all, we have already seen a number of cases in which the more natural reading of the statute is not the one intended by the legislature. Perhaps the most striking examples were discussed in connection with the and/or rule in chapter 2.

As these cases suggest, the application of the rule of lenity is not always possible to predict. In principle, it could have changed the outcome of Brown's sentence and Hardin's conviction.

RICO—LENITY AND THE MEANING OF WORDS

Many of the cases that invoke the rule of lenity do so because of the ambiguity of particular words, as opposed to syntactic ambiguity. What generally happens is that a statute prohibits certain categories of behavior by certain categories of people or entities. The battle arises over whether a particular event or a particular actor falls within the categories that the statute defines. Vagueness in word meaning provides a constant source of dispute over significant legal issues. We will discuss the nature of the problem more fully in chapter 4. At this point, I will limit myself to presenting some interesting examples that involve the rule of lenity.

I can think of no better source of disagreement over the meaning of words in a statute than the federal Racketeer Influenced and Corrupt Organization Act: RICO.[27] Enacted as Title IX of the Organized Crime Control Act of 1970, RICO's stated purpose was

> to seek the eradication of organized crime in the United States by strengthening the legal tools in the evidence-gathering process, by establishing new penal prohibitions, and by providing enhanced sanctions and new remedies to deal with the unlawful activities of those engaged in organized crime.[28]

Congress's effort to achieve these goals is an immensely complicated statute calling for criminal penalties and allowing civil lawsuits by those injured as a result of violations of the statute.

There has been an enormous amount of litigation over the meanings of virtually every substantive word in RICO. The case law has prompted a law review literature so extensive that we now have RICO bibliographies,[29] and the *Index to Legal Periodicals* has a "Civil RICO" heading, along with other legal topics such as constitutional law and criminal law.

The heart of RICO is section 1962 of the criminal code. Section 1962(c), for example, provides:

> It shall be unlawful for any person employed by or associated with any enterprise engaged in, or the activities of which affect, interstate or foreign commerce, to conduct or participate, directly or indirectly, in the conduct of such enterprise's affairs through a pattern of racketeering activity or collection of unlawful debt.[30]

Other provisions of section 1962 make it illegal to invest money derived from a pattern of racketeering activity in an enterprise; to acquire any interest in an enterprise through a pattern of racketeering activity; and to conspire to violate any of the above. Both criminal (section 1963) and civil (section 1964) penalties are provided for violators of section 1962.

In essence, the statute attempts to characterize the behavior in which organized crime engages, imposing serious penalties for violators (twenty-five thousand dollars and/or twenty years plus forfeiture of any "interest" acquired[31]). Much of the extensive RICO litigation has been about the fit between the words of this powerful law and its stated purpose: the eradication of organized crime in the United States.

Many of RICO's terms are defined in a glossary contained in the statute.[32] With respect to the section quoted above, the glossary defines *person, racketeering activity, enterprise, pattern of racketeering activity,* and *unlawful debt.* Briefly, a *racketeering activity* is a "chargeable" or "indictable" offense contained in a list, which includes murder, arson, mail fraud, wire fraud, securities fraud, and bribery.[33] A *pattern of racketeering activity* requires at least two acts of racketeering activity within ten years.[34] Thus, for example, someone who is a member of an arson ring that burns buildings in order to collect insurance money and then invests the funds in some legitimate business "enterprise" has violated RICO, provided that the various commissions of arson fit within the definition of a pattern of racketeering activity.

But what about a member of an arson ring who has not invested the insurance proceeds in a legitimate business? Is he employed or associated with an enterprise as required by Section 1962(c) quoted above? In *United States v. Turkette,*[35] decided in 1981, the Supreme Court answered this question affirmatively in its first adventure with RICO. At issue was the definition of "enterprise," which the statute defines as follows:

> "[E]nterprise" includes any individual, partnership, corporation, association, or other legal entity, and any union or group of individuals associated in fact although not a legal entity.[36]

Novia Turkette had been convicted of numerous crimes, including RICO, for his role as a member of an arson and narcotics ring. On appeal, the court of appeals reversed the RICO conviction, holding that the word "enterprise" means only some legitimate enterprise, and cannot merely be the arson ring of which Turkette was held to be a member. The Supreme Court reversed again, reinstating the conviction by a 8–1 vote. It held that the definition of "enterprise" was unambiguous in its breadth, which includes all associations, and therefore refused to apply the rule of lenity.[37] The Court held:

> There is no restriction upon the associations embraced by the
> definition: an enterprise includes any union or group of individ-
> uals associated in fact. On its face, the definition appears to in-
> clude both legitimate and illegitimate enterprises within its
> scope; it no more excludes criminal enterprises than it does legit-
> imate ones.[38]

Only Justice Stewart disagreed, stating that the court of appeals had it
right. The lower court had concluded that "enterprise" could only encompass legitimate organizations since illegal associations exist only by virtue of
the crimes they commit. Congress, the court had reasoned, could not have
intended proof of a pattern of racketeering activity to provide automatic
proof of an enterprise.[39] In addition, the court had concluded that the principal purpose of RICO was prevention of infiltration by organized crime
into legitimate business, a purpose consistent with the narrower reading of
enterprise.

The majority of the Supreme Court rejected both of these arguments. It
argued that while proof of an enterprise and of a pattern of racketeering activity may sometimes overlap, they are still separate elements of the crime.
For example, an arson ring that has thus far committed only one act of arson
has not engaged in a pattern of racketeering activity, even though it may be
an enterprise. The Court further held that the legislative purpose of RICO is
best fulfilled by getting at organized crime at its source.

As a doctrinal matter, the Supreme Court's decision makes sense. It inter-
prets RICO to prohibit racketeering through an organized criminal association.[40] But it is wrong to say that "enterprise" could not be understood to
include only legitimate businesses. Generally speaking, that is how the word
is used, and the statute's definition is not really very helpful. With the rule of
lenity as a threat to the reasonable inferences it had drawn, it became important for the Court to find the statute clear as a matter of law. And it did.
Interestingly, the court of appeals decision that the Supreme Court reversed
found that the "plain meaning" of the definition of "enterprise" supported
the position rejected by the Supreme Court.[41]

Two years after *Turkette,* the Supreme Court decided in *Russello v. United
States*[42] that the rule of lenity did not apply to another RICO term: "interest." In another case involving an arson ring, Joseph C. Russello was convicted of RICO violations for his role in an organization that burned
buildings in order to collect insurance proceeds. For one of the buildings, it
was found that Russello collected more than $340,000. The government

requested forfeiture of this amount—Russello's share (apart from thirty thousand dollars paid to a helpful insurance company official)—under the following provision in RICO:

> Whoever violates any provision of section 1962 of this chapter
> . . . shall forfeit to the United States (1) any *interest* he has ac-
> quired or maintained in violation of section 1962 . . . [43] (Em-
> phasis added)

The issue before the Court was whether the word "interest" applied to the defendants' share of the proceeds, or whether it had to refer to an interest in something else, in this case, an interest in the enterprise. At the time *Russello* was decided, the courts around the United States were divided on the question, some holding that the defendants' share of the take constituted an acquired "interest," and others holding that it did not. In this case, a three-judge panel of the court of appeals had read the statute as not calling for forfeiture of Russello's share, but the full Court of Appeals for the Fifth Circuit overruled the original panel by a 16–7 vote.[44]

The Supreme Court, in a unanimous opinion, sided with those courts that had interpreted the word "interest" broadly to include a defendant's share of the take. Again, the opinion is an earnest and sensible one in its result, but linguistically questionable. The Court cited a number of RICO provisions in which the statute refers to interest in an enterprise[45] and inferred that if Congress had wanted to so limit the forfeiture provision of section 1963(a)(1), it would have done so. It also noted that section 1963(a)(2) requires forfeiture of all interests in a RICO enterprise, however acquired. Since these interests properly include interests in a RICO enterprise that have been illegally acquired, the narrow reading of "interest" would render the statutory language in question entirely superfluous.[46] Other, economic arguments further bolster the Court's decision, providing additional justification.

Is the language really clear? Of course not. That is exactly why the courts were in such disagreement with one another. Without the benefit of statutory and historical context, my first reading was the one rejected by the Court. While "interest" can be understood very broadly, we generally construe it to refer to partial ownership of property that is co-owned (e.g., an interest in a baseball team; an interest in a piece of real estate, etc.). But to enable the Court to sidestep the rule of lenity, it had to find the language clear, which once again it did, quoting partial entries from dictionaries to support its analysis.[47]

To make matters a little more complicated, RICO contains an admonition: "The provisions of this title shall be liberally construed to effectuate its remedial purpose."[48] This flies in the face of the rule of lenity and the considerations that underlie it. A court faced with a RICO case must decide between the narrow construction prescribed by the rule of lenity and the broad construction that Congress instructed.

The Supreme Court has been very cautious with the issue of liberal construction. In *Turkette*, the Court acknowledged the provision, but stated that it would have reached the same result "with or without this admonition."[49] In *Russello*, the Court stated that as far as it knew, RICO is the only substantive federal criminal statute containing such a directive,[50] but used that fact only in its discussion of RICO's legislative history.

This conflict between the rule of lenity and the statute's admonition that it be construed broadly was apparently resolved in *Sedima, S.P.R.L. v. Imrex Co., Inc.*,[51] a 1987 Supreme Court case. *Sedima* was a civil lawsuit brought by one business against another, claiming damages as a result of RICO violations. Again construing the statute broadly, the Court noted that it is possible to apply the rule of lenity to criminal RICO cases ($1961 and $1962) but to interpret broadly the provision permitting civil suits ($1964).[52] But section 1964 permits plaintiffs to sue only those who violate section 1962. How one can construct a coherent jurisprudence interpreting section 1962 narrowly while interpreting broadly section 1964, which incorporates section 1962, is a mystery that the Court does not address, much less solve. In chapter 4, we will look at some more RICO mysteries. We now turn to the interpretation of insurance policies—which supplies another set of interesting linguistic arguments that favor one party over another. Again, we will see various courts struggling to find or to avoid finding ambiguity.

The Linguistics of Insurance Policies

Mrs. Anderson is not the only one in California to have benefited from some questionable linguistics, as we shall see. Another rule has been used creatively by the courts to justify holding insurance companies liable. That rule says that ambiguities in an insurance policy are to be resolved against the insurance company.

THE JACOBER ACCIDENT

Warren Jacober had purchased his automobile insurance policy from State Farm. On July 2, 1968, he was killed as a passenger in his own car after it struck a power pole. The car was being driven with Jacober's permission by a Roger Dell. The other passengers, three of Jacober's children and two of Dell's, were injured. Warren Jacober's wife, Joyce Jacober, and their children sued Dell for wrongful death. Prior to the resolution of that lawsuit, State Farm filed its own action, seeking a judicial declaration that it was not obligated under Warren Jacober's policy to defend the lawsuit against Dell, and that it would not have to pay damages if Dell was found liable for the accident. Named in State Farm's suit were the Jacobers, the Dells and Dell's insurance company: Volkswagen Insurance Company. At issue was the interpretation of several interrelated provisions of the State Farm Policy, which are presented below:

> The Insurance:
> [State Farm agrees] to pay on behalf of the insured all sums which the insured shall become legally obligated to pay as damages because of . . . bodily injury [including death] *sustained by other persons* . . . caused by accident arising out of the ownership, maintenance or use . . . of the owned automobile . . . (Emphasis added)

The policy defines bodily injury to include death.

> The Insured:
> The unqualified word "insured" includes *(1) the named insured,* and (2) if the named insured is a person or persons also includes his or their spouse(s), if a resident of the same household, and (3) if residents of the same household, the relatives of the first person named in the declarations, or of his spouse, and *(4) any other person while using the owned automobile, provided the operation and the actual use of such automobile are with the permission of the named insured or such spouse and are within the scope of such permission.* and (5) . . . (Emphasis added)

> The Exclusions:
> [Insurance does not apply] to bodily injury to the insured or any member of the family of the insured residing in the same household as the insured.

State Farm argued that while Dell was an insured under definition (4) above, the policy does not cover him since the person who died is also an insured under the policy: the named insured. Since the policy covers only injuries sustained by "other persons," and Warren Jacober as an insured is not in the class of other persons, the policy does not cover Dell for the death of Warren Jacober. Moreover, State Farm argued, the exclusion clause specifically denies coverage for bodily injury to the insured. Since Warren Jacober is the named insured, the policy does not cover injuries to him. State Farm lost and appealed to the Supreme Court of California. That court affirmed.[53]

First, the court held that the insurance does cover accidents in which the named insured is injured as a passenger in the car. The policy is concerned with two classes of people: *the insured* and *other persons*. The court reasoned that the words "the insured" in the insuring clause can be understood as referring to whichever member of the class of insured people is subject to liability in the particular accident. Since in this case only Dell is subject to liability, the other categories of insured people do not count as "the insured" in this clause, at least under one reading of the policy. Those who are not "the insured" in this sense gain potential status as "other persons." Warren Jacober, the court held, was the named insured but not "the insured" and therefore a potential "other person." Although this is not the only way to interpret the insuring clause of the policy, the court applied the principle that unless a policy clearly and unambiguously excludes an individual the exclusion is ineffective.

Justice Sullivan dissented. To him, the policy is not ambiguous. Reading the insuring clause as having only a single interpretation, he concluded:

> The term "other persons" therefore stands in contrast to the term "insured"; and "other persons" means those *not* having the status of an insured. The terms are mutually exclusive. It is crystal clear that under the insuring clause, State Farm is bound to insure the named insured and the driver only with respect to bodily injuries sustained by persons *other* than the named insured or the driver. It is an ineluctable conclusion from the foregoing that the policy does not insure against claims for personal injuries or death made by the named insured or his heirs.[54]

To see better the ambiguity in the insuring clause perceived by the majority, let us look at the language a little more formally. The policy requires the insurance company "to pay . . . all sums which the insured shall become legally obligated to pay . . . [to] other persons." The ambiguity is brought out in (7) and (8) below:

(7)   For every x, if x is a member of i (the class of insured individuals), and x does not equal y, then the company will pay . . . all sums which x shall become legally obligated to pay [to] y.

(8)   For every x, if x is a member of i (the class of insured individ-
      uals), and for every y, if y is not a member of i, then the
      company will pay . . . all sums which x shall become legally ob-
      ligated to pay [to] y.

The difference between (7) and (8) reflects different possible interpretations of "other persons." It can mean either a person other than the one
making the claim, as reflected in (7), or a person not a member of the class
of insured individuals, as reflected in (8). The court found the policy
ambiguous.

   Secondly, using essentially the same argument, the court held that the exclusion in the policy for injury to "the insured" has a sensible interpretation in which "the insured" means the member of the class *the insured* who is
subject to potential liability in this particular case, and who has invoked the
protection of the insurance policy. Although State Farm vigorously argued
that the exclusion for "the insured" can only be read to mean *any* insured on
the list, the majority disagreed, applying the principle that "'[i]f semantically permissible, [an insurance] contract will be given such construction
as will fairly achieve its object of securing indemnity to the insured for the
losses to which the insurance relates.'"[55] Again, Justice Sullivan disagreed,
accusing the majority of subverting the language of the policy. He concluded that "[t]he effect of the majority's position is to remove the term
'named insured' from the definition of an 'insured' stated in the polic[y]."[56]

   The dissent raised an interesting point. From the perspective of Mr. Dell,
the driver, it makes some sense to interpret the policy as did the majority.
The definition of "the insured" is a shifting one, depending on who is at
fault in operating the car. But, as Justice Sullivan points out, from the point
of view of Warren Jacober at the time that he bought his insurance policy,
this interpretation makes no sense whatsoever. It is almost inconceivable
that someone could buy an insurance policy that excludes "the insured"
from coverage and believe that he is not excluded from coverage.

   This notion, that reference should be determined with respect to the perspectives of the speaker and the individuals mentioned in the sentence, finds
support in the linguistic literature, as reflected in the work of Susumu
Kuno,[57] who has developed a linguistic notion of *empathy*. Justice Sullivan
is arguing in essence that the majority has created ambiguity in the exclusionary clause of the policy by a shift in empathy from the named insured to
the driver, an illegitimate shift if the policy is to be viewed as a contract between State Farm and Warren Jacober.

Despite the force of Justice Sullivan's argument, the policy probably is ambiguous. Ambiguity resulting from shifts in empathy, even unfair shifts, is ambiguity nonetheless. But this problem had only a short-lived effect on the jurisprudence of insurance law in California. In *California State Automobile Ass'n Inter-Insurance Bureau v. Warwick,*[58] the Supreme Court of California in 1976, three years after deciding *Jacober,* was faced with the following exclusionary clause in a case factually similar to *Jacober:*

> This policy does not apply . . . to liability to [*sic*] bodily injury to any insured.

The court took only a few pages to uphold the exclusion in this policy. By substituting "*any* insured" for "*the* insured," the insurance company had eliminated the ambiguity that the majority had found in Warren Jacober's policy. California insurance policies now use the word *any,* and this issue no longer arises in legal disputes between insurance companies and their insured. When such battles are fought on linguistic grounds, it should not be surprising that the party with control over the language ultimately wins the war.

IGNORING LANGUAGE—PARTRIDGE

Wayne Partridge, a hunting enthusiast, had a homeowner's insurance policy and an automobile insurance policy, both issued by State Farm Insurance Company. As the court in *State Farm Mutual Automobile Insurance C. v. Partridge*[59] described, one day in July 1969, Partridge filed the trigger mechanism of his pistol to give it a hair trigger action. On July 26th, Partridge was driving his car in the countryside with two friends, Vanida Neilson and Ray Albertson, hunting jackrabbits by shooting through the open windows of the car as Partridge drove along. The court continued:

> On the occasion in question here, Partridge spotted a running jackrabbit crossing the road and, in order to keep the rabbit within the car's headlights, Partridge drove his vehicle off the paved road onto the adjacent rough terrain. The vehicle hit a bump, the pistol discharged and a bullet entered Vanida's left arm and penetrated down to her spinal cord, resulting in paralysis. At the time of the accident, Partridge was either holding the gun in his lap or resting it on top of the steering wheel pointed at Vanida.

Ms. Neilson sued Mr. Partridge, seeking $500,000 for personal injuries suffered as a result of Partridge's negligence. Partridge's automobile insurance policy contained a fifteen thousand dollar limit, and his homeowner's policy a twenty-five thousand dollar limit. State Farm recognized its obligation to pay under the automobile policy, and gave Ms. Neilson a check for fifteen thousand dollars. It further brought suit against both Partridge and Neilson, seeking a judicial declaration that the homeowner's policy did not cover Partridge for liability under these circumstances. State Farm lost and appealed to the Supreme Court of California, where it lost again.

At issue were the following two provisions of the homeowner's policy:

> The Insurance:
> The Company agrees to pay on behalf of the Insured all sums which the Insured shall become legally obligated to pay as damages because of bodily injury or property damage, to which this insurance applies, caused by an occurrence.
>
> The Exclusions:
> This policy does not apply . . . To Bodily Injury or Property Damage Arising Out of the Ownership, Maintenance, Operation, Use, Loading or Unloading of . . . Any Motor Vehicle Owned or Operated By, or Rented or Loaned to, any Insured.

The word "occurrence" in the insuring clause is defined broadly in the policy and was not in controversy. Neither was the obligation of State Farm to pay the fifteen thousand dollars under the automobile policy in question.

In determining that the homeowner's policy does provide coverage in this case, the court initially pointed to the language of the exclusion for bodily injury arising out of use of an automobile. The court cited authority to the effect that "arising out of " is to be interpreted broadly when it is contained in an insuring clause and restrictively when it is contained in an exclusion. However, while hinting at its ability to find ambiguity almost anywhere, the court did not ultimately rely on linguistic argumentation.

Ignoring the language of the policy, the court based its decision on the fact that the injury to Ms. Neilson was the direct result of two separate negligent acts: altering the pistol and operating the car in an unsafe manner. Since the insurance policy unquestionably covers injury resulting from the first of these acts, the court held that the insurance company cannot escape liability because of the second. The court presented a hypothetical case in which Partridge, instead of using the gun himself, had lent it to a friend who had misused it in the friend's own automobile. Clearly Partridge would have been covered for his role in the accident. The court reasoned that insurance coverage should not be governed by whether the insured commits only one of two acts, or whether he commits both of them himself. Thus the holding: "[W]e believe that coverage under a liability insurance policy is equally available to an insured wherever an insured risk constitutes *a* concurrent proximate cause of the injuries."[60]

Two of the six justices dissented. Relying on the language of the policy, the dissent argued that the exclusion clause in the policy itself should govern the outcome of the case, and that the exclusion clause says nothing to indicate that coverage can be revived when use of an automobile is not the *only* cause of an accident. In essence, the dissent engaged in the type of argumentation employed in *Anderson* and *Jacober*.

The principle espoused by the majority in *Partridge* has broad ramifications. For example, should an exclusion for fraud in a lawyer's malpractice insurance policy be rendered ineffective if the lawyer is found to have both acted negligently and committed fraud? The law requires the insurance company to pay. Even the dissent in *Partridge* agreed that under certain circumstances, in which the excluded cause is "remote, incidental, or dependent,"[61] a policy should be construed as offering coverage even when the policy read literally would exclude coverage. In one such case, a woman afflicted with a debilitating cancer died in a fire. The insurance policy in question excluded coverage for injury caused in whole or in part by disease or mental infirmity. The court in that 1945 case, *Brooks v. Metropolitan Life Insurance Co.,*[62] rejected the insurance company's argument that the victim would not have perished had she been healthy enough to escape, placing the death within the exclusion clause of the policy.

In the discussion of both *Anderson* and *Jacober,* I presented evidence that courts stack the deck against insurance companies, relying on the availability of technically possible, but implausible readings of provisions in the policies to establish the existence of ambiguity that will be construed against the insurer. In *Partridge,* we see that the deck is not only stacked linguistically. To the extent necessary to achieve certain results, technical analysis of the language is abandoned entirely in favor of broad policy considerations. Perhaps the decisions in all of these cases are the best ones possible under the circumstances. Even if we assume so, the result is reached at the expense of selective use of linguistic analysis in such a way as to compromise the analytical integrity of the system producing the decisions.

Understanding Ambiguous Contracts

The rule that ambiguities in insurance policies are to be construed against the insurance company is actually a special case of a broader rule: ambigu-

ities in a contract are construed against the party that prepared it.[63] The rule
stacks the deck against the party that controlled the language in controversy.
Here, we again can see that courts are regularly faced with the question of
whether to apply the rule at all. And since ambiguity leads to a particular
result, courts argue about whether contractual terms are ambiguous.

To examine the rule's application, let us look first at a 1984 case in which a
court was asked to interpret an arbitration agreement between doctor and
patient requiring that malpractice claims be submitted to arbitration. In
Baker v. Sadick,[64] Diana Baker brought an arbitration proceeding against
her physician, Dr. Sadick, after complications arose following surgery,
which led to additional surgery. The arbitrators not only awarded damages
to compensate Ms. Baker, but also awarded punitive damages in the amount
of $300,000. At issue was whether the arbitrators had the power to award
punitive damages. The court held that they did.

Under California law, punitive damages can be assessed for intentional
wrongdoing, but not for negligence. In her complaint, Ms. Baker alleged
intentional wrongdoing (fraudulent inducement to submit to surgery; unnecessary surgery; falsification of medical records) as well as negligence. The
question before the court was whether the arbitration agreement permitted
arbitration of the claims of intentional wrongdoing for which the punitive
damages would be legitimate, or whether the agreement covered only
claims of negligence. The court began with a related substantive rule of construction, which promotes the policy of favoring arbitration as a means of
dispute resolution: ambiguities in an agreement concerning the scope of arbitration are to be resolved in favor of arbitration. It then looked at the language of the contract, the relevant section of which reads in part:

> It is understood that any dispute as to medical malpractice,
> that is as to whether any medical services rendered under this
> Contract were unnecessary or unauthorized or were improperly,
> negligently or incompetently rendered, will be determined by
> submission to arbitration as provided by California law . . . [65]

This contractual language is required by law in California when a doctor
asks a patient to sign an agreement to arbitrate. But the same statute that
requires this language applies by its own terms to allegations of "professional negligence," which the statute defines as "a negligent act or omission
to act by a health care provider in the rendering of professional services."[66]
This would seem to limit arbitrations to negligence claims, and not to claims

of intentional wrongs. Furthermore, there is no mention, in either the agreement or the statute, of punitive damages.

The court held that the language of the agreement contrasts with the definition of "professional negligence," creating an ambiguity. It then applied the "general rule respecting standard form agreements [that] any ambiguities are to be resolved against the draftsman,"[67] in this case, the doctor. The court focused on the fact that it was the stronger party who was trying to limit the scope of his own agreement.

Of course, it is not entirely fair to attribute to Dr. Sadick the role of draftsman since he (or his lawyers) only adopted the language that a statute says must be used. Neither is it accurate, for that matter, to say that the agreement is ambiguous in the way that the court suggests. The arbitration clause is vague with respect to its scope. The statutory language, if anything, tends to indicate that the agreement was only intended to cover negligent acts. But since prior to signing the agreement Ms. Baker was made privy only to the agreement—not to the statute books—she is at least as innocent as the doctor in the matter.

The principle that contracts are to be construed against the drafter has its roots in notions of distributive justice. This becomes more clear if we examine cases in which this principle conflicts with other legal principles for resolving ambiguity, many of which are not result-oriented. For example, the *parol evidence rule* ordinarily prohibits a court from looking at evidence extrinsic to the language of a contract when the parties intend the written contract to constitute their whole agreement. On the other hand, when a contract is ambiguous, courts do look at the parties' conduct and relationship to one another in an effort to construe the contract consistent with the intentions of the parties at the time that they entered into it. But this effort is at odds with the principle that ambiguities in a contract are interpreted against the drafter. Given the choice between investigating the parties' intentions through extrinsic evidence or simply resolving ambiguity against the drafter, what will a court do?

The answer is that sometimes courts take one option and sometimes the other, and the less equal the parties' bargaining power the more likely that the ambiguity will be resolved against the drafter. This generalization is illustrated in *Tahoe National Bank v. Phillips*,[68] a 1971 case decided by the Supreme Court of California. That case involved a dispute between Beulah Phillips and a bank that had lent money for real estate development to a group of which she was a member. At the time of the loan, Ms. Phillips signed an agreement entitled "Assignment of Rents and Agreement Not to Sell or Encumber Real Property." The agreement called for her not to dispose of certain property, and to assign rents received to the bank. But the property encumbered by the agreement was not the development under construction, but rather, Ms. Phillips's house. When she defaulted on this and other loans, the bank sued, and tried to foreclose on Ms. Phillips's house, claiming that the agreement was actually an "equitable" mortgage. The trial court agreed with the bank, but on appeal the Supreme Court reversed, ruling in Ms. Phillips's favor.

Nowhere did the agreement say it was a mortgage, allowing foreclosure on the house if the loan was not paid, and Ms. Phillips testified that she did not think it was. But at trial, the bank had been permitted to introduce evidence extrinsic to the agreement showing that it should be construed as a mortgage. The Supreme Court determined that the contract on its face could not be "reasonably construed" as a mortgage. To the extent that the contract was ambiguous, the court had this to say:

> The rule of resolving ambiguities against the drafter "does not serve as a mere tie-breaker; it rests upon fundamental considerations of policy." . . .
>
> In the present case, we conclude that to permit a creditor to choose an allegedly ambiguous form of agreement, and then by extrinsic evidence seek to give it the effect of a different and unambiguous form would be to disregard totally the rules respecting interpretation of adhesion contracts, and to create an extreme danger of over-reaching on the part of creditors with superior bargaining positions. . . . It is only "poetic justice" if such ambiguity is construed in favor of the borrower.[69]

The considerations announced by the California Supreme Court in *Tahoe* are not the only ones when it comes to the relationship between the rule calling for the resolution of ambiguity against the drafter and the rule permitting the introduction of extrinsic evidence when a contract is ambiguous. Just as we saw in chapter 2 in connection with the last antecedent rule, exactly the opposite principles exist as well. In 1979, a federal appellate court was faced with this problem in *Board of Trade of San Francisco v. Swiss Credit Bank*,[70] a case governed by the law of California. The dispute involved the construal of a letter of credit issued by the bank. The letter of credit called for the bank to pay a named party (Arrays) for goods shipped by a bank customer (North American) upon presentation by Arrays[71] of "full set clean on board bills of lading . . . " i.e., shipping documents. When documents were presented for payment for an initial shipment, the bank paid, although it questioned whether ocean shipment, rather than the air shipment that occurred, was required. When this happened a second time, the bank refused to pay, claiming that "full set clean on board bills of lading" requires ocean shipment. A bank officer testified that "clean on board" normally refers to ocean shipments. An "air waybill" is the equivalent document when air shipment is involved.

The trial court ruled against the bank. But the court of appeals reversed, holding that a trial should be held on the meaning of "clean on board bills of lading."[72] As for the interpretive principles, the court's reasoning is difficult to reconcile with that in the *Tahoe* case:

> Arrays also contends that even if the letter of credit is ambiguous, any ambiguity should be construed against the issuer . . .
> [W]e conclude that even if the rule is applicable to letters of credit, it is premature to apply the rule in the context of this appeal. A trial is necessary to determine whether the ambiguity is real or imagined and, if an ambiguity exists, its extent. A rule for construing contracts against the author is not an alternative to construing the contract as the parties intended. It is to be applied after the court has inquired into the intent of the parties, and then only if its meaning remains uncertain.[73]

In other words, to adopt the language of the *Tahoe* court, the rule that ambiguities in contracts are to be construed against the drafter is a "tie-breaker," exactly the opposite of what the Supreme Court of California had held.

Another California appellate court has more recently taken the same position as did the *Swiss Credit Bank* court, not applying the *Tahoe* rule. In a 1985 decision, the court in *Rainier Credit Co. v. Western Alliance Corp.* stated:

> This rule [that an ambiguity in a contract will be construed against the drafter] is to be used only when there is no extrinsic evidence available to aid in the interpretation of the contract or where the uncertainty cannot be remedied by other rules of interpretation . . . The rule remains that the trier of fact will consider any available extrinsic evidence to determine what the parties actually intended the words of their contract to mean . . . Only in those instances where the extrinsic evidence is either lacking or is insufficient to resolve what the parties intended the

terms of the contract to mean will the rule that ambiguities are resolved against the drafter of the contract be applied.[74]

Again, the interpretive principle is a "tie-breaker."

Of course, it is possible to rationalize these cases. *Baker* and *Tahoe* clearly involved one party's presenting a take-it-or-leave-it contract to another. The *Rainier* case did not, and the *Swiss Credit Bank* case falls somewhere in the middle. But the flavor of these cases is that there exists a grab bag of principles, all available to the court in any case. The court will choose one or more in order to justify doing what it considers fair. And hypotheses as to when one available principle should be applied instead of another one quickly lose whatever intellectual force they may have in the abstract when one examines their application to a particular case.

Finally, let us return to Cass Sunstein's proposal that courts should carry out policy in part through a clearly articulated set of substantive rules of interpretation, favoring one or another party under different circumstances.[75] From the examples that I have presented, we can see that courts already use these sorts of principles in justifying their decisions, although the principles that stack the deck do not form a coherent whole. Naturally, it can only advance the cause of thoughtful decision making to debate openly which of these principles are to be taken seriously, and what the hierarchical relationship among conflicting principles should be. Sunstein's work itself takes us a long way toward this goal.

As the cases show, however, judges regularly take advantage of these interpretive principles to justify their decisions, even when the application of them is highly suspect from a linguistic perspective. Judges try to do justice, but at times feel constrained to play games with language in order to justify the justice they do, which undermines the very legitimacy for which they strive. Because there will always be cases that make us want to take advantage of an interpretive principle that does not clearly apply, or to avoid one that does, I anticipate that the sorts of problems discussed in this chapter will continue regardless of what progress is made in developing the substantive principles.

4 | When the Language Is Clear

WE HAVE seen that courts become animated over linguistic issues when the law provides for a particular result in resolving the ambiguity of a statute, insurance policy, or contract. Not surprisingly, the law speaks also of what should happen when a document under dispute is *not* ambiguous. The legal principle that addresses this situation is called the "plain language rule" or "clear language rule," which states that when the language is clear, courts have no authority to go beyond the words of a statute or contract, but must apply the clear language of the document to the facts before them.

The rationale for this rule is straightforward, and mirrors the reasoning behind the rule of lenity, discussed in chapter 3. It is the business of the courts to effectuate the will of the legislature in interpreting statutes and to effectuate the agreement between the parties in interpreting contracts. What better way to learn what the legislature or parties had in mind, the argument goes, than to read what they said in the statute or contract.

The problems with the plain language rule are twofold. First, as we saw in the application of the rule of lenity and its kin, it is not always easy to tell when a statute is ambiguous. This is especially true when lawyers for both sides tug at the court, one party explaining how clear and precise the language is, the other showing it to be a muddled mess. Forty years ago, Edward Levi wrote: "It is only folklore which holds that a statute if clearly written can be completely unambiguous and applied as intended to a specific case."[1] Yet courts will soon complete another half century of telling this tale. In this chapter we will explore how and why they do so.

The second problem with the plain language rule is that courts are reluctant to apply it even when the language is clear and unambiguous. This is because events sometimes occur that seem to fit within the category of happenings covered by statutory language, but application of the statute to the facts would be unfair, or remote from the statute's purpose, or both. To avoid the plain language rule in these circumstances, courts have developed a battery of auxiliary rules and principles limiting its application. But as with the last antecedent rule discussed in chapter 2, there really is no theory that dictates in any coherent manner when to apply the plain language rule and when to apply the auxiliary rules. Occasionally courts admit this, but most often they either apply or refuse to apply the plain language rule without much analysis.

Here, we will look at these problems from several perspectives. First, I will discuss, from a linguistic point of view, what it means for language to be clear, and what causes language not to be clear. Second, I will examine Supreme Court cases interpreting RICO, a federal statute that has engendered considerable debate about the relationship between its purpose and its language. RICO is a statute directed at fighting organized crime, although it does not mention organized crime in its text. Not surprisingly, this state of affairs has engendered enormous debate about the statute's meaning, triggering both the plain language rule and the auxiliary interpretive principles to which I referred earlier.

The remainder of the chapter will compare the use of the plain language rule and another principle that says to look past the plain language when the language of the statute does not carry out the intentions of the legislature. In keeping with what we have seen already, these opposing principles exist side by side, without any rules for when to apply one and when to apply the other. I will try to explain why this happens, taking into account both the linguistic perspective and recent proposals by legal scholars.

How Plain Can Language Be?

Let us begin by asking how clear statutes can be. Can the meaning of a statute ever be plain? If not, should the plain language rule be abandoned altogether as nothing more than a formal opportunity for judicial subterfuge?

To address these questions, we return to the description of our knowledge of language outlined in chapter 1. As I pointed out there, many aspects of interpretation derive from formal relationships among the various elements in a sentence, about which we have tacit knowledge. To take a very simple example, in "the snake crawled into the hole," our knowledge of English, acquired during childhood without formal training, tells us that the sentence has a subject, "the snake," that it has a predicate, "crawled into the hole," that "into the hole" is a prepositional phrase that is part of the predicate and describes where the snake crawled, and that the entire predicate is being asserted about "the snake." These facts seem to us simple and uncontroversial only because this aspect of interpretation occurs automatically, without any thought going into it. In fact, the linguistic relationships of which we have tacit knowledge are very complicated.[2] Nonetheless, processing of sentences occurs so rapidly that we are not capable of watching it in progress even if we try.

The very existence of the plain language rule reflects at some intuitive level a high degree of confidence in people's potential to communicate successfully. Much of interpretation is indeed clear, and we all recognize it as so. When we engage in conversation, we come away believing that we have understood what was said and that in turn we were understood. Linguistic theory tells us that this intuition is in large part based in biological fact, as the few examples I have presented illustrate. No one reading "the snake crawled into the hole" thinks that the sentence means "the leopard ate the snake," or "the federal government should require automobile manufacturers to install airbags in all new cars." It is therefore very tempting for judges and legal theorists to put their faith in the language that a statute or a contract contains in order to maintain the belief that a rule of law is operating, and that the will of the legislature or the will of the contracting parties has been given its due deference. Even critics of the plain language rule acknowledge its attractiveness,[3] a fact to which we return at the end of this chapter.

Despite linguists' enthusiasm about the extent to which our knowledge of language makes interpretation entirely uncontroversial, many legal theorists with diverse political orientations have reached the common conclusion that language in fact is not plain.[4] In certain respects, they are right. Consider first the problem of structural ambiguity. In chapters 2 and 3 we saw a number of instances in which the words of a sentence may be assigned more than one syntactic structure, and in which the different syntactic structures are associated with different meanings. For example, the Supreme Court decisions in *Yermian* and *Liparota*,[5] discussed in connection with the rule of lenity, involved ambiguity in the scope of adverbs, and the decision in *Brown*,[6] the death penalty case, depended on the scope of adjectives, which is also sometimes ambiguous.

A related interpretive problem occurs when a sentence with a given syntactic structure can have more than one logical form associated with it.[7] Consider (1):

(1)   Each of the lawyers thought that he should conduct a thorough
       cross-examination of the witness.

In (1), *he* can be interpreted in two different ways. First, it can be interpreted as a variable, connected to the phrase *each of the lawyers*. Under this interpretation, the sentence means that lawyer$_a$ thought that lawyer$_a$ should conduct a thorough cross-examination, lawyer$_b$ thought that lawyer$_b$ should conduct a thorough cross-examination, etc. Alternatively, we can interpret *he* as an ordinary pronoun, referring to some particular individual, perhaps a lawyer who was just beginning to cross-examine the witness. In this second reading, lawyers watching the cross-examiner have reached a consensus about how he should proceed. Whether we select the first or second reading of the pronoun, and if we select the second, how we choose the appropriate antecedent for the pronoun, all depend on the context in which the sentence is uttered. Thus, while the syntax of (1) is clear, the logical relations among its elements are ambiguous.

Next consider (2):

(2)   The litigation team worked through the night, except for a twenty-minute break to eat a sandwich.

How many sandwiches were eaten, and by whom? Seemingly simple structures like this have complicated, but predictable semantic possibilities.[8] We saw other instances of this phenomenon in chapter 2 in connection with the interpretation of *and* and *or*.

There exists a third set of instances in which language ceases to be plain, and these account for most of the problems that arise in the legal context. The problem arises, as we saw in Chapter 3, when a statute or other legal document makes reference to a category of things or events, and a dispute arises over whether a particular thing or event in question fits into the category.

Philosophers of language have long written about the difficulties that we have with categorization. Wittgenstein, for example, wrote about our inability to state necessary and sufficient conditions for something to be a "game."[9] Quine used the word "mountain" as his example,[10] and Putnam chose the word "jealousy," among others.[11] Legal philosophers rely on their own set of examples, most notably H. L. A. Hart's discussion of the word "vehicle" in the context of a hypothetical law that proscribes bringing vehicles into public parks. Does a child's toy automobile count? What about a war memorial that incorporates tanks used in World War II?[12]

Among the most interesting work in this area is that of Ray Jackendoff, especially his book *Semantics and Cognition*.[13] Jackendoff makes several points relevant to the discussion here. First, when it comes to questions of categorization of things into types of things, people's judgments often become indeterminate at the margins. To take another classic example, also discussed by Wittgenstein and others, our concept of color enables us to identify as such an object that is bright red, and to identify as not red an object that is, say, white. But when it comes to shades that are between red and orange, or between red and violet, our judgments become tentative, and we simply stop knowing whether an object is properly called red or not. As Jackendoff puts it, "fuzziness is an inescapable characteristic of the concepts that language expresses."[14]

Moreover, this fuzziness is not easily resolved by introspection. To return to my earlier example, "the snake crawled into the hole," assume that for some reason it becomes important to prove that the thing that crawled into the hole was really a snake. Perhaps there is a law prohibiting the ownership of snakes, or some similar reason for caring. If I were called to testify as a witness at a trial that depended on the snakehood of the crawler, having seen the animal crawl into the hole, I would be unable to explain how I knew that the animal was a snake. That is, I cannot explain what makes a snake a snake. In fact, not only can I not explain it, but I do not consciously know what makes a snake a snake. (Nor do I know at any level of conscious awareness what makes a dog a dog, for that matter.) I would merely have to say that I know what a snake looks like, and what I saw was a typical snake, as far as I am concerned. The same holds true for other concepts. I cannot, with any degree of confidence, recite the necessary and sufficient conditions for something being a game, or a vehicle, etc. There may be some words for which this task is relatively easy (e.g., "sister" means female sibling), but in large part, as Jackendoff accurately concludes, generic categorization is a matter of induction and intuition, which we are sometimes not able to make with any degree of certainty, and are rarely able to describe.[15]

Nor can we ordinarily rely on experts to clarify concepts for us. Focusing again on the snake, suppose that I am mistaken in my characterization of what happened. The creature that I saw crawl into the hole looks exactly like a snake, but zoologists would agree that it is not a snake. Rather, it is a legless lizard that looks like a snake.[16] In this case, an expert would save the day, assuming that the judge hearing the case is inclined to bow to the literal meaning of the statute.

But this example does not take us very far. For one thing, even within biological research, there is substantial debate over taxonomic decisions about whether a given animal is a token of a particular animal type.[17] Categorization at the margins becomes fuzzy for experts, just as it does for the rest of us. More significantly, expertise is irrelevant to most of the problems of categorization that face us in everyday life, and in the legal context in particular.[18] There is no expert with the expertise to tell us whether the word "vehicle" in Hart's example should be interpreted to include such things as bicycles, toy automobiles, etc. While I can call a bicycle a vehicle, I can also use the word "vehicle" when I only intend to include motor vehicles. As Jackendoff points out, we seem to rely on notions of typicality and centrality in deciding whether to include a thing or event in a category. These notions do not force us to adopt any particular position with respect to bicycles, although we would have no question about the statute's application to functioning trucks and automobiles.

When we speak of clarity in construing the concepts expressed by statutes, we are not really making statements about the clarity of the concepts themselves. Rather, we are expressing judgments about the goodness of fit between the statutory concept and the thing or event in the world that is the subject of dispute.[19] Seeing a truck drive through the park, we say that Hart's statute banning vehicles from the park is clear and that the driver violated the statute. By this, however, we do not mean to say that the word "vehicle" does not become fuzzy at the margins. Rather, we mean that a truck is such a typical token of the category *vehicle* that there should be no controversy about the applicability of the statute to the situation at hand.

There exist other interpretive problems, which relate largely to construing ambiguous and indeterminate linguistic expressions within a discourse. While I will not dwell on these here, they are of some importance. Our need to understand the context in which utterances are made in order to choose among multiple possible interpretations is beyond dispute, and forms the substance of the field of pragmatics.[20] The interpretation of pronouns, when our knowledge of language leaves open more than one possible antecedent, is an example that we have already seen. Others include choosing a particular sense of a word when more than one exists.[21] We use the word "snake," for example, to mean a sneaky person who should not be trusted. I doubt that many readers, however, construed my earlier example as meaning that such a person crawled into a hole.

In the discussion that follows, we will see courts invoking the plain language rule in the face of all of these problems. We should keep in mind, however, that there are many cases in which these interpretive difficulties do not arise. In these instances, the syntax is unambiguous, and the events and things in the world fall obviously enough within the categories that the statute defines. These cases renew our confidence in the prospect of plain language, even in the face of the many critics who say that language cannot be plain. It is the critics, however, who have the right to be confident when abuses of the plain language rule occur, such as those illustrated below.

The "Plain Language" of RICO

Cases construing the federal Racketeering Influenced and Corrupt Organization Act illustrate many of the problems with the notion of plain language. We begin with a case in which the Supreme Court found language plain, despite a structural ambiguity. We then move to some difficult cases in which the Court had to grapple with the indeterminacy of various concepts necessary to understanding RICO.

WHEN THE LANGUAGE AND ITS OPPOSITE ARE BOTH PLAIN

The most interesting application of the plain language rule in a RICO case is *Sedima, S.P.R.L. v. Imrex Company, Inc.,*[22] touched on in chapter 3 in connection with the rule of lenity. *Sedima* involved the interpretation of several of the terms in section 1964, the provision in RICO that permits lawsuits by individuals against RICO violators. The statute provides:

> Any person injured in his business or property by reason of a violation of section 1962 of this chapter may sue therefor in any appropriate United States district court and shall recover three-fold the damages he sustains and the cost of the suit, including a reasonable attorney's fee.[23]

Before the enactment of RICO, the *Sedima* case would have been an ordinary business dispute, in which one party to a contract accused the other of cheating. Sedima was a Belgian corporation that had an agreement with Imrex, an American company, through which Imrex would supply electronic parts to Sedima for resale to a European customer. Sedima and Imrex were then to split the profits. But when Sedima became convinced that Imrex was sending inflated bills, and thereby collecting for nonexistent expenses, it sued Imrex in federal court. The lawsuit alleged breach of contract and other such claims, and it also alleged RICO violations based on mail and wire fraud. Recall that to prove a RICO violation, one must demonstrate that a defendant engaged in a "pattern of racketeering activity," which requires the commission, in a pattern, of two or more acts of racketeering activity within a ten-year period. The statute lists mail fraud and wire fraud among the acts of racketeering activity.[24] Imrex apparently had used both the mail and the telephones in submitting the allegedly inflated bills.

At issue in *Sedima* was the question of what it means to be "injured . . . by reason of a violation of section 1962." Sedima argued that it means only that a plaintiff be injured by virtue of a defendant having committed two acts of racketeering activity, sufficiently related to one another to constitute a pattern. Thus, injury by two acts of mail fraud (e.g., mailing two inflated bills) is sufficient to prove entitlement to RICO's treble damages, provided that the two acts are committed in a pattern. Imrex, on the other hand, argued that a plaintiff must show more than ordinary business injury resulting from the predicate acts themselves. Rather, it must show a "racketeering injury," an injury resulting from having been victimized by the pattern of racketeering, and not just from the predicate racketeering acts that make up the pattern.

This dispute was of great moment in the legal community, and in the business world generally. For while mail fraud and wire fraud are both crimes, private lawsuits have never been allowed under the criminal statutes outlawing these activities. Perhaps even more significant, the securities statutes, under which private lawsuits are allowed, have evolved over the past fifty year s to place some rather difficult obstacles in front of plaintiffs suing under them. Civil RICO, if applied as broadly as Sedima was asking, would serve to undercut much of this history, by permitting securities fraud plaintiffs to sue in federal court if they allege two acts of mail or wire fraud, thereby evading the securities law obstacles. Moreover, the successful plaintiff would collect treble damages plus attorney's fees. In fact, at the time that *Sedima* was decided, a recent report on civil RICO had found that "40% of the reported cases involved securities fraud and 37% involved common-law fraud in a commercial or business setting [like the *Sedima* case]." "Only 9% of all civil RICO cases have involved allegations of criminal activity normally associated with professional criminals."[25]

Both the trial court and the court of appeals agreed with Imrex, holding that some sort of "racketeering injury" must be alleged in a civil RICO case, distinct from the injury caused only by the predicate acts themselves. As the Supreme Court noted, these opinions were part of a plethora of decisions on these and related RICO issues, reflecting tremendous diversity in attitudes and approaches toward the statute by the various judges.

In a 5–4 decision, the Supreme Court reversed. The majority opinion, written by Justice White, held that the plain language of the statute requires nothing more than proof of injury caused by two or more related instances of racketeering activity, including mail or wire fraud. Justice Marshall, who wrote a dissenting opinion, also concluded that the language of the statute is clear, but read the language to mean that a racketeering injury is required. Justice Powell also wrote a separate dissenting opinion. Both sides wrote that the history of the statute's enactment supported its position as well.

The disagreement among the justices on the Supreme Court can be attributed to an ambiguity in the statute that none of them admits is present.[26] Although both of the proposed interpretations are possible, each side is wrong in its assertion that the language is clear. Thus, in an interesting voting paradox, the justices agreed 9–0 that the language is plain, but disagreed 5–4 about what it means.

The majority stated its position as follows:

> A reading of the statute belies any such requirement [of racketeering injury]. Section 1964(c) authorizes a private suit by "[a]ny person injured in his business or property by reason of a violation of section 1962." Section 1962 in turn makes it unlawful for "any person"—not just mobsters—to use money derived from a pattern of racketeering activity to invest in an enterprise, to acquire control of an enterprise through a pattern of racketeering activity, or to conduct an enterprise through a pattern of racketeering activity. Sections 1962(a)–(c). If the defendant engages in a pattern of racketeering activity in a manner forbidden by these provisions, and the racketeering activities injure the plaintiff in his business or property, the plaintiff has a claim under Section 1964(c). There is no room in the statutory language for an additional, amorphous "racketeering injury" requirement.[27]

The Court went further, chiding the court of appeals whose decision it reversed for not recognizing how plain RICO's language really is:

> Given the plain words of the statute, we cannot agree with the court below that Congress could have had no "inkling of [section 1964(c)'s] implications. . . . Congress' "inklings" are best determined by the statutory language that it chooses, and the language it chose here extends far beyond the limits drawn by the Court of Appeals.[28]

The majority reasoned that if (a) a defendant engages in a pattern of racketeering activity *and* (b) the activities injure the plaintiff, then the plaintiff has a claim under section 1964. This reading assumes that injury by a "pattern" of racketeering activity is the same as injury by the set of racketeering activities that make up the pattern. The reading, however, is only one of at least two possible interpretations of the statute. To see how this is so, consider the following sentences:

(3)   A series of rainstorms damaged the house.

(4)   A gang of teenagers intimidated the neighbors.

(5)   A flock of geese landed on the pond.

Each of these sentences is ambiguous. For example, (3) may mean that a series of rainstorms occurred, each rainstorm causing independent damage to the house. Or it may mean that a series of rainstorms occurred, and that the house was damaged in some way by virtue of their cumulative effect on the building. In this second reading, it is entirely possible that none of the individual rainstorms damaged the house on its own. Let us call these the distributive reading and nondistributive reading, respectively. In (4), the nondistributive reading, in which it is the fact that the teenagers are in a gang that caused the intimidation, is the more natural one. It is possible, but less natural to understand the sentence as meaning that teenager$_1$, teenager$_2$, etc., each intimidated the neighbors. In (5), the distributive reading is the more natural, although the two readings do each paint their own picture of the event. What makes one reading more natural in a particular sentence appears to be the contextual relationship between the group term and the predicate of the sentence.

What causes the ambiguity? The phrase "pattern of racketeering activity" is structurally ambiguous. "Pattern of racketeering activity" is a noun phrase, which by definition must have a noun as its "head." For example, in "the empty courtroom," *courtroom* is the head, and *the* and *empty* are various kinds of modifiers. In "the table in the courtroom," *table* is the head, and the prepositional phrase "in the courtroom" is a complement that further modifies *the table*.

As Elizabeth Selkirk has pointed out,[29] noun phrases like those in (5)–(7) are ambiguous with respect to which noun is the head. *Series* may be the head in (5), in which case *of rainstorms* is a complement, or *rainstorms* may be understood as the head, in which case *a series* is a modifying measure phrase. These possibilities yield the nondistributive and distributive readings, respectively. To put the matter more intuitively, the structure of the noun phrase permits us to say that the noun phrase is about a series, or that the noun phrase is about rainstorms. These possibilities correspond to the alternative readings that I introduced above.

Exactly the same analysis applies to "pattern of racketeering activity." If we understand *pattern* to be the head of the noun phrase, then *of racketeering activity* is merely a complement that modifies *pattern*, and we understand the expression nondistributively. If, on the other hand, we take *activity* to be the head, *pattern* becomes merely a modifying measure phrase, and we interpret the phrase distributively, focusing on the activities themselves—not the pattern.

In *Sedima*, the majority acknowledges only the distributive reading of the expression "pattern of racketeering activity." The Court's reasoning is that to be injured by reason of a violation of section 1962 is to be injured by a "pattern of racketeering activity," which is to be injured by each racketeering activity individually. To these justices, *activity* is the head of the phrase.[30] The reading is parallel to the interpretation of (3) in which damage by a series of rainstorms is understood to mean separate damage by each storm, a legitimate interpretation, but not the only one, as we have just seen.

The four dissenting justices argued for the nondistributive reading, concluding that the language is clear:

> In summary, the statute clearly contemplates recovery for injury resulting from the confluence of events described in § 1962 and not merely from the commission of a predicate act. The Court's contrary interpretation distorts the statutory language under the guise of adopting a plain meaning definition, and it does so without offering any indication of congressional intent that justifies a deviation from what I have shown to be the plain-meaning of the statute.[31]

This interpretation is consistent with "pattern" being the head of its noun phrase, "pattern of racketeering activity."

Of course, each side in *Sedima* brought out bits and pieces of the legislative history. For example, the majority pointed out that Congress stated specifically that RICO should be interpreted "liberally to effect its remedial purposes." The dissent retorted that its remedial purposes were specifically identified as the eradication of organized crime, and that broad interpretation of RICO to do mischief to the structure of the relationship between federal and state law (many of the predicate acts identified in the statute are state law violations) and to the federal securities laws falls way outside the intent of Congress.

How to interpret these provisions presents a difficult doctrinal question. But one thing is clear: the statute is not clear. To the extent that the Court is telling us that one result or the other is a necessary consequence of the plain language of the statute, we are experiencing efforts to mask a set of complicated and contingent inferences.

UNDERSTANDING PATTERNS: RICO AS AN UNCLEAR STATUTE

A more recent foray into RICO by the Supreme Court admits the statute's lack of clarity, at least in part. In *H.J. Inc. v. Northwestern Bell Telephone Co.*,[32] the Court was confronted with an issue that *Sedima* skirted: Exactly what is a "pattern of racketeering activity?" The case was brought by customers of Northwestern Bell, a telephone company in Minnesota. The customers charged that officers of Northwestern Bell had over a period of time illegally influenced the Minnesota government commission in charge of setting telephone rates, by making cash payments to the state commissioners, among other things. Both the trial court and the United States Court of Appeals agreed that the case should be dismissed because the complaint alleged only a single scheme to influence the commissioners, and that a "pattern of racketeering activity" requires proof of at least two schemes.

The Supreme Court unanimously reversed, although the Court was divided 5–4 as to the grounds for the reversal. Recall from our discussion of *Sedima* that RICO defines "pattern of racketeering activity" as "requir[ing] at least two acts of racketeering activity" within a ten-year period.[33] The statute says nothing more. In the majority opinion, Justice Brennan admitted the paucity of plain language:

> The text of RICO conspicuously fails anywhere to identify, however, forms of relationship or external principles to be used in determining whether racketeering activity falls into a pattern for purposes of the Act.[34]

In fact, Justice Brennan chided Congress for not clarifying the statute and for choosing instead to let the courts interpret Congress's imprecise words.

Nonetheless, relying on "a common-sense, everyday understanding of RICO's language and Congress' gloss on it,"[35] the Court formulated a rule: "[T]o prove a pattern of racketeering activity a plaintiff or prosecutor must show that the racketeering predicates are related, *and* that they amount to or pose a threat of continued criminal activity."[36] As for continuity, the Court held that "[p]redicate acts extending over a few weeks or months and threatening no future criminal conduct do not satisfy this requirement."[37] Applying this rule to the case before it, the Court decided that the allegations against Northwestern Bell and others met the Court's new standard, and reinstated the lawsuit.

Justice Brennan's effort to divine a "common-sense, everyday understanding" of the statute from its language is actually an effort to decompose the word "pattern" into what he apparently believes are its component concepts. The effort fails, as do most efforts at lexical decomposition.[38] First, there is no reason to conclude that relatedness plus continuity really do form the component parts of patternhood. For example, there is nothing in the word "pattern" that requires continuity, except for a period long enough to permit formation of the pattern itself. Consider the following:

(6)   During the three weeks that he was on drugs, John exhibited a pattern of violent behavior that we had not seen before and have not seen since.

(7)   The two-week outburst of burnings formed a pattern: only buildings that had not been occupied for two months were torched.

Each of these examples uses the word "pattern" acceptably. That is, as native speakers of English, we accept (6) and (7) as grammatical, and therefore consistent with our knowledge of English in the sense discussed in chapter 1. Yet, these sentences use the word "pattern" in the context of a series of events that took place over a very short period of time—which is exactly what the majority opinion says that RICO does not cover. Nor would it do to substitute other concepts for relatedness and continuity. Exactly the same types of problems would arise. We will always be able to find examples of patterns and nonpatterns that challenge the proposed components.

A second problem with Justice Brennan's analysis is that it merely postpones the difficult interpretive problems. Even if we agree to decompose *pattern* to mean relatedness plus continuity, we need to know when two events are related and when they are continuous. But *relatedness* is at least as indeterminate a concept as is *patternhood,* and *continuity* is not much better. Try, as an experiment, to define *relatedness* meaningfully so that your definition has predictive force. You will fail.

The problems that the Court faced in construing the word "pattern" in RICO are, in fact, unavoidable. They result from the imperfect match between concepts conveyed by the words in a statute and the virtually infinite variety of events that can occur in the world. As hard as we may try to avoid the indeterminacy of concepts at the margins, we will not succeed. No one drafting RICO or any other statute could conceivably imagine every hypothetical set of events, and decide in advance whether they form a pattern. Our knowledge of language, as discussed in chapter 1, simply does not answer all of these questions.

Nor should this be surprising in light of the discussion at the beginning of this chapter. If concepts like *vehicle* and *mountain* fray at the edges, why should *pattern* be any easier? As a second experiment, arbitrarily select two events from your own experience. Almost invariably, it will turn out that by looking at the events abstractly, you will be able to discern a pattern, and by looking at them microscopically, you will be able to see them as events isolated from each other.

Justice Scalia's concurring opinion in *H.J. Inc.* recognized some of these problems. He agreed that the statute does not require proof of multiple schemes of illegal activity. That is, the multiple acts can be part of the same scheme. However, Scalia found the language of the statute so indeterminate, and the majority's guidelines for its application so uninformative, that he conjectured that RICO may be unconstitutionally vague, suggesting that he would seriously entertain such a challenge to the statute in a later case.[39]

Both the majority and concurring opinions marveled at the extraordinary range of RICO interpretations that judges have proposed over the years. As Justice Scalia observed, the majority's "common-sense, everyday" interpretation of this vague statute will most likely help this tradition of inconsistent judicial positions to continue. While we will no doubt see more pronouncements about the clarity of RICO, we see from *H.J. Inc.* that the justices on the Supreme Court know better.

Turkette and *Russello* Revisited: Some More Fuzzy Concepts

To see further difficulty that courts have with the plain language rule in the context of RICO, let us return to *United States v. Turkette*,[40] the Supreme Court's first adventure with RICO. Recall from the previous chapter that the Court in *Turkette* would not apply the rule of lenity in construing the definition of "enterprise" in RICO,[41] deciding instead that the relevant statutory language was not ambiguous. The specific issue was whether RICO's prohibition against investing illegally acquired money to further an "enterprise" should be construed to bar distribution of money to the members of an arson ring. Eschewing the rule of lenity, the Court instead applied the following interpretive principles:

In determining the scope of a statute, we look first to its language. If the statutory language is unambiguous, in the absence of "a clearly expressed legislative intent to the contrary, that language must ordinarily be regarded as conclusive." . . . Of course, there is no errorless test for identifying or recognizing "plain" or "unambiguous" language. Also, authoritive administrative constructions should be given the deference to which they are entitled, absurd results are to be avoided and internal inconsistencies in the statute must be dealt with. . . . We nevertheless begin with the language of the statute.[42]

While the Court listed and briefly considered numerous auxiliary principles (the legislative intent rule, the administrative decision rule, the absurd result rule, and the internal inconsistency rule), it basically applied the plain language rule, while also confirming that the result was neither absurd nor contrary to a clearly expressed legislative intent. But as we saw in chapter 3, there is nothing the least bit clear about what the word "enterprise" means in RICO. While we do have a sense of a typical enterprise, I would be extremely hard pressed to state the necessary and sufficient conditions for membership in the class of enterprises.

As a matter of logic, the Court was forced in *Turkette* either to hold that the meaning of "enterprise" is clear and unambiguous, or to reverse Turkette's conviction. As noted in chapter 3, the Court's reading of "enterprise" fits well into RICO's legislative scheme. Racketeers who invest in illegal enterprises are no less racketeers than those who invest in legitimate ones. By holding that the language of RICO is clear, the Court was able to accomplish its goal of construing the statute consistent with the Court's vision of RICO's philosophy. In fact, the Court *had* to declare the statute clear to do so.

Exactly the same problem arose in *Russello v. United States*,[43] also discussed in chapter 3. Recall that the issue in *Russello* was whether the RICO provision requiring forfeiture of a RICO violator's "interest" in an enterprise included his share of the take from money acquired through the illegal activities of an arson ring. The concept *interest* does not necessarily include money that has been distributed to a person from a business, whether that business is legal or illegal. Like *enterprise, interest* becomes a fuzzy concept at the margins. Nonetheless, the Supreme Court invoked the plain language rule, as its only available antidote to the rule of lenity.

THE Court's interpretation of the statute in these cases reflects an earnest effort to mold sensible doctrine out of a complicated and somewhat vague statute. But like the last antecedent rule discussed in chapter 2 and the rule of lenity discussed in chapter 3, the invocation of the plain language rule and the auxiliary principles of construction to explain RICO lapses into a weak attempt to demonstrate the necessity of holdings reached through a far more elaborate and contingent set of inferences. The Supreme Court in *Turkette* could easily have reached the conclusion that the definition of "enterprise" is not very clear, and could therefore have applied the rule of lenity to reach the opposite result. The same holds true for *Russello*. In *Sedima*, the minority of four justices presented a coherent alternative interpretation of the structurally ambiguous statute, more attractive in a number of respects. While the result in *H.J. Inc.* may follow reasonably enough from the language of the statute, the Court's reasoning is a perfect illustration of the intuitive nature of our understanding of concepts. In all of these cases, the Court took whatever information was available to reach the best decision it could, taking into account the words of the statute, the legislative history, judicial precedents, related statutes, and anything else that could help. The decisions are intelligent and defensible, but by no means necessary. To the extent that the cases rely on judgments as to whether particular events and things are tokens of the categories used in the statute, our cognitive capacity takes us no further.

When Is Plain Language Enough?

As we have already seen, courts are selective in applying the plain language rule. Although one legal writer declared the rule to be dying about fifteen years ago,[44] the RICO cases discussed above demonstrate that the rule is still alive, although perhaps not well.

The status of the plain language rule is most frequently called into question when the language of a statute, applied literally to a dispute before a court, would result in an outcome seemingly at odds with the legislature's purpose for enacting the statute in the first place. When this happens, the court must decide whether to rely on the statute or to rely on what it believes the statute was intended to accomplish. We saw all of these considerations sneaking their way into RICO analysis, especially in *Turkette*. In many cases, however, one or the other rule is simply set forth as the only rule, with no real explanation for the rejection of its opposite.

The question of what information judges should consider in interpreting statutes is currently a topic of considerable discussion in the legal literature.

Some would focus primarily on the original intent of the legislature that enacted the statute.[45] Others adhere to the text to the extent possible,[46] often quoting Holmes's pronouncement: "We do not inquire what the legislature meant; we ask only what the statute means."[47] A number of theorists propose that judges take advantage of whatever they can, including the record of legislative history, the language of the statute, how the statute can best fit into the current body of law as a whole, and so on.[48] Before discussing these approaches, let us look at a few cases in which the plain language rule conflicts with other principles.

For example, in *Train v. Colorado Public Interest Research Group, Inc.,*[49] which the Supreme Court decided in 1976, a citizens' group sued the federal Environmental Protection Agency (Train was its administrator) for failing to regulate the discharge of radioactive materials into the waterways. The relevant statutes required the EPA to regulate "pollutants," and the statute defined "pollutant" as including "radioactive materials."[50] The EPA's refusal to act was based on the notion that another government agency, the Nuclear Regulatory Commission (NRC), is in charge of regulating the discharge of the relevant radioactive materials under the Atomic Energy Act.[51] The plaintiffs, environmentalists, wanted the EPA to regulate the discharges, since under the relevant statutes, the EPA would be forced to adopt tougher standards than had the NRC.

Writing for a unanimous Court, Justice Marshall refused to rely exclusively on the plain language of the statute. Rather, quoting from a particular line of cases, the Court held:

> When aid to construction of the meaning of words, as used in the statute, is available, there certainly can be no "rule of law" which forbids its use, however clear the words may appear on "superficial examination."[52] (Citations omitted)

Applying this principle, and reviewing an enormous amount of legislative history, the Court concluded that the EPA should not be regulating the discharge of these radioactive materials; rather, the NRC should be doing so.

Justice Marshall's statement that "there certainly can be no 'rule of law'" forbidding the use of extrinsic aids to statutory construction is curious. There certainly can be such a rule of law, and that rule of law is the plain language rule.

Two years after deciding *Train,* the Supreme Court decided *Tennesee Valley Authority v. Hill,*[53] in which the majority (including Marshall) returned to the plain language rule. That case, known as the "snail darter case," involved interpretation of the Endangered Species Act of 1973. The act requires that the Secretary of the Interior identify endangered species, and all federal departments and agencies take whatever action is necessary to provide for the conservation of any that are identified. In particular, it requires that federal agencies

> tak[e] such action necessary to insure that actions authorized, funded, or carried out by them do not jeopardize the continued existence of such endangered species and threatened species or result in the destruction or modification of habitat of such species . . . [54]

At issue in *Hill* was whether the Tennessee Valley Authority (TVA) could activate a dam that would lead to the destruction of the snail darter's habitat. The snail darter is a small fish. The dam was begun before the Endangered Species Act was enacted, although the effect of the project on the snail darter was not discovered until after the enactment of the statute. By the time that the matter came to court, the dam was virtually completed, and more than $100 million had already been spent on the project.[55] During the period between the statute's enactment in 1973 and the Supreme Court's decision in 1978, Congress continued to appropriate money for the dam project.

The District Court had ordered that construction continue, after which the Court of Appeals had reversed, stopping the project. The Supreme Court, in a 6–3 decision, agreed with the appellate court, and ordered that construction of the dam be halted. Chief Justice Burger wrote the majority opinion. In justifying its decision, the Court applied the plain language rule:

> One would be hard pressed to find a statutory provision whose terms were any plainer than those of §7 of the Endangered Species Act. Its very words affirmatively command all federal agencies "to *insure* that actions *authorized, funded,* or *carried out* by them do not *jeopardize* the continued existence" of an endangered species or "*result* in the destruction or modification of habitat of such species."[56]

Although the majority also evaluated the statute's legislative history, the Chief Justice explained that this excursion was only for the purpose of rebutting statements made in the dissenting opinion. As far as the majority was concerned, "it is not necessary to look beyond the words of the statute" to come to the conclusion it reached.[57] With respect to the fact that Congress had continued funding the dam even after the enactment of the Endangered Species Act, the majority relied on a canon of statutory construction that disfavors interpreting later congressional action to repeal earlier action, especially when the later action is limited to the appropriation of funds.[58]

Not surprisingly, Justice Powell's dissenting opinion tried to find ambiguity in the statute, arguing that the language was not at all plain. In particular, the dissent took the position that the word "actions" in the statute should be construed as referring only to prospective actions, and not to actions that are already in progress. Since the dam was already under construction at the time that the statute was enacted, its completion by TVA should not be considered an "action" under the statute.

It is virtually impossible for me to conceptualize the closing of a dam gate that will result in an enormous flood as not being an action. Justice Powell does have a point, however. Consider what we do to throw a ball. I think that everyone would agree that throwing a ball is an action. When we say, "he threw the ball," we describe someone's action. But this action consists of a series of different muscular events. First, we grasp the ball. Then, we move our arm back, and finally snap it forward, releasing the ball at just the right moment. Now, consider the period during which we move our arm back. Is this itself an action? Consider further a portion of the arm motion backward, say, the middle third of this motion. Can we call this portion of the toss an action? I think not. It is thus possible to distinguish between events that form part of an action and events that are themselves actions. Powell seems to be saying that the completion of the dam was like a portion of the action of throwing a ball, which we would not ordinarily consider to be an action.

Here, again, the judgments are intuitive, and not subject to much analysis.[59] However, my clear intuition is that the completion of the dam is not like an intermediate portion of the activity of throwing a ball, at least not in the sense that I just described. What was left to complete the dam was a discrete set of activities, the most important of which was to close the gate. Returning to our ball thrower, assume that he is receiving and responding to the instructions of a coach: "First, grasp the ball." He grasps the ball. "Now, move your arm back." He moves his arm back. "Now, snap your arm forward, and release the ball." He does this. Here, it is natural to regard each instruction as calling for an action, although each of these new actions is part of the larger action of throwing a ball. To the extent that the ball-throwing analogy applies, it applies in this second sense far more closely than in any way that would be helpful to Justice Powell's position. If I had to vote on linguistic grounds, my vote would be with the majority.

Any intellectually satisfying argument against application of the Endangered Species Act to completion of the TVA dam, then, must find a way around the plain language of the statute. Resort to legislative intent is not available here either, as it was in *Train,* because the legislative history of the act, as Chief Justice Burger pointed out in the majority opinion, largely contains statements about a national priority of protecting the earth's species from extinction.

In his own dissenting opinion, Justice Rehnquist observed that as part of their equitable power, courts always have discretion in deciding whether to issue an injunction, even if the law has been violated. The District Court that first heard the case and refused to issue the injunction, the argument continues, did not clearly abuse this discretion. Therefore, its decision should be respected, and the TVA should be permitted to complete the dam.

Analytically, Justice Rehnquist's dissent is far more successful than Justice Powell's. For he asks the question head on: Even when the language of a statute is clear, how much attention do the courts have to pay to it?[60] Rehnquist's approach would permit courts, even in matters of enormous importance, to exercise judgment independent of the words of an applicable statute before issuing an injunction. His position is a radical one, since it would permit courts to engage in a cost/benefit analysis whenever the Endangered Species Act is invoked, despite the strong national policy in favor of conservation that the statute represents. Probably for this reason, it received only one vote, despite its coherence.

Ronald Dworkin, in his discussion of the snail darter case, attempts to avoid the issue by acknowledging the importance of plain language, while at the same time rejecting the notion that language can be plain outside of contextual considerations.[61] Dworkin argues that we conclude that language is plain only after we analyze the statute and apply it to the facts. This is probably true enough, at least when it comes to evaluating the clarity of concepts expressed by language. For example, the Endangered Species Act contains the word "destruction." *Destruction,* like other concepts, becomes fuzzy at the margins. There may be instances in which it is difficult to tell whether what we see is destruction, or merely extensive damage falling short of destruction. Moreover, destruction can refer to the process of destruction or to its result. Yet, in reading the Endangered Species Act in the context of the snail darter case, we do not notice this indeterminacy in the meaning of "destruction" since it is not relevant to the issue at hand: the meaning of "actions." Thus, when the majority says that the language of the act is plain, it can really only mean that the language is sufficiently clear with respect to the language in dispute. It cannot mean to say that the language of the statute is clear in some absolute sense. In fact, such a statement would be untrue.

But this point is not sufficient to let Dworkin off the hook. Once he concedes that courts have an obligation to pay attention to the language of the statute, he is committed to taking the additional step—taken in both Burger's majority and Powell's dissenting opinions—of asking whether closing the gate of the dam can reasonably be seen as anything other than an action. Although Dworkin devotes most of a chapter of his *Law's Empire* to the snail darter case, nowhere does he discuss the language of the statute. Rather, he equates disagreement about the correct decision with disagreement about statutory language, and infers from this disagreement that the language is not clear.[62]

Dworkin's approach to statutory interpretation is to interpret the statute in a manner "that follows from the best interpretation of the legislative process as a whole,"[63] likening a statute to an ongoing chain novel whose history continues right up to the present. He thus concludes that the case was wrongly decided, principally because Congress's funding of the project after the snail darter issue arose provides strong evidence that continuing the dam would allow the Endangered Species Act to fit best into the body of laws as a whole. Certainly, Dworkin's point as to the reasonableness of stopping construction has some force. The point, however, is in conflict with the plain language of the statute. By failing to deal with this fact, Dworkin, too, falls short of providing a satisfying escape from the majority decision.

Since these cases were decided, the Supreme Court has refused to apply the plain language rule in some instances,[64] while applying it enthusiastically in others,[65] along the lines that I have described. Interestingly, with the 1986 appointment of Antonin Scalia to the Supreme Court, the principle has gained in prominence as a rule of interpretation and as an issue of contention.[66]

Justice Scalia takes the plain language rule very seriously. In fact, he has frequently written concurring opinions, agreeing with the Court's conclusion, but criticizing the majority for looking unnecessarily at legislative history and the like when the language of the statute in dispute is clear.[67] Although he most often votes with the conservatives on the Court, his analysis of statutory language has led him to vote the other way on a number of occasions, sometimes in dissent.[68]

An instructive debate between Justices Scalia and Stevens over the plain language rule arose recently in *West Virginia University Hospitals, Inc. v. Casey,*[69] which the Court decided in 1991. In that case, WVUH, which op-

erates a hospital in West Virginia near the Pennsylvania border, sued the
governor of Pennsylvania (Casey) and other Pennsylvania government officials. In dispute was the legitimacy under certain federal statutes of newly
published reimbursement schedules in which the Pennsylvania government
set forth how much WVUH would receive for providing medical services to
indigent residents of Pennsylvania. WVUH won that suit, and requested
that the defendants be ordered to reimburse it for its attorney's fees, under
section 1988, a federal statute that permits courts to award costs, including
"a reasonable attorney's fee" to the prevailing party in a suit in which a party
has successfully sued a government agency to enforce certain rights.[70] The
question that the Supreme Court had to decide in *Casey* was whether section
1988 permitted the court to award more than $100,000 in expert fees as
part of the "reasonable attorney's fee."

Writing for the majority in a 6–3 decision, Justice Scalia's opinion held
that the statute does not permit the awarding of expert fees. Scalia's principal argument was that other statutes that call for the shifting of attorney's
fees either specifically mention expert fees, or have generally been interpeted
by the courts as not permitting the recovery of expert fees. As for WVUH's
argument that the legislative history of section 1988, including the texts of
various committee reports, reflects a congressional desire to afford citizens
the opportunity to recover their costs in vindicating their rights in court,
Justice Scalia responded:

> As we have observed before, however, the purpose of a statute
> includes not only what it sets out to change, but also what it re-
> solves to leave alone. . . . The best evidence of that purpose is
> the statutory text adopted by both Houses of Congress and sub-
> mitted to the President. Where that contains a phrase that is
> unambiguous—that has a clearly accepted meaning in both leg-
> islative and judicial practice—we do not permit it to be ex-
> panded or contracted by the statements of individual legislators
> or committees during the course of the enactment process. . . .
> "[W]here, as here, the statute's language is plain, 'the sole func-
> tion of the court is to enforce it according to its terms.'"[71] (Cita-
> tions omitted)

The majority similarly rejected WVUH's argument that even if Congress
did not include expert fees in section 1988, the omission was inadvertent,
and had Congress considered the matter, they certainly would have included
them.[72]

In dissent, Justice Stevens focused on another case interpreting section 1988, one in which the Court had construed "reasonable attorney's fee" to include charges for the work of law clerks and paralegals employed by a law firm, in addition to that of attorneys.[73] Similarly, Stevens pointed out, courts routinely permit the recovery of a lawyer's out of pocket disbursements, such as travel, telephone bills, and the like, even though these expenses are not, strictly speaking, attorney's fees. He reasoned that as far as interpreting the statute is concerned, there should be no difference between these charges on the one hand, and expert fees on the other.[74]

With respect to Justice Scalia's argument about the plain language of the statute, Justice Stevens made the following point:

> In recent years the Court has vacillated between a purely literal approach to the task of statutory interpretation and an approach that seeks guidance from historical context, legislative history, and prior cases identifying the purpose that motivated the legislation.
>
> . . . .
>
> In the domain of statutory interpretation, Congress is the master. It obviously has the power to correct our mistakes, but we do the country a disservice when we needlessly ignore persuasive evidence of Congress' actual purpose and require it "to take the time to revisit the matter" and to restate its purpose in more precise English whenever its work product suffers from an omission or inadvertent error.[75]

Criticizing his colleagues for "those occasions . . . when the Court has put on its thick grammarian's spectacles and ignored the available evidence of congressional purpose and the teaching of prior cases construing a statute,"[76] Justice Stevens pointed out many instances in recent years in which Congress has enacted legislation to repudiate decisions of the Supreme Court. These repudiations, according to Stevens's analysis, invariably occur when the Court has attempted to rely on the literal language of a statute, rather than on some effort to make sense of the statute in light of other facts, such as the legislative history, subsequent legislation, and so on. In fact, although Justice Stevens does not mention it, the snail darter case led to new legislation setting up procedures to permit more flexible review of exemptions under the Endangered Species Act.[77]

As a linguistic matter, our knowledge of language tells us nothing about whether or not the phrase "a reasonable attorney's fee" should be interpreted to include fees paid to experts. Lawyers regularly advance the fees paid for experts and then bill their clients for reimbursement. The expression "reasonable attorney's fee" may mean a reasonable fee paid to the attorney, which would include expert fees (as well as fees for paralegals, law clerks, telephone bills, travel, etc.), or it may mean a reasonable fee for the services of the attorney only, which would exclude everything except for the attorney's personal charges.

In general, possessive modifiers, like *attorney's,* can have a range of relationships with the nouns that they modify.[78] The expression *a girl's hat* can mean a hat that some girl owns, or a hat that is intended for girls to wear, rather than boys, or perhaps women. Consider other examples: *my book, the student's desk* and *Bill's wallet.* The last of these examples can mean many things under different circumstances, including the wallet that Bill carries, the wallet that Bill designed, the wallet for which Bill has made a down payment, the wallet that Bill wishes he could afford, etc. *Attorney's fee,* similarly, can refer to either the fee charged by the attorney or the fee for the attorney's time. In short, the language is not plain.[79]

Casey, then, is a case in which the Court was faced with an unwanted indeterminacy in a statute (although none of the justices acknowledged the problem). As I hope to have shown earlier in this chapter, such indeterminacies are inevitable. Moreover, as we saw from the reactions of the dissenters in the snail darter case, statutory language is sometimes undesirably clear. Future events sometimes fit squarely within the meanings of the words used in a statute, whether or not the enacting legislature, or any other legislature, for that matter, would have wanted them to.[80] These problems are inevitable too.

Because of these difficulties, which arise as the result of limitations in our linguistic capacity, the plain language rule has its limits,[81] despite the good reasons for supporting it that Justice Scalia articulates. Although communication is largely a successful enterprise, when the issue is the fit between an event and a statutory category, or the relationship between a possessive and a noun, the enacting legislature may simply not have taken care of the situation, whether or not the language seems clear. Thus, on purely cognitive grounds, we should prefer an approach to statutory interpretation that gives considerable deference to the statutory language, but encourages us to inquire into other factors, such as legislative history and the current legislative corpus, to insure that the language of the statute makes sense as the basis for the exercise of state power.

As I noted earlier, a number of theorists, including Dworkin, Posner, and

Eskridge, have recently proposed methods of statutory interpretation that take into account these various factors.[82] Justice Stevens's dissent in *Casey* reflects this perspective as well, as does Justice Marshall's statement in *Train* that "there certainly can be no 'rule of law'" forbidding us from using available information to help us understand a statute, regardless of how clear the language appears to be.[83] Of course, the more flexible the approach the less certain the result. For instance, while Eskridge would initially emphasize the text, Dworkin focuses on the entire history of the statute and how it fits into the current legislative scheme, and Posner would place more weight on the preenactment history of the statute.[84] These differences in focus can no doubt lead to different results. Moreover, there is plenty of room for disagreement about how each factor plays out in a particular case, as *Casey* illustrates. Despite the problems of predictability, however, these approaches appear to be better than steadfast adherence to the plain language rule, in that they permit judges to acknowledge and deal with interpretive problems that arise as a result of the limits of our linguistic capabilities.

THROUGHOUT this chapter, we have seen the Supreme Court wavering between the plain language perspective of Justice Scalia and the broader interpretive perspective of Justice Stevens and others. Justice Stevens himself pointed out this ambivalence in *Casey*. Courts at times rely heavily on what they perceive to be plain language even where ambiguity exists. At other times, they refuse to rely on language that they recognize is clear. But there are many instances in which, for the reasons discussed above, language is not and cannot be clear. To the extent that courts fail to sort all of this out, whether intentionally or not, they subject themselves to criticism for using the plain language rule improperly as a means for justifying decisions made on entirely different grounds.

5 | Too Much Precision

SEARCHING OUT plain language in statutes is not the only occasion on which judges and lawyers focus on clarity in legal documents. As the reader has already seen, the very fact of ambiguity can determine important legal rights. And litigants are not shy about raising these issues. For when people enter the legal system winning quickly becomes an obsession, and litigants will use any argument that a court will listen to in order to advance their cause. One need only recall Mrs. Anderson's successful battle against her insurance company.[1]

Lawyers are acutely aware that any ambiguity in a legal document can lead to litigation down the road. In my own experience as a lawyer, at any given time I have several cases in which parties are fighting over the meanings of various documents, often agreements into which they had entered when they were on friendlier terms, each party attempting to prove that the other had not done what he was supposed to have done according to the language of the documents. No lawyer wants to risk being on the losing side of cases like those discussed in the earlier chapters of this book. Consequently, lawyers do what they can to make it impossible for opposing parties (and subsequently, judges) to interpret documents that they draft contrary to their clients' interests.

In an effort to accomplish this goal of superprecise writing, lawyers, without serious criticism from judges, have over the years attempted to create their own special syntax, one which is just like English syntax but more precise. As we will see directly, the effort is doomed to failure. After all, the litigants and their lawyers are human too, and are constrained by their knowledge of language (in the sense that I described in the first chapter's discussion of Chomsky's work), just as the rest of us are. No matter how hard they try, lawyers cannot remove from judges the chore of matching events in the world with the language in documents and answering the question "who is right?" when the parties disagree about the relationship between the two. And of course, once judges accept the task, they also accept the pressure to speak decisively and within the bounds of accepted legal doctrine, which leads us back to the phenomena discussed earlier.

Failure to achieve its goal of extraordinary precision is not the only problem facing this legal syntax. Specialized legal writing, or "legalese," as it is sometimes called, sounds so pompous and silly that it is now literally against the law to use it in certain contexts. Many states have passed laws requiring that leases, insurance policies, loan agreements, and other documents intended for nonlawyers be written in "plain English," so that "normal people" can understand them. While I generally support these legislative efforts, the best that we can expect from them is to maintain the status quo that I described in the first chapters. Laws that spring from the failure of legal syntax to add clarity or precision leave judges with the task of interpreting ordinary syntax, no easy feat.

In this chapter we will examine this effort to create a legal language more precise than ordinary English and the reaction against it. There are no real winners. The effort fails and the reaction does little to address the core difficulties with the legal system that lead to the problems that have been the theme of this book.

The Quest for Precision

Without question, the best catalogue of how lawyers attempt to write more precisely and why these attempts fail is the thirteenth chapter of David Mellinkoff's book, *The Language of the Law*.[2] Mellinkoff, whose book is as entertaining as it is interesting, concedes that there exists a small domain in which legal language really is particularly precise: the use of terms of art with specialized technical definitions. This, he argues, has had the unfortunate side effect of encouraging legal writers to believe that legal language is by its nature more precise than ordinary English:

> Outside the academy, no profession of words has a longer history of practical effort devoted to refining language. . . . Lawyers spend more time talking about being precise than others similarly addicted to words—politicians and the clergy, for example. Listening to these discussions about precision, and contrasting their own concern with the indifference of the street, law students and lawyers come to the effortless conclusion that with so much interest in precision, there must be a lot of it around.[3]

Mellinkoff also describes a shyness that comes over lawyers who even contemplate straying from the language that judges have accepted in the past:

> Buttressing all the other reasons for belief in the precision of the language of the law is fear. The fear not merely of changing, but of being weakened by doubt of the correctness of a whole pattern. For the profession, this is no ordinary conservative fear. Lurking in the dark background is the always present, rarely voiced lawyer's fear of what will happen if he is not "precise"—in the way that the law has always been "precise." Consider, you lawyers, " . . . 'plain and simple' language . . . " and " . . . the possible liability of lawyers for negligence who use too much of it." . . .
>
> That is the fear that freezes lawyers and their language. It is precise now. We are safe with it now. Leave us alone. Don't change. Here we stay till death or disbarment.[4]

The fear that Mellinkoff describes is a real one. Lawyers routinely use language that has been used successfully before simply because it is likely to accomplish its goal. I confess that I have personally done so more than once, knowing that the formulas grate on the ear, but taking comfort in the collective experience that tells me that they will work.

But Mellinkoff is also correct that a lawyer's nervousness should not be misconstrued as an ability to write precisely. Ironically, as Mellinkoff points out, there exist many legal terms that are intended to convey nothing other than imprecision.[5] One such term is the *reasonable man,* a fictitious person against whose behavior our conduct is measured in determining whether we should be held liable for having caused injury to others. The late William Prosser, the leading American commentator on the law of torts, noted that "[t]he conduct of the reasonable man will vary with the situation with which he is confronted. . . . Under the latitude of this phrase, the courts have made allowance not only for the external facts, but for many of the characteristics of the actor himself, and have applied, in many respects, a more or less subjective standard."[6] Other expressions, such as *substantial* and *satisfactory,* also have their place in legal writing, as Mellinkoff notes.

We are thus left with a body of writing that calls itself precise, but reserves the right to be as imprecise as it wishes, when the situation calls for imprecision. This state of affairs is widely criticized by lawyers and nonlawyers alike, who recognize much of legal language as arrogant and empty hocus-pocus.

In fact, the peculiarities of legal language have become a symbol of the inaccessibility of the law to ordinary people and of the extraordinary expense of legal services. To many, I imagine, the lawyer is some sort of bizarre translating device: The lawyer is presented with a problem in the actual world, such as an automobile accident. He translates this easily understood problem into some sort of incomprehensible jargon. The judge then rules, and the incomprehensible jargon is translated into dollars owed, or prison terms, or something else that can once again be understood. For all of this translation back and forth, the lawyer charges a healthy fee. Some critics go so far as to claim that legal language is a plot perpetrated by lawyers to create the false impression that their services are needed so that the legal profession can fleece the rest of society.[7]

I will not here attempt to catalogue all the differences between legal language and ordinary speech. This has been done by Mellinkoff and others.[8] Rather, I will limit myself in this chapter to several observations about lawyers' efforts to create some sort of superprecise dialect of English and about the strident and passionate backlash against these efforts. As an initial example, we will look in some detail at the attempt by lawyers and other legal writers to avoid using pronouns in order to add precision by reducing ambiguity.

PRONOUNS, PRECISION, AND THE LAW

Even though lawyers may be sincere in the quest to be precise, the labor of creating a specialized syntax to accomplish the task is generally misguided. The problem results from lawyers' ignoring the fact that our ability to speak and understand is largely defined for us by the internalized set of rules for our language that we acquire as children. As we saw in chapter 1, linguists refer to this body of knowledge, applied by all of us unselfconsciously and with great rapidity in everyday speech, as a generative grammar. Much of peculiar legal syntax can be seen as a futile attempt to plug up certain gaps in our internal rule systems, reducing the number of possible interpretations that a sentence in a legal document may have.

With this in mind, we should not be surprised that lawyers hate pronouns. Pronouns have little inherent meaning, acquiring their interpretation from the context in which they are used. The lengths to which lawyers will go to avoid using them make for some of the silliest and most irritating examples of "legalese."

The problem with pronouns is that it is not always clear from the language, or even the context, which of a number of possible antecedents is the intended one.

Consider, for example, the following:

(1)   Burger told Mason that *he* was likely to win the case.

(2)   Della told Perry that *he* was likely to win the case.

In (1), the pronoun *he* can refer to either *Burger* or *Mason* (prosecutor Hamilton Burger and defense attorney Perry Mason are both male), or to someone not mentioned in the sentence at all. Burger can be bragging about his own likelihood of success, he can be conceding that Mason might win, or he can be talking about some case other than one in which he and Mason are adversaries. As for referential possibilities outside the sentence, there are no limits at all. (2), on the other hand, is limited by the fact that *he* is a masculine pronoun and *Della* is a woman's name. *He* cannot refer to Della. Otherwise, (2) has the same referential possibilities as (1).

In chapter 2, we looked at some cases in which the interpretation of pronouns in sentences like (2) was in issue. That is, a pronoun with a certain gender was used in a document, and the court had to decide how seriously to consider this fact in determining who could and could not be an antecedent to the pronoun. We saw this issue arise in the contexts of a drug case, tax cases, and cases interpreting trusts. But there are factors other than gender that determine what the possible antecedents of a pronoun are. By examining some of these, we can see how elements of legal syntax may best be seen as an unsuccessful attempt to reduce the extent of ambiguity of reference through peculiar syntactic devices, which have a nasty, legal flavor.

Pronouns and the Fifth Amendment

A number of factors that contribute to the ways in which we understand pronouns show themselves in the Fifth Amendment to the Constitution. The relevant passage is presented below:

> Nor shall any person be subject for the same offence to be twice
> put in jeopardy of life or limb; nor shall be compelled in any
> criminal case to be a witness against himself.

There has been a century of debate over the question of who or what counts as a "person" for purposes of deciding who receives the protection of the Fifth Amendment.[9] Just about every other concept in the Fifth Amendment has also received extensive attention in the courts. For example, the circumstances under which two prosecutions constitute "double jeopardy" is the subject of a substantial body of judicial decisions;[10] the extent to which administrative proceedings count as "criminal cases" for Fifth Amendment purposes has been the subject of case law;[11] and whether a grant of immunity from prosecution makes self-incrimination impossible has been an issue.[12] But one question has not seriously arisen: the relationship between *himself* and *any person*.[13]

This omission should be surprising, since just about everything else has been brought to the courts for determination. But our tacit knowledge as speakers of English of the rules governing the structure of our language has left this rather complicated syntactic structure of the Fifth Amendment beyond debate. Let us look briefly at what it takes to understand this passage to see just how sophisticated our tacit knowledge really is.

First, we must recognize that the expression

> Nor shall be compelled in any criminal case to be a witness against himself

is in the passive voice. Missing is the agent who is doing the compelling. That is, we understand the phrase to mean "nor shall be compelled *by someone*" Since the Constitution is about the powers of government, and the Fifth Amendment is specifically about limits in government's exercise of power, we infer that "government" or "federal government" is the implied agent.

Second, this expression is missing its subject. We are not told here to whom the expression "shall be compelled in any criminal case" applies. Therefore, we must ask the question, who shall not be compelled to be a witness? In fact, we recognize this omission as we process the sentence, and assign to the subject position the expression "any person," the subject of the preceding clause, which protects "any person" from being put in double jeopardy. We do all of this automatically, without any awareness of the process at all, unless it is brought to our attention, as it is here. Similarly, we understand that "any person" is also the subject of "to be a witness against himself," which is another clause without a subject.

Third, we must reach an understanding of what *himself* means in the Fifth Amendment. Again, entirely unself-consciously, we determine that *himself* is connected to *any person*, the implied subject of the phrase, which actually appears only in the preceding phrase.

We can represent this entire array as follows, where we use subscripts to indicate which elements are understood to corefer, and [e] to represent a position that is empty, but for which we infer meaning:

> Nor shall [any person]$_i$ be subject for the same offence [e]$_i$ to be twice put in jeopardy of life or limb; nor shall [e]$_i$ be compelled

[by government] in any criminal case [e]$_i$ to be a witness against himself$_i$.

In reading the Fifth Amendment, then, we automatically recognize that "be compelled" has no subject, and assign "any person" to that position; that "to be a witness" has no subject, and assign "any person" to that position; and that "himself" needs an antecedent, and assign "any person" as the antecedent of "himself".

In fact, the antecedent of "himself" is assigned by virtue of our previous assignment of "any person" as the implicit missing subject of the clause containing it: " . . . to be a witness . . . ." As (3) and (4) illustrate, the antecedent of a reflexive must be part of the clause containing the reflexive:

(3)   Perry asked Della to excuse himself.

(4)   Perry asked Della to excuse herself.

Both (3) and (4) are understandable, but only (4) is a grammatical sentence of English. In both instances we understand *Della* to be the subject of "to excuse," but only in (4) is *Della*, a woman's name, an appropriate antecedent for the reflexive. All of these facts, and many other related facts, are the subject of detailed investigation by linguists, who have been studying these sorts of structures in many languages in an attempt to come to an understanding of the properties of human cognition that make certain interpretations necessary, others possible, and still others impossible.[14]

Returning to (1), repeated below, we can understand the ambiguity in the reference of pronouns by using the same formalism.

(1)   Burger told Mason that he was likely to win the case.

Pronouns, unlike reflexives, are not assigned a particular subscript, or "referential index," as this notation is called in the linguistic literature, when we hear or read them in a sentence. Rather, as shown in (5), several referential possibilities exist.

(5)   Burger$_i$ told Mason$_j$ that he$_{\{i,j,k\}}$ was likely to win the case.

In (5), *he* can refer to *Burger,* to *Mason,* or to someone not mentioned at all, *k,* as discussed above. Here again, there exist principles, applied automatically and known only subconsciously except to those who study them, that limit our assignment of antecedents to pronouns, as illustrated by (6):

(6)   He told Mason that Burger was likely to win the case.

In (6), *he* cannot refer to *Mason* or to *Burger*. But even in (6), the pronoun is otherwise free to refer to anyone else, creating a potential ambiguity of reference. Thus, while we automatically "index" reflexives as we hear them to match particular local antecedents, we refrain from "indexing" pronouns in certain ways, but are otherwise free to interpret pronouns as referring to any antecedent.[15]

All of this leads to a single conclusion: If ambiguity of reference carries potentially disastrous consequences for a writer, it is better to avoid using pronouns, although reflexive pronouns would do just fine.[16] In fact, legal writers do try to avoid using pronouns and other such forms.

Below, we will look at several examples in which the legal writer attempts to narrow the range of possible interpretations of sentences through peculiar syntactic devices, with the goal of limiting the opportunity for misunderstanding resulting from ambiguity of reference. In the course of this discussion, we will see first that these devices occur only where the operative linguistic principles underdetermine reference, indicating confidence in those principles at some unconscious level of mental activity, and second that these efforts are largely unnecessary in that they fail to achieve their purpose, making the language of the law more mysterious (and sometimes laughable) than precise.

Devices to Limit Ambiguity of Reference in Legal Language

Party of the First Part. Returning to our discussion of the sentences presented in the last section, if it were actually possible to utter the subscripts (or indices) of the potential antecedents, and the intended subscript of the pronoun, the ambiguity of reference would disappear in many cases. The sentences in (7) through (9) illustrate this point.

(7) $Burger_i$ told $Mason_j$ that he_i was likely to win the case.

(8) $Burger_i$ told $Mason_j$ that he_j was likely to win the case.

(9) $Burger_i$ told $Mason_j$ that he_k was likely to win the case.

In both (7) and (8), the subscripts within the sentence are sufficient to determine the antecedent of the pronoun. In (9), on the other hand, we must know from prior discourse the expression to which the subscript k has been assigned, if such an expression exists. Of course, in natural speech, we do not use referential indices, nor could we. To prove this, the reader should try for just a few minutes to speak using these indices. It will be virtually impossible, even with enormous concentration.

In drafting contracts, lawyers sometimes define the contracting individuals in advance as "the party of the first part" or "party of the second part," and then refer to the individuals throughout as names containing these "referential indices." In essence, the legal writer gives each party a number, and then uses the number instead of the party's name to refer to that party. Except for the number, all of the parties have the same name. While the expression "party of the first part" has an archaic ring to it, a search for this language in a computerized database of legal decisions (LEXIS) reveals that it was quoted by courts throughout the United States in hundreds of cases during the 1980s. I do not know any lawyers who use this device, but it apparently is not entirely out of fashion.

Two examples are presented below:

(10) . . . and the party of the second part is to build and maintain
       the fence along the road by the Large Swamp and half of the
       fence of the Little Round Swamp, and the party of the first part
       to build and maintain the other half of the fence.[17]

(11) . . . the party of the first part does hereby covenant with the
       party of the second part that so long as the party of the second
       part or its successors or assigns shall maintain a garage on the
       site of said existing garage. . . .[18] (Emphasis added)

In (10), where there is only one mention of each party, the use of "party of the first part" achieves nothing. If the writer had simply called these people by their names (the case is called *Gray v. Handy*), nothing would have been lost.

Notice that in (11), on the other hand, this linguistic device seems to accomplish some reduction in ambiguity in that a pronoun in the place of the second "party of the second part" would not be sufficient to specify a particular antecedent. The principles discussed above would allow it to have as its antecedent either of the two parties mentioned in the first clause.

As (11) also illustrates, however, legal writers are sometimes willing to use a pronoun when its referent is obvious, and when not using the pronoun would make the language too cumbersome. The presence of *its* in (11) is completely inconsistent with the use of "party of the first part" and more generally with the proposition that pronouns must be eliminated from legal writing for the sake of additional precision. In this instance, of course, it is clear that the drafter intended *its* to refer to *the party of the second part*. Even those who most desperately want to use *legal* syntax sometimes succumb to their knowledge of *English* syntax.

Interestingly, when linguistic principles limit to one the possible antecedents of a pronoun, that pronoun is always used. This occurs when a reflexive appears with only one possible antecedent in its local environment, as we saw in reviewing the Fifth Amendment. Examples are presented below:

(12) It is the intention of the party of the first part to reserve unto *herself* during the full term of her natural life the right of possession and occupancy in and to the said real estate.[19] (Emphasis added)

(13) The party of the first part reserves unto *himself* the unrestricted right to put the park and waterfront . . . to any lawful uses desired.[20] (Emphasis added)

Nowhere have I encountered examples in which "the party of the first part" occupies the position of a reflexive pronoun. This reflects a sensitivity to the difference between reference dictated by grammatical principles and reference established on the basis of context. Again, this sensitivity is entirely automatic and unself-conscious.

While it seems, then, that *party of the first part* reduces ambiguity in some cases (such as (11)), it does so only with respect to the ambiguity that would be present if a nonreflexive pronoun were used instead. We will see that there are less legalistic ways of accomplishing this task.

Replacing Pronouns with Names. For the most part, repeating the names of individuals referred to accomplishes the same precision as does *party of the first part*. When a name is used more than once in the same syntactic domain, noncoreference is sometimes preferred, as illustrated by (14), which is a little awkward if we wish to understand both occurrences of *John* to refer to the same person.

(14) John told us that John had been overworked.

However, when context dictates that both occurrences of the name refer to the same individual, we do understand them as coreferring, as (15) illustrates.[21]

(15) What a witness! Even Glenn's mother wouldn't believe Glenn.

The use of names instead of pronouns should be effective in reducing referential ambiguity when the pronoun could have had more than one potential antecedent, but the two occurrences of the same name could have only one referent in the discourse in which the sentence occurs. Below are presented two examples from actual cases, in which this device is used.

(16) It is stipulated that "Elliott advised Gilligan that . . . Elliott was . . . going to sell as much as was left to certain of his friends" after Gilligan took what he wanted of the $2,500,000 remaining after Elliott's wife took $500,000.[22]

(17) The Government points to the provisions of the revenue acts imposing upon the beneficiary of a trust the liability for the tax upon the income distributable to the beneficiary.[23]

Only in (16) does the avoidance of pronouns reduce ambiguity at all. In (17), there would have been only one possible antecedent for a pronoun replacing the second occurrence of *the beneficiary.*

We can conclude from all of these examples that using *party of the first part* accomplishes no more precision than does the use of names instead of pronouns, assuming that each name has only one possible referent. In a sense, calling someone the "party of the first part" only renames that individual. If there is only one Jones in the universe of discourse, then assigning a number to Jones and calling him Smith makes the name no more identifiable.[24] The appearance that a special legal term is required in order to define individual rights with scientific accuracy helps to foster the notion that there is a rule of law operating in some objective fashion. The legal term, however, is no more precise than a name.

Said and Same. Finally, let us consider the use of two words whose function supposedly is to limit the class of possible referents to a noun phrase. The word *said,* derived from *aforesaid,* can be traced to the early English period. David Mellinkoff comments that *said* "is currently more popular than *aforesaid,* because lacking the Old English *afore said* is not twice as archaic as it could be."[25] Mellinkoff accurately points out the difficulty with *aforesaid:*

> If there is only one possible reference for *aforesaid,* it is usually unnecessary—as when an answer refers to the only action there is, "the action aforesaid." If *aforesaid* can by any chance refer to more than one thing, or to nothing, its long history of uncertain reference marks it as dangerous. In either case, no aid to precision.[26]

Consider the following examples:

(18) The decree of the court below fixing and determining the specific amount to be distributed to stockholders is affirmed. In other respects, except as to the allowance of costs, the said decree is reversed.[27]

(19) In December 1923 when the petitioner, then unmarried, and S. S. Kresge, then married, were contemplating their future marriage, he delivered to her 700 shares of the common stock of the S. S. Kresge Company. The shares were . . . to be held by the petitioner "for her benefit and protection in the event that the said Kresge should die prior to the contemplated marriage."[28]

I chose these excerpts because the presence of "said" seems especially anomalous. However, anyone reading legal documents will find the word added frequently in current writing as well. While *said* does have the effect of limiting reference to something mentioned earlier in the discourse, it does nothing else. Thus, one could never utter (20) without the prior discourse necessary to bring the phone into the conversation.

(20) Said telephone rang twice while you were in the shower.

Not surprisingly, I have never seen *said* narrow the class of antecedents that would have been available if *the* were used instead. In written language, the only way to justify using any definite description is by mentioning it earlier in writing, since gesturing and shared experience are unavailable.

Used as special proforms, the words *such* and *same* do no more work than does *said*. Consider (21):

(21) And for such surface space as it may take for the purpose aforesaid said party of the second part or his successors in title agree to pay before taking same . . . the sum of thirty dollars per acre.[29]

This example is an encyclopedia of legal double talk. "This space" or some similar description would have left no more uncertainty than "same" does, and would have sounded far less legalistic. The antecedent for *same* is derivable from context. It plays the same role as *said*.

IN THIS section, I have presented illustrations of several linguistic devices used in legal writing presumably to reduce ambiguity that remains after the application of the principles discussed in the previous section. Only one, the use of names where pronouns might ordinarily be used, has any positive effect at all, and this device is the one that is not peculiarly legalistic. More than fifty years ago, a commentator on legal language wrote: "The law wraps itself in solemn, mystical, and equivocal phrases, which can be construed any way a headachy judge pleases."[30] The devices discussed above serve more to mystify than to clarify, making reactions like this one appropriate even today. In short, the quest for precision through the creation of a special syntax ends in failure.

Using Special Words

At the same time that the law fails to achieve precision through the use of special syntactic structures, it attempts to accomplish clarity and precision through the use of a technical vocabulary. For a variety of reasons, the use of specialized words is far more defensible than the use of the syntactic devices that we saw above. Significantly, though, disputes arise about the relationship of these technical words with events in the world, just as they arise about the relationship between nontechnical words and events in the world. When this happens, the judge is faced with exactly the same problems that we have seen many times in this book.

I have no animosity toward the use of technical vocabulary. The law is often complicated, and like most complicated fields, practitioners have developed a special set of words with which to communicate. As a general matter, a technical vocabulary should serve to reduce confusion by permitting those in a field to discuss a particular phenomenon without having to describe it separately each time reference to it is made.

The development of technical legal terminology serves just this purpose. We have seen many of these terms in this book. For example, contract law speaks of "consideration"; the criminal law has a "*mens rea*" requirement; the federal racketeering statute defines "enterprise." Other examples abound. In tax law, measurement of capital gains requires computation of a "basis;" to prove fraud one must demonstrate that a defendant acted with "scienter" (discussed below); and the securities laws restrict the amount of stock that an "affiliate" is permitted to sell. For that matter, the securities laws require us to understand what is and what is not a "security"—no easy task.[31] Each of these terms is defined either by statute or by judges' decisions in cases, or by both.

Despite their utility, the presence of technical words is an undemocratic feature of an institution that is supposed to treat everyone equally. As helpful as these words may be to those enmeshed in debate about the nuances of legal doctrine, the technical vocabulary is only alienating to those not familiar with it. The question that we should ask, then, is whether the law would become more democratic, more accessible to those without formal legal training, if we were to eliminate this technical vocabulary and describe all legal concepts with ordinary words on every occasion. I believe that such a step would be a step backward in clarity, and would do nothing to make complicated legal rules more accessible without study.

For example, lawyers reading this book already know that to prove fraud a plaintiff must prove that the defendant acted with "scienter," which is defined very loosely as "intent to deceive." Of course, we could eliminate the word scienter entirely from legal discourse (by passing a law making it illegal to use the word since it is not "plain English") and substitute for it the expression "intent to deceive" in every instance in which "scienter" had appeared.

However, "intent to deceive" is not really an accurate definition of scienter in all cases. Courts have interpreted the requirement of scienter to reflect different states of mind in different circumstances, and the use of the expression "intent to deceive" would sometimes be misleading.

In fact, the substance of the scienter requirement, as applied by the courts, really is a complicated business, no matter what vocabulary is used. How much intent is needed to meet the scienter requirement has been the subject of extensive discussion in legal decisions, and the requirements differ subtly from jurisdiction to jurisdiction. Must a defendant desperately want to deceive another, or is a disregard of the truth of a statement enough to hold a defendant liable for fraud? Do we have an obligation to learn the truth if we have greater access to the facts than people with whom we are dealing? These sorts of questions are at the core of the law of fraud, and they would exist whether or not we use the word scienter. Probably a more accurate definition of scienter is, tautologically, "the state of mind required to prove fraud, which usually is intent to deceive."[32] But, like all tautologies, this definition tells us very little.

Thus my first point about technical vocabulary and the accessibility of the law to nonlawyers: much of the law would not be accessible to those who do not study it carefully regardless of whether technical terms are used. By "careful study" I do not mean that formal legal education is needed. Anyone can learn the law (to the extent that it exists) by reading it and reading about it. But no one can learn its subtleties and complexities without devoting time and effort. In all but the clearest cases, I would not advise a client as to whether a fraud was committed without reviewing what judges had said in similar situations, and even then my answer might well be that different courts can come to different conclusions depending on how the judge views the case as a whole. It would be wrongminded to say that lawyers and judges have schemed to make understanding the law of fraud unavailable to the general public by introducing words like "scienter." As far as I can tell, the introduction of the word scienter has nothing to do with what is difficult about the law of fraud. To the contrary, it makes discussion of the law of fraud a little easier.

Of course, I do not mean here to defend the use of every idiotic legal expression, under the rubric of a technical legal vocabulary. Mellinkoff reminds us of "fit and proper," "by and with," "force and effect," "give, devise and bequeath," and other gems.[33] Many peculiarly legal expressions that add nothing to meaning stay alive through the inertia of legal writers. But it is simply not the case that all legal terminology is part of some sinister plot to obscure the law to the public.

My second point is related to the first: while a technical vocabulary can focus our attention on certain concepts, the technical words become just as unclear at the fringes as do any other words. For example, as a general matter, gratuitous promises are not enforceable in courts as contracts, but promises made for "consideration" are. Essentially, only when the recipient of a promise suffers some legal detriment can he or she expect help from the courts. But what is a legal detriment for purposes of defining "consideration?" In chapter 1, we saw a case in which Cardozo ruled that a college's promise to use a gift only for certain purposes was enough to qualify as consideration.[34] What about instances in which the parties to an agreement say that their action is in consideration for one dollar, or some other nominal amount, just to create the impression that there has been consideration? Or instances in which the detriment is real, but it is something that the recipient of the promise had a legal obligation to do anyway?

As we have seen, most of the problems associated with judges' construal of words in legal documents result from the difficulty in determining whether the word in question applies to the events in dispute. The goodness of fit between a concept and the events that occur in the world is as a rule no better for concepts expressed by technical words than it is for those expressed by ordinary ones, a fact that limits the benefits of a technical vocabulary. On the other hand, the goodness of fit is in principle no worse for technical words than it is for ordinary ones. Thus, technical words should be useful exactly to the extent that they are able to represent the core of concepts that would not be expressed as easily without them.[35] It seems to me that words like "scienter" and "consideration" do this, as do many other technical legal words.

There is a substantial rebellion against all of this legal language. Let us now look at that rebellion and ask what it professes to accomplish and what it can accomplish.

The War against Legal Language

The sound of legal language offends just about everyone. When someone accuses a friend of sounding like a lawyer, the remark is most likely meant as a playful insult, meaning something like, "you have just spoken at great length, but have said nothing of substance." Perhaps sometimes the insult is not playful.

In recent years, campaigns have been waged against the demon legalese, much the way campaigns have been waged against other evils that are perceived as worthy of extermination, such as drug use and pornography. The war has taken two forms: an impassioned law review literature, begging lawyers to stop speaking and writing nonsense, and a series of statutes making it illegal to do so in certain types of documents, such as leases, insurance policies, and loan agreements. By and large, I subscribe to this movement. But for reasons that I will explain below, we should expect the movement's success to bring about very little change in the legal world.

The most serious attack on legalese is that lawyers continue to use it in order to make their otherwise unneeded services appear indispensable. Consider the following statement by George Gopen:

> In teaching lawyers how to clarify their language, I have often heard them express the fear that if their prose were to lose its arcane, ponderous, and technical qualities, their clients would be likely to protest the stunningly high costs incurred. . . .
>
> Here perhaps is the core of the matter: It is in the lawyer's self-interest to keep legal prose unreadable. If money, power, and prestige are all protected by keeping the layperson confused and awestruck, why should any lawyer voluntarily opt for clear, concise, communicative prose?[36]

Despite Gopen's statement that the lawyers he has taught readily admit that they write as they do to impress clients, I doubt that the corruption about which Gopen writes is really the driving force behind much of legal language. Rather, I believe the fear of abandoning successful formulas, which Mellinkoff describes, and simple inertia are the heart of the matter. Lawyers are often conservative people in a conservative profession. While, as Gopen suggests, professionalism may indeed enter the lawyer's psychology when he decides how to write a particular document, it is certainly possible for an individual to want to "sound like a lawyer" for reasons other than attempting to justify unnecessary legal work to clients. I know many lawyers who routinely write phrases such as "said agreement" into legal documents that their clients ordinarily will not see. These lawyers most likely are attempting to be precise and to sound professional to the other lawyers and judges to whom they are communicating. While the language that they use is neither precise nor attractive, they seem to me to be motivated by considerations very different from dishonesty and greed.[37]

As a solution, Gopen applauds the plain language legislation that has been enacted and recommends expanded education in writing for both law students and practicing lawyers. No one can seriously deny that additional training would benefit the legal profession and those who have contact with it. Much of legal writing is simply bad writing. Although lawyers make their livings writing, many have never studied or thought seriously about how to write well. Moreover, lawyers, like others, vary in talent when it comes to writing skills.

But I fail to see how eliminating all of the "party of the first part"s and "said agreement"s, either through education or legislation, will solve any of the more serious linguistic problems facing our legal system. In particular, the linguistic games described earlier in this book do not result from peculiar legal syntax or vocabulary. Rather, they grow from the temptation of judges to create the illusion that the interpretation of language is more definitive than it really is. Judges do this because of the pressure on them to sound authoritative and to limit the range of the argumentation in their opinions to that which is permitted by the doctrine of the day. If the plain language movement had already achieved one hundred per cent success, I might not have written this chapter—but I would have written the rest of this book.

Among the most expansive criticisms of legal language, apart from Mellinkoff's, is Robert W. Benson's 1985 article "The End of Legalese: The Game is Over."[38] Benson not only picks on some of the ugliest features of legal language, drawing support from Shakespeare, the Marx Brothers, and his own collection of incomprehensible examples, but he subjects legal texts to standardized tests of comprehensibility, demonstrating the impenetrability of legal writings to ordinary eyes and ears.

Benson raises a serious issue. Many documents intended for consumption by nontrained individuals are simply not understood. Of the texts that he presented to groups of subjects, a sixth grade text and a substantively simple plain language jury instruction were the only documents that passed muster.[39] Sadly, Benson's study found that excerpts from *The Los Angeles Times* were as difficult as certain legal texts, although other legal texts were the most opaque of all. If the members of a jury do not understand the judge's instructions to them, how can we expect them to follow the law in reaching a verdict? Do we even have a rule of law apart from basic notions of fairness shared by the mainstream of a community?

Along these lines, Charrow and Charrow's[40] excellent earlier work on the comprehensibility of jury instructions, which Benson discusses in his article, had found that even jury instructions rewritten into plain language can be relatively difficult for jurors to understand, based on the comprehensibility tests that they used. While rewriting the instructions led to a marked increase in comprehension (41 percent to 59 percent), it still left a large percentage of the material not understood.[41] This is what we might expect when we deal with concepts that are at times both unfamiliar and complicated.[42]

Although Benson focuses most of his article on the improvement that comes with clearer language, we should not lose sight of the fact that some of the difficulties with legal concepts come from their substance, and not only from the quality of the language used to describe them. Benson is probably correct in attributing the difficulty that his experimental subjects had understanding a *Los Angeles Times* article to the unfamiliarity of the material it contained. Imagine the difficulty that a judge must have trying to make sure that a jury understands the concept of scienter. For this reason, we can never close the gap entirely.

This is not to say that we have no obligation to do the best we can to make ourselves understood, an obligation at the heart of plain language legislation. To see both the benefits and the limits of plain language laws, let us look briefly at New York's version:

> Every written agreement . . . for the lease of space to be occupied for residential purposes, or to which a consumer is a party and the money, property or service which is the subject of the transaction is primarily for personal, family or household purposes must be:
> 1. Written in a clear and coherent manner using words with common and every day meanings;

2. Appropriately divided and captioned by its various
sections.[43]

New York's plain language law grew chiefly out of a concern over the in-
comprehensibility of consumer credit contracts[44]—contracts under which a
consumer buys, say, an automobile or a refrigerator on credit, agreeing to
make monthly payments, which include interest. If the payments are not
made, the purchased item may be repossessed. Obviously, the people who
most frequently suffer the consequences of these contracts are the poor.
Wealthy people pay cash for their refrigerators.

Prior to the legislation, the various rights and procedures described in
many of these contracts were nearly impossible to understand. The plain
language statute gives people buying on credit a better opportunity to see
what they are getting themselves into. The same holds true for those signing
residential leases.

While we should not deceive ourselves into thinking that plain language
will ever make much of a practical difference in the lives of those that it is
supposed to help, it is conceivable that some consumers will refer to their
contracts (that by now are often enough quite old and may be lost). If they
do, they may see, for example, that the proper procedures have not been
followed, learn how to enforce their rights, and take action. Understanding
the contract is especially important when it comes to any legal right that a
consumer can preserve by curing his default, perhaps by becoming current
in his payments by a certain deadline.

With respect to leases, very much the same holds true. In trying to write a
lease in "plain language," we encounter the problem that we discussed
above in connection with technical legal words, such as "consideration" and
"scienter." For example, leases require tenants to "take good care of" the
premises.[45] When landlords and tenants begin to fight about the duty of the
tenant to make repairs, no list of circumstances can be exhaustive enough to
predict what a court will consider fair in every situation, and the expression
"take care of" is not much help. On the other hand, certain "clear" lease
provisions do appear to have made their way into the minds of tenants. For
example, in my experience, New York tenants are very much aware of the
landlord's obligation to put a security deposit in a separate account and to
return the money to the tenant with interest. The plain language law should
be given some credit here.

Finally, the plain language laws have caused an ironic, unwanted consequence. Recall from chapter 3 the principle that stacks the deck in favor of the nondrafter of an ambiguous contract. This principle is applied especially in instances in which the bargaining power between the drafter and the other party is skewed. As we saw, courts sometimes apply this rule aggressively to aid the underdog. In essence, plain language legislation serves to reduce the impact of this principle. The consumer creditor or landlord sensitive to what courts are calling ambiguous need only make adjustments in the plain language forms that are printed in bulk, and sooner or later their language will receive the court's stamp of approval. We saw in chapter 3 that insurance companies have known for years how to make these subtle adjustments. The irony of plain language legislation is that it has forced landlords and consumer creditors to clarify form contracts and leases for their own good, sometimes provoking judges, in turn, to find ambiguity where none exists, for the sake of doing justice.

How Much Better Can We Do?

To summarize, legal language contains many peculiar devices which serve to create the appearance of precision while in fact they decrease clarity. Our ability to express ourselves precisely is defined in large measure by our knowledge of language. At times, this knowledge limits interpretation to only one possibility. In the sentence "the cat killed the mouse," we know that *the mouse* is the direct object of the verb *killed*. And we know that in fact the cat killed the mouse. We may have trouble determining whether a particular rodent is indeed a mouse or something else, but we certainly know that *the mouse* is the direct object, and not the subject of the sentence. And we know that as the direct object, the mouse is what was killed, not the killer.

To the extent that our knowledge of language leaves open the interpretation of certain structures or words, legal writers have attempted to compensate by creating their own vocabularies and their own syntax. As I hope to have shown above, this syntax is basically a failure. "Said agreement" and "party of the first part" do nothing to make legal language more precise than devices we use in ordinary speech. Even if legal writers are sincere in their efforts, they might as well stop.

With respect to the meanings of words, the situation is a bit more complicated. Some technical legal words serve useful purposes, just as do technical words in any active field. But at the margins, technical words have no more clarity than do ordinary words. That is, we cannot alter our cognitive capacity to extrapolate from the core meanings of particular words just by inventing new words. Consequently, interpretation becomes indeterminate as we stray from the central concept that the word was invented to convey, a point made by Wittgenstein, among others.[46]

With all of this as background, can we do anything to improve legal language? Of course we can. The legal profession, judges and lawyers alike, can heed the critics and engage in an all out effort to write more clearly, with fewer unnecessarily legalistic expressions. But we should keep in mind that doing so will never be sufficient to make natural language any more precise than our cognitive capacities permit. That is, as we saw in chapter 1 and again in this chapter, some aspects of language are clear and determinate, others are not.

The temptation to create the impression of determinacy has its roots deeply embedded in our system, and will not evaporate even if the plain language movement becomes a complete success. Nonetheless, the added accessibility of legal documents written in plain English does help to inform those people who read the documents of the extent to which their lives are in their control, a positive contribution, in my opinion. A world in which judges and lawyers write plainly is a better world—but only a slightly better one.

6 | Some Problems with Words: Trying to Understand the Constitution

OUR KNOWLEDGE of language stems largely from our biological endowment as human beings. Put simply, we are stuck with whatever communicative endowment we have inherited, just as we are stuck with the strengths and weaknesses of our other intellectual functions, such as depth perception, the perception of color, etc. We can, of course, strive to use our language capacity better, as the plain language laws require, but we cannot expand it past what our biology allows.

It would be a mistake, however, to focus all of our attention on the fact that our knowledge of language often leaves us with more than one available interpretation of a text or utterance, since our knowledge of language works to limit severely the possible ways in which we can interpret the sentences that we hear and read. It is just not the case that any utterance can mean anything, a point that should be intuitively clear. In fact, as we saw in chapter 3, language is sometimes less ambiguous than some would want it to be, and judges are at times under pressure to find ambiguity where none exists.

Without doubt, most legal battles over language are battles over the meanings of words: Did the defendant's state of mind constitute "scienter"? Is an arson ring an "enterprise" as defined by RICO, the racketeering statute? Does a college's promise to use a donation for certain purposes constitute "consideration"? Similarly, dispute about the scope of various fundamental rights that the Constitution guarantees frequently takes the form of debate about the meanings of the words in the Constitution.

We have already seen some disputes about word meaning in chapters 3, 4, and 5. Almost invariably, the disagreement concerns whether some unexpected event in the world comes within the scope of some word in a document, such as a statute or a contract, that defines people's rights or obligations. In this chapter, we will look at several battles over the meanings of words in the Fourth and Fifth Amendments to the Constitution, focusing on decisions of the Supreme Court of the United States. In each instance it should become clear that the linguistic features of the word help to define the issues that constitute the legal debate, but do not resolve them. Yet, judicial opinions are often drafted to imply that the relationship between the meaning of the word in question and the events in the world is entirely self-evident, beyond dispute.

Analytically, this is a mistake. For the linguistics of words, like the linguistics of sentence structure, serves to confine interpretation, but fails to provide a perfect match between the language that we use and all of the peculiar events that occur in the world. That is, our knowledge of words (known by linguists as the "lexicon") provides an arena in which the fundamental legal battles are fought.

Below I will discuss three examples of constitutional issues that involve the meanings of words: What is a "person"? What does it mean to be a "witness against oneself"? And what is a "search"? In each instance, it is possible to investigate the extent to which our knowledge of language limits possible meanings, but leaves open certain interpretative possibilities. It is exactly within this interpretative space that the legal disputes occur. Yet, for the reasons that I discussed earlier, the disagreement rarely takes the form of open debate in judicial opinions. Rather, it takes the form of mutually inconsistent pronouncements about what the words of the Constitution must mean, in an effort to speak authoritatively about the matter.

We begin by looking at who and what the Constitution regards as a person. We will soon discover a doctrinally sensible, but theoretically incoherent body of law.

People, Corporations, and Other Creatures

WHAT IS A CORPORATION?

It is a maxim of American law that a corporation is a "legal" or "artificial" person. What makes it so? In some cases, the answer is quite simple. Recall that RICO, the federal racketeering statute, defines a person as anything that can own property, which quite clearly includes corporations, since the law permits corporations to own property.[1] Therefore, if we were to limit inquiry into the meaning of the word "person" to statutes that carry their own definitions, there would be very little to say, at least in most cases.

But the Constitution has no glossary. Not only does the Constitution not define words like "person" or "citizen," but the corporation as we know it today did not even exist in the late eighteenth century when the Constitution was written. The Constitution regularly speaks of "citizens" and "persons." The Fourth Amendment refers to "the right of the *people* to be secure." The Fifth Amendment guarantees that no *person* shall be compelled to be a witness against himself, and grants the right to due process to *persons*. Article III extends federal judicial power to disputes between *citizens* of states, and Article IV grants the *citizens* of different states the privileges and immunities of each state.

As laws restricting the powers of corporations were relaxed, especially during the nineteenth century, more and more cases reached the courts in which it had to be determined whether or not a corporation should count as a person, vested with the rights and obligations of natural persons and citizens. Morton Horwitz, a legal historian, and Sanford Schane, a linguist, have written insightfully about the Supreme Court's reaction to this problem.[2] I rely heavily on their work in the discussion that follows.

To take an early example, in 1809, the Supreme Court, in *Bank of the United States v. Deveaux*,[3] had to determine whether the federal courts were permitted to decide a controversy between a Pennsylvania corporation and a Georgia tax collector. Article III of the Constitution defines what sorts of controversies make up the federal judicial power. Included are controversies "between Citizens of different States." The issue in *Deveaux* was whether the tax collector and corporation were citizens of different states. If so, the case could be heard in federal court. If not, the Pennsylvania corporation would have to sue the Georgia tax collector in the Georgia state courts, a less appealing prospect since the state court might have a bias toward its own tax collector. The decision rested on whether a corporation could be viewed as a "citizen" of any state.

Chief Justice Marshall, writing for the Court, granted the corporation access to the federal courts, holding that a corporation is nothing other than a group of individuals associated with one another. Since the individuals are citizens, their mutual association should not keep them out of court, even though the corporation itself is "a mere creature of the law,"[4] existing only because statute books allow it to exist.

In later cases, the Court was forced to go even further in order to maintain corporate access to the federal courts. The problem surfaced when the shareholders of a corporation were from a variety of states, including the state of which the opposing party was a citizen. Is the dispute still a controversy between citizens of different states? In 1844, the Supreme Court decided in *Louisville, Cincinnati & Charleston Railroad Co. v. Letson*[5] that the federal courts have jurisdiction as long as an opposing party does not live in the same state as the corporation's place of residence. The citizenship of the corporation's shareholders, so instrumental in *Deveaux*, no longer mattered. The corporation was seen not as an association of its shareholders, but rather as a person, albeit an artificial one. Since *Letson* was decided, the courts have taken some peculiar turns, but the law today has not changed very much: for purposes of determining the jurisdiction of the federal courts, a corporation is a citizen of the state in which it is incorporated (as well as of the state in which it has its principal place of business).[6]

Thus, in two cases, we have seen the Supreme Court announce three different views of corporate identity: a corporation is a mere creature of the law; a corporation is a group of its members; and a corporation is a "legal" person. By early in the twentieth century, the Supreme Court was repeatedly adopting the "person theory" of corporate identity for the various constitutional provisions whose definition of "person" or "citizen" had reached the Court. Again, I refer the reader to the interesting writings of Morton Horwitz and Sanford Schane (see note 2) for much more detail, and for political analysis.[7]

In deciding these cases, the Supreme Court set for itself an intellectual trap. Once the Court committed itself to a particular perspective on corporate identity for the purpose of justifying its decision in one case, it could rule differently in another only by promoting a different perspective. In so doing, the Court would necessarily rob the first case of its intellectual force, since there is no theory explaining why the features that were so instrumental in the first decision could not carry the day in the second. If, on the other hand, the Court were in this second case to stay with the original theory of corporate identity for the sake of consistency, it could do so only at the expense of forsaking what it considered to be a just result. This is exactly the problem of which Cardozo warned in *The Growth of the Law*.

We saw just this sort of dilemma in earlier chapters in connection with the application of interpretive principles.[8] At the root of this problem is the fact that a judge's vision of justice in each case operates independently of the interpretive principles that he adduces to justify his decisions. The interpretive principle that was so helpful just last year may become a haunting nuisance when the next case arises this year. In short, while there may be three distinct views of corporate identity, there is no theory, including linguistic theory, that forces us to select any one over another.

The problem surfaced most dramatically when the Supreme Court had to decide whether a corporation is a person for purposes of the Fourth and Fifth Amendments. Since the beginning of this century the rule has been that a corporation is not a person afforded Fifth Amendment protection.

Ironically, the case that established this rule is the same case in which the Court determined that a corporation is a person entitled to Fourth Amendment protection against illegal searches and seizures. Let us see how the Court arrived at this peculiar doctrinal array.

CORPORATIONS, THE LEXICON, AND THE FIFTH AMENDMENT

The Fifth Amendment says in part:

> No person . . . shall be compelled in any criminal case to be a witness against himself, nor to be deprived of life, liberty, or property without due process of law; nor shall private property be taken for public use without just compensation.

In *Hale v. Henkel,*[9] decided by the Supreme Court in 1906, Edwin Hale had been served with a grand jury subpoena demanding that he testify and produce extensive records of the corporation of which he was an officer. The grand jury was investigating Hale's company and others regarding criminal violations of the antitrust laws. When he refused to testify and refused to produce the documents, Hale was held in contempt and put in prison. He sued for a writ of *habeas corpus,* claiming that he was being incarcerated in violation of his constitutional rights. His case made its way to the Supreme Court, where he lost.

Of the many arguments that Hale made, one of them was that he could not be compelled to produce the documents since they might incriminate the corporation. At first, the Court brushed this argument aside, saying that it need not reach the question of whether a corporation is a person since Mr. Hale was not himself a corporation, and the Fifth Amendment protects only against compelled testimony against *oneself*—not against others.

But this begs the question. One can only determine whether a corporation is protected by the Fifth Amendment by deciding whether its employees have a right to refuse to testify to avoid incriminating the corporation. Recognizing this logic, the Court changed course and addressed the issue of whether a corporation is a person subject to Fifth Amendment protection. The Court was systematic, first explaining to us what it means to be a person as far as the law is concerned:

> . . . The individual may stand upon his constitutional rights as a citizen. He is entitled to carry on his private business in his own way. His power to contract is unlimited. He owes no duty to the State or to his neighbors to divulge his business, or to open his doors to an investigation, so far as it may tend to criminate him.

He owes no such duty to the State, since he receives nothing therefrom, beyond the protection of his life and property. His rights are such as existed by the law of the land long antecedent to the organization of the State, and can only be taken from him by due process of law, and in accordance with the Constitution. Among his rights are a refusal to incriminate himself, and the immunity of himself and his property from arrest or seizure except under a warrant of the law. He owes nothing to the public so long as he does not trespass upon their rights.[10]

The focus, of course, is on the natural rights of people, emphasizing the limited role that government may play in our lives. (Government, in fact, had already asserted itself quite forcefully in this case, having locked Mr. Hale behind bars.) Corporations, on the other hand, are by their nature very different creatures, according to the Court:

Upon the other hand, the corporation is a creature of the State. It is presumed to be incorporated for the benefit of the public. It receives certain special privileges and franchises, and holds them subject to the laws of the State and the limitations of its charter. Its powers are limited by law. It can make no contract not authorized by its charter. Its rights to act as a corporation are only preserved to it so long as it obeys the laws of its creation. There is a reserved right in the legislature to investigate its contracts and find out whether it has exceeded its powers. It would be a strange anomaly to hold that a State, having chartered a corporation to make use of certain franchises, could not in the exercise of its sovereignty inquire how these franchises had been employed, and whether they had been abused, and demand the production of the corporate books and papers for that purpose.[11]

Because of this dissimilarity between people on the one hand and corporations on the other, Mr. Hale was to remain in jail.

But the Court could not stop there. Mr. Hale had also argued that the subpoena violated the corporation's Fourth Amendment right "of the people" to be immune from unreasonable searches and seizures:

The right of the people to be secure in their persons, houses, papers, and effects, against unreasonable searches and seizures, shall not be violated, and no Warrants shall issue, but upon probable cause, supported by Oath or affirmation, and particularly describing the place to be searched, and the person or things to be seized.

By issuing the subpoena that compelled production of the papers, Hale argued, the government planned to search the company's papers for evidence of a crime. Thus, service of a subpoena comes within the scope of the word "search." The Fourth Amendment speaks only of the right of the people. Is a corporation a person as far as the Fourth Amendment is concerned? Using the group and person theories of corporate identity, the Court said yes:

> . . . A corporation is, after all, but an association of individuals under an assumed name and with a distinct legal entity. In organizing itself as a collective body it waives no constitutional immunities appropriate to such body. Its property cannot be taken without compensation. It can only be proceeded against by due process of law, and is protected, under the Fourteenth Amendment, against unlawful discrimination. . . . Corporations are a necessary feature of modern business activity, and their aggregated capital has become the source of nearly all great enterprises.[12]

The determination that the Fourth Amendment offered the corporation constititutional protection led the Court to the additional question of whether the search was an "unreasonable" one. The Court held that it was unreasonable because the subpoena was excessively broad in what it sought to examine, reasoning that a search warrant similarly worded would not be valid. But the Court also held that this excess in government action did nothing to excuse Mr. Hale, who continued to be held in contempt of court.

We now see all three views of corporate identity—"creature," "group," and "person"—in the same case without even a hint that the interpretive principles underlying this array are in conflict. This is not to say that the Court was not motivated by legitimate concerns. In several passages the Court focused on a significant practical issue that explains its decision. If everyone employed by a corporation could refuse to testify or otherwise cooperate in a government investigation into the corporation's criminal activity, then it would become almost impossible to penetrate the goings on inside a corporation engaged in committing crimes. One can easily imagine individuals deciding to incorporate in order to immunize their behavior from government scrutiny. The theme of preventing the corporate form from obstructing government inquiry continues today. For example, courts have been willing to force corporations to hire an agent to produce documents and to testify when every employee of a corporation with sufficient knowledge has asserted his own privilege against self-incrimination and has refused to testify when a subpoena is issued to a corporation.[13]

When it comes to the Fourth Amendment, very different considerations apply. The Fourth Amendment protects against unreasonable invasion by the police into people's affairs, rather than against compulsion to come forward. Law enforcement activities can proceed effectively even with the obligation to obtain a search warrant before seizing a corporation's papers. The same could not be said if a corporation were permitted to hide behind the Fifth Amendment's immunity, as described above.

Two of the justices in *Hale v. Henkel* dissented, directing their attention to the peculiar asymmetry between the Court's understanding of personhood in the Fifth Amendment on the one hand and the rest of the Constitution on the other. Quoting Chief Justice Marshall, they observed: "The great object of an incorporation is to bestow the character and properties of individuality on a collective and changing body of men."[14] In essence, the dissenters would hold that corporations are afforded Fifth Amendment rights using some hybrid of the group and person approaches to corporate identity.

Significantly, linguistic theory is of no help here. As much as our internal system of knowledge of language tells us about the meaning of the Fifth Amendment (see chapter 5), it does not force us to adopt any particular view of corporate identity. In fact, the word "corporation" has linguistic features that are consistent with all three approaches to corporate identity: creature, group, and person, making it easy for courts to adopt any of them. For example, as Schane points out, even though a corporation may consist of a group of people, we always use the grammatical singular in speaking of corporations.[15] Thus, we may say (1a), but we cannot say (1b):

(1)   a. The jury have been sequestered.
      b. The corporation have been subpoenaed.

Rather, like "person," "corporation" has the characteristics of a noun that names a single entity. This, as Schane concludes, makes it especially easy for courts to equate corporations and persons, although, of course, it does not necessitate any such conclusion. Recognizing a corporation as a single entity is also consistent with the creature theory.

On the other hand, the word "corporation" has certain linguistic features that are in keeping with the group theory.[16] Consider, for example, (2), which might be part of a fictional press release:

(2)   Cleanair Corporation voted yesterday to censure companies
        whose furnaces emit dioxins into the air.

The announcement is ambiguous with respect to who voted. It may mean that the members of the board of directors of Cleanair Corporation voted to censure polluters. This is consistent with the "group" interpretation. The words "Cleanair Corporation" are being used to represent a group: the members of the board of directors of Cleanair Corporation. On the other hand, (2) would make just as much sense if Cleanair Corporation were a member of, say, a committee comprised of corporations whose mission it is to determine how the corporate world should react to environmental issues. Cleanair Corporation has cast its vote in favor of censure. This understanding is consistent with both the creature and person theories. And if the committee were to consist of both individuals and corporations, with each person or entity getting one vote, then the announcement would be consistent with only the person theory of corporate identity.

When the Supreme Court decides whether it should deem a corporation to be a person for purposes of construing a particular provision of the Constitution, it decides whether to focus on those features that the two words have in common or on the dissimilar features. Of course, there is no theory articulated for how the Court should adjust its focus, and linguistic theory does not necessitate any particular result.[17] Consequently, cases like *Hale v. Henkel* are possible, where even in the same opinion the Court relies on divergent perspectives. Interestingly, if linguistic principles, counter to fact, did dictate a particular outcome in these cases, the great likelihood is that the entire issue would go unnoticed, much the way the interpretation of *himself* in the Fifth Amendment goes unnoticed.

WITH respect to corporate personhood and the Fifth Amendment, nothing much has changed since 1906, although details have been filled in. For example, in *Wilson v. United States*,[18] decided in 1911, the Supreme Court held that the individual in possession of corporate documents may not avoid production of them by asserting his personal Fifth Amendment privilege even if the content of the documents would tend to incriminate the individual. Some thirty years later, the Court applied similar principles to labor unions and their officials.[19] And in 1974, in *Bellis v. United States,* the rule was expanded to hold that the members of a small partnership, a law firm, cannot use their personal privilege against compelled self-incrimination to avoid producing the partnership's financial records.[20]

By the time *Bellis* was decided, the "collective entity rule," as the principle of *Hale v. Henkel* has come to be called, had become sufficiently entrenched that the Court had long since abandoned as unnecessary its efforts to discuss in philosophical terms the distinctions between people on the one hand and the various forms of association on the other. Rather, the Court was concerned with whether the organization's existence was sufficiently distinct from that of the individual wishing to assert the privilege. Justice Douglas dissented in *Bellis,* arguing that a law partnership with three partners was merely "an aggregate of individuals and not . . . a separate entity," quoting from a court decision on partnership law from Pennsylvania, the state in which Mr. Bellis's partnership practiced law.[21] The majority, in contrast, had decided that the difference between a small corporation and a small partnership should have no legal significance as far as the application of the Fifth Amendment is concerned. But everyone entered the debate on the same grounds: if a partnership is deemed an entity with existence independent of its members, then the partnership itself has no Fifth Amendment right against compelled self-incrimination, and neither do its members with respect to the production of partnership property.

It has now been so long since the *Hale v. Henkel* doctrine was adopted that law students today learn as a matter of simple fact that the Fourth Amendment protects corporations but the self-incrimination clause of the Fifth Amendment does not. As we have seen, though, the distinction has its roots in inconsistent treatment of the words "person" and "corporation." Here again, the substantive political basis for the scheme of rules is as sensible as the linguistic underpinnings are faulty.

Testimony and the Act of Speech

The Supreme Court has recently created a linguistic issue out of a second phrase in the Fifth Amendment: "No person shall be compelled . . . *to be a witness against himself.*" What does it mean to be a witness against oneself? As we will see, the Court has interpreted this phrase as prohibiting government from forcing an individual to engage in a testimonial or communicative act. This, of course, leaves the Court with the question of which acts are testimonial or communicative. Here, linguistic theory does provide a partial answer, as I will show below, after introducing the notion of *speech acts*. However, as I also hope to demonstrate, whether we regard any particular act as testimonial or communicative depends crucially on how we characterize the act. Unfortunately, neither the theory of speech acts nor any other theory, for that matter, tells us how to characterize acts that government attempts to compel individuals to do. As a result, we are left with judicial opinions that make confident pronouncements about what falls within the ambit of the Fifth Amendment, but never reveal that the result depends crucially on the court's characterization of government behavior.

THE CURRENT STATE OF THE FIFTH AMENDMENT

Witnesses are routinely compelled to do two things: to testify and to produce documents, which explains why the Court in *Hale v. Henkel* analyzed the application of the Fifth Amendment both to Mr. Hale's refusal to testify and to his refusal to produce corporate books and records.[22] This understanding of what it means to be a witness against oneself can be traced back to 1886, when the Supreme Court held in *Boyd v. United States* that "any forcible and compulsory extortion of a man's own testimony or of his private papers to be used as evidence to convict him of a crime"[23] would violate that person's Fifth Amendment rights. It was reaffirmed in virtually all of the cases discussed in the last section, through the 1974 decision of *Bellis v. United States*.[24] The Court in those cases had no need to ask whether the Fifth Amendment prohibited compelled production of documents, but only who or what had the benefit of this prohibition.

In 1976, all of this changed with the Supreme Court's decision in *Fisher v. United States*,[25] a case that took the compelled production of certain papers outside the scope of the Fifth Amendment. By examining *Fisher* and other cases that establish the current state of Fifth Amendment doctrine, we can see how linguistic analysis has entered the realm of Fifth Amendment law, making current doctrine appear to be only natural. To do so, we must first turn to some cases that set the stage for *Fisher*.

In *Schmerber v. California*,[26] decided in 1966, the Supreme Court affirmed the conviction of Armando Schmerber for driving while intoxicated. Following a car accident, Schmerber was taken to a hospital for treatment of injuries. There, the police instructed a doctor, over Schmerber's objection, to extract blood for analysis of alcohol content. The test results became evidence on which Mr. Schmerber was convicted. He appealed, claiming that his Fifth Amendment rights had been violated.

Justice Brennan wrote the majority opinion in this 5–4 decision. In a jurisprudentially significant passage, he wrote:

> We hold that the privilege protects an accused only from being compelled to testify against himself, or otherwise provide the State with *evidence of a testimonial or communicative nature,* and

that the withdrawal of blood and use of the analysis in question in this case did not involve compulsion to these ends.[27] (Emphasis added)

The *Schmerber* Court reaffirmed the Court's commitment to the principle of *Boyd* that the compelled production of one's personal papers is communicative, and therefore unconstitutional, despite its holding that the extraction of blood is not. Likening the situation to a 1910 case in which the Court had upheld requiring a defendant to don a blouse worn by the perpetrator of a crime,[28] Justice Brennan distinguished between compelling communicative acts on the one hand and compelling bodily acts on the other. In addition, he noted that the Fifth Amendment has been construed to permit government to compel individuals to submit to fingerprinting and photography, and to make a particular gesture that a witness remembers the perpetrator to have made. The dissent disagreed with Justice Brennan's analysis, reasoning that the word "witness" should not be construed so narrowly.

Within a year of deciding *Schmerber,* the Supreme Court decided that the Fifth Amendment did not prohibit government from compelling handwriting exemplars[29] and voice exemplars for identification,[30] where the defendant was compelled to repeat the words that the victim said that she had heard during the crime. Thus, by 1976 when the Supreme Court decided *United States v. Fisher,* the Fifth Amendment scorecard showed protection against compelled testimony and document production, and no protection against compelled blood analysis, donning of a garment, and production of voice and handwriting exemplars.[31]

In *Fisher,* the Court reversed itself on the issue assumed in *Hale v. Henkel,* holding that the Fifth Amendment does not protect against government's compelling the production of certain papers either. This essentially brought to an end the ninety-year reign of *Boyd v. United States* as the law on this matter, although the official death of *Boyd,* as we shall see, was not announced for a few more years.

The subpoena in *Fisher,* which was issued as part of an investigation into income tax payments, sought the defendant's production of his accountant's workpapers, which the defendant had obtained from the accountant and had promptly turned over to his attorney. The Court held that neither the taxpayer nor any one else had been compelled to say anything, and that the Fifth Amendment, therefore, did not apply. Speaking for a majority of seven, Justice White wrote:

A subpoena served on a taxpayer requiring him to produce an accountant's workpapers in his possession without doubt involves substantial compulsion. But it does not compel oral testimony; nor would it ordinarily compel the taxpayer to restate, repeat, or affirm the truth of the contents of the documents sought. Therefore, the Fifth Amendment would not be violated by the fact alone that the papers on their face might incriminate the taxpayer, for the privilege protects a person only against being incriminated by his own compelled testimonial communications.[32]

Justice White further noted that had the papers been authored by Mr. Fisher himself, and not by Mr. Fisher's accountant, the same reasoning would have applied, since the only act being compelled was the act of production itself.[33]

Justice Brennan, who wrote the majority opinion in *Schmerber,* the blood case, wrote a bitter concurrence in *Fisher,* obviously unhappy about where his own reasoning had taken the Court. He agreed with the holding in the case because the subpoenaed papers were really those of an accountant, sent to Mr. Fisher and eventually turned over to a lawyer. Reacting to the majority's view that only the act of production was compelled, however, Justice Brennan wrote:

> Obviously disclosure or production of testimonial evidence is also compelled, and the heart of the protection of the privilege is in its safeguarding against compelled disclosure or production of that evidence.[34]

He further marveled at a rule of law that would not permit compelling a witness to disclose the contents of his mind, but would permit compelling him to produce a scrap of paper on which he wrote the contents of his mind. Historically, Justice Brennan pointed out, the Fifth Amendment had its roots in a British jurisprudence that rightly drew no such distinction.[35] Thus, analysis of the "original intent" of the drafters, to the extent ascertainable from historical investigation, appears to support Brennan's view that the Fifth Amendment is to be given broader scope to prohibit governmental coercion.[36]

The final blow to *Boyd* came eight years later in 1984, when the Court decided *United States v. Doe.*[37] I will call this case *Doe*$_1$ since I have already made reference to another case with the same title, *Doe*$_2$ (see note 31). The facts in *Doe*₁ were very similar to those in *Fisher*, except that the papers sought by the government were not an accountant's papers, but rather the defendant's own business papers. Relying on *Fisher*, the Court, in a 6–3 decision, had little difficulty holding that the compelled production of these papers did not violate the Fifth Amendment. Even though the content of the papers may be incriminating, the Court reasoned, no one forced the defendant to write incriminating papers in the first place.

Again, the Court noted that the act of producing the documents may itself have testimonial or communicative elements, since production is a tacit admission that the papers are the ones that were called for in the subpoena, that they were in the defendant's possession, and that they are authentic. In a brief concurrence, Justice O'Connor wanted to leave no doubt as to what this decision means:

> I concur in both the result and reasoning of Justice Powell's opinion for the Court. I write separately, however, just to make explicit what is implicit in the analysis of that opinion: that the Fifth Amendment provides absolutely no protection for the contents of private papers of any kind. The notion that the Fifth Amendment protects the privacy of papers originated in *Boyd v. United States*, . . . but our decision in *Fisher v. United States* . . . sounded the death knell for *Boyd*.[38]

In what reads as a hopeless attempt to limit the Court's ruling, Justice Marshall wrote in dissent that the Court has still not ruled on the Fifth Amendment's protection of papers of a personal, as opposed to a business, nature. Justice Marshall is correct, but the thrust of *Fisher* and *Doe*₁ would allow for no such distinction.[39]

Finally, in 1988, the Court decided a case in which questions of corporate identity and self-incrimination collided. In *Braswell v. United States*,[40] the Court was faced with a challenge to a subpoena that had been issued to an individual who personally ran and owned two small corporations, demanding that he produce the books and records of the corporations. The defendant, Braswell, refused, relying on his Fifth Amendment rights. Recognizing that *Fisher* and *Doe*₁ held that the content of the documents was not privileged since no one compelled anyone to write them, Braswell asserted only that the act of producing the documents might incriminate him personally. That is, the Court in *Braswell* had to decide whether a person could assert his own Fifth Amendment claim with respect to the act of producing a corporation's documents. The Court held 5–4 that he could not.

In an opinion written by Chief Justice Rehnquist, the Court relied heavily on the rule of *Hale* and *Bellis,* that collective entities have no Fifth Amendment rights, and individual corporate custodians required to produce corporate documents must do so. The Court refused to adopt the defendant's position that he was personally being compelled to engage in communicative or testimonial acts by virtue of his production of the documents.

Having decided the Fifth Amendment issues, the Court took a peculiar turn at the end of the opinion. It concluded by holding that while the custodian of corporate records may not resist a subpoena based on his own Fifth Amendment privilege, the individual's act of production cannot be used in a subsequent trial as evidence against him personally, since he is acting only as the agent of the corporation, and not in his individual capacity. Thus, a jury may be told that the corporation produced the incriminating documents, but not that the individual produced them.[41]

Justice Kennedy explained the difficulty with the Court's reasoning, writing in dissent on behalf of himself and three others:

> The majority gives the corporate agent fiction a weight it simply cannot bear. In a peculiar attempt to mitigate the force of its own holding, it impinges upon its own analysis by concluding that, while the Government may compel a named individual to produce records, in any later proceeding against the person it cannot divulge that he performed the act. But if that is so, it is because the Fifth Amendment protects the person without regard to his status as a corporate employee; and once this be admitted, the necessary support for the majority's case has collapsed.
>
> Perhaps the Court makes this concession out of some vague sense of fairness, but the source of its authority to do so remains unexplained. It cannot rest on the Fifth Amendment, for the privilege against self-incrimination does not permit balancing the convenience of the Government against the rights of a witness, and the majority has in any case determined that the Fifth Amendment is inapplicable.[42]

In the future, *Braswell* may be used to argue for the abandonment of the act of production doctrine altogether, limiting Fifth Amendment protection to compelled testimony only. Whether it will be so used remains to be seen.[43]

Speech Acts: Linguistics and the Fifth Amendment

The current Fifth Amendment doctrine, as we have seen, requires us to ask two questions when faced with a challenge to government-compelled acts: first, whether the person or entity asserting the privilege has rights under the Fifth Amendment (e.g., corporations do not); and second, whether the act that the government attempts to compel is protected by the Fifth Amendment, that is, whether the act is self-incriminating and testimonial or communicative in nature. If these questions are answered affirmatively, then the Fifth Amendment prevents government compulsion.

The question of what is testimonial or communicative can be seen as a linguistic issue. To see how this is so, we must turn to the theory of speech acts, first developed by the philosopher John Austin, and outlined in his 1969 book, *How to Do Things with Words*.[44]

Linguists concern themselves largely with the structure and meanings of sentences. But speaking can be seen as more than some necessary way of getting out an intended meaning. Speaking can be seen as an act in and of itself. In some instances, the act of speaking and the act of doing are the same. The classic example is, "I now pronounce you husband and wife." Provided that this is uttered under the right circumstances (Austin describes certain "felicity conditions" which define in part what these circumstances are), to say this sentence is to accomplish a marriage, just as nonverbal acts accomplish other results, such as lifting a switch to turn on a light.

Uttering some verbs, such as "pronounce," has the quality of performing the act of the verb just by saying it. Austin called these verbs *performatives*. To better see the special status of performatives, compare the following two sentences:

(3)   I hope that you arrive early.

(4)   I insist that you arrive early.

Of "hope" and "insist," only "insist" is a performative. In uttering (3), the speaker is reporting on his state of mind. The sentence will be true if the speaker really does hope that you arrive early, and it will be false if he does not. When someone utters (4), on the other hand, he is indeed insisting just by speaking the sentence. He may not mean it, but when someone says that he insists that something happen, then he has insisted that it happen by virtue of having said so.

Similarly, in a court room, when a lawyer says, "I object," he has objected because to say "I object" is to object. "Object," in other words, is another performative. To complete the story, when the judge says "sustained" or "overruled," he too has engaged in a speech act, the results of which are to accomplish exactly what he has said. "Sustain" and "overrule" are also performatives.

The relationship between the law and the theory of speech acts has not gone unnoticed. For example, Schane, whose work on the meaning of "person" was discussed above, has also written on the relationship between contract law and the performative verb "promise," pointing to similarities between the lines drawn by the law as to which promises are enforceable and the taxonomies of speech acts developed by philosophers of language and linguists.[45] Danet, in a thorough piece, relates different kinds of speech acts to particular legal phenomena,[46] and Tiersma has written an extremely interesting article relating speech act theory to the law of defamation.[47]

Underlying the Fifth Amendment is the rejection of a government whose police force has the right to beat confessions out of those accused of committing crimes. If we view the Fifth Amendment as granting a privilege of protection against government compulsion of communicative or testimonial acts, then the essence of the Fifth Amendment is to protect us against being forced to engage in self-incriminating speech acts or their equivalent. Confession is the most severe example, but lesser statements can also be self-incriminating, as we shall see.

Admissions

How can we tell whether what the government is trying to make us do constitutes a self-incriminating testimonial act? This question goes to the heart of Fifth Amendment doctrine, and can be answered in part by reference to the theory of speech acts. English has a verb, "admit," that by and large means to perform a communicative act against one's interest. To testify against oneself is to "admit" wrongdoing. By asking whether acts that government seeks to compel can properly be seen as "admissions," and by looking more closely at the properties of "admit," we can begin to structure the debate over the scope of the Fifth Amendment.

"Admit" is a performative. Consider the following example:

(5)   I admit that I haven't filed tax returns for the last five years.

By uttering (5), I actually engage in an admission. But it is no more necessary to use the word "admit" to admit than it is to use the word "say" to say. Uttering (6) is just as much an admission as is uttering (5).

(6)   I haven't filed tax returns for the last five years.

Moreover, admissions are statements against the interest of the speaker, not against the interest of someone else. Example (7) would be a very peculiar utterance, and (8) makes sense only if the speaker is speaking on behalf of the corporation mentioned in the sentence:

(7)   I admit that you haven't filed tax returns for the last five years.

(8)   I admit that the corporation hasn't filed tax returns for the last five years.

All of these characteristics are known to us tacitly as speakers of English. Like other aspects of our knowledge of language, we learned them without any specific training. Indeed, the kinds of facts discussed here are generally considered so "obvious" that they would never even appear in a dictionary.

"Admit" has other relevant properties. Not only can one admit without using the word "admit," but one can admit without speaking at all:

(9)   The FBI agent asked who in the room was the drug pusher.
       John stood up, thereby admitting that he was the one.

This phenomenon is not unique to admitting. The philosopher John Searle presents a number of examples of acts that can be performed by speech or otherwise:

> I may make estimates, give diagnoses and draw conclusions in saying "I estimate", "I diagnose", and "I conclude", but in order to estimate, diagnose or conclude it is not necessary to say anything at all. I may simply stand before a building and estimate its height, silently diagnose you as a marginal schizophrenic, or conclude that the man sitting next to me is quite drunk. In these cases, no speech act, not even an internal speech act, is necessary.[48]

Admitting can thus be seen not only as a speech act, but simply as an act, with speech being the primary way in which the act is performed.

Similarly, when admitting is an act of speech, the speech can imply the substance of what is admitted, without stating it directly:

(10) John admitted that he had begun drinking again when he complained that Budweiser does not taste as good as it used to.

Not all acts are admissions. Ordinarily, admitting requires some intention on the part of the actor to communicate something through his action. For this reason, (11) seems odd at best:

(11) Bill admitted that he had stayed up all night by sleeping through the movie.

But the intention to communicate need not be an intention to communicate against one's interest. One can blurt something out, thereby admitting something, without intending to do so, as (12) illustrates.

(12) Bill admitted that he was at the scene of the crime when he announced that he had spent the night with his girlfriend, who, as we now know, was herself at the scene that night.

However, admitting does seem to imply the revelation of something private. It would be very strange to say "I admit that you and I are sitting next to each other," or similar statements that are obvious to the hearer without any investigation at all.

We now see that we can admit either by speech or by other actions, although we admit principally through words. Our intention must be to communicate, generally something private. An admission is contrary to the speaker's interest, although we may not fully realize in advance that what we are communicating will be self-damaging. Again, we utilize these properties of "admit" in everyday speech without any real awareness of them, unless they are specifically brought to our attention. In short, "admit" is a word that describes a self-damaging communicative act, the very act that the Fifth Amendment tells us we cannot be forced to perform.

Admitting by Bleeding

In its opinions, the Supreme Court recognizes the relationship between the Fifth Amendment and government's forcing people to admit. In fact, the Court's application of the act of production doctrine in *Doe₁* was motivated by a recognition that to produce documents would be to admit. The trial court had determined:

> With few exceptions, enforcement of the subpoenas would compel [respondent] to *admit* that the records exist, that they are in his possession, and that they are authentic. These communications, if made under compulsion of a court decree, would violate [respondent's] Fifth Amendment rights . . . [49] (Emphasis added)

The Supreme Court adopted these findings. It repeated the significance of admitting in *Braswell:* "By producing the records, respondent would *admit* that the records existed, were in his possession, and were authentic"[50] (emphasis added).

We can test an act to determine if it is an admission by asking whether, as speakers of English, we can properly say that we have admitted something by performing the act. To begin with an easy case, let us consider an individual who has testified that he committed a murder. We can certainly utter (13) as a well-formed sentence:

(13) Bill admitted that he murdered John by testifying that he committed the crime.

Thus, testifying that he committed the crime can be properly seen as an admission.

But if (13) is well-formed, then (14) is also well-formed, and (14) describes unconstitutional governmental compulsion:

(14) The government compelled Bill to admit that he murdered John by forcing him to testify that he committed the crime.

In this way, we can judge whether a particular instance of government compulsion violates the Fifth Amendment. If the defendant's act can be understood as an admission, then the government may reasonably be seen as violating the Fifth Amendment whenever it compels the admission by forcing a witness to perform the act. The test relies on our intuition, as speakers of English, as to whether we can "admit by doing x."[51]

As we begin to consider some of the more controversial Fifth Amendment cases in this way, something both interesting and unsettling occurs. In many instances, it becomes difficult to tell whether or not a compelled act is an admission. This is true for two reasons. First, whether an act qualifies as an admission depends on how we describe it, and acts can be described in many different ways. Second, as we have seen with the meaning of "corporation" and as we will see later in our discussion of the word "search," our knowledge of the lexicon leaves open certain possibilities for interpretation, and it is within these gaps that legal debate over the meanings of words occurs. When it comes to admitting, the same holds true.

The difficulty becomes immediately apparent when we attempt to reexamine in linguistic terms the blood test case, *Schmerber v. California.*[52] Recall that in *Schmerber,* the Supreme Court held that the police may, within the bounds of the Fifth Amendment, compel an individual to submit to a blood test to determine whether his blood alcohol level rendered him legally intoxicated. Using the test that we developed above, let us first ask whether one can admit being drunk by voluntarily producing blood.

(15) Frank admitted that he was intoxicated by putting out his arm to allow the doctor to take blood.

(16) Frank admitted that he was intoxicated by turning over a sample of his blood.

(17) Frank admitted that he was intoxicated by turning over a sample of his blood, which he knew to be alcohol-laden.

Of these three sentences, (17) strikes me as the best by far. Sentence (16) is somewhat marginal, and (15) does not seem to me to use "admit" properly. The issue is whether, in each sentence, Frank is attempting to communicate anything by his actions. Recall that *admit* requires an intention to communicate, either verbally or by other means. In (15), even if Frank is intoxicated, and even if he wants everyone to find out, it is very hard to construe presenting an arm for a blood test as a communicative act.[53]

In (17), on the other hand, turning a sample over to the authorities may be much more easily seen as a communicative act. It is as though someone asked: "Are you legally intoxicated?" and he answered: "Of course. See for yourself: analyze this blood."Sentence (16) is not as good as (17) because it lacks the description of the blood that makes the act self-incriminating.

In *Schmerber*, the Supreme Court viewed the compulsion as requiring Schmerber to submit to something much closer to (15) than to (17). For example, the Court focused on how Schmerber was only being forced to undergo a minor medical procedure. Since (15) is not easily seen as an admission, the Court held that the Fifth Amendment was not violated.

It is not always simple to decide whether an act is both self-damaging and communicative in nature. Nonetheless, it would have been difficult in this case for the Court to have characterized the compulsion as forcing an act of communication. Although (17) describes an act of communication, the sentence seems remote from what was really happening in *Schmerber*, where the debate focused on whether the government should be allowed to extract physical evidence of a crime from within a defendant's body. Sentence (17) describes a situation in which a defendant already has a blood sample, and must decide whether to produce it in order to convey a message. Thus, while we can admit by bleeding, it was at least reasonable for the Court to conclude in *Schmerber* that the blood test was not the compulsion of a communicative act.

The "admit" test also helps focus the issues in cases dealing with the production of documents, *Fisher*[54] and *Doe*$_1$.[55] Recall that these were the cases in which the Supreme Court, relying on *Schmerber,* overruled *Boyd,* holding that the Fifth Amendment does not protect against the compelled production of incriminating documents. Consider the following:

(18) The defendant admitted that he had filed false tax returns by
      giving government agents his financial records, which were in-
      consistent with the information he had written on his returns.

I have little trouble with (18) because one may communicate by showing someone a piece of paper that has on it information of interest to the recipient. Recall Justice Brennan's concurrence in *Fisher.* Once again, if (18) is an appropriate utterance, then so is (19), and (19) describes a violation of the Fifth Amendment.

(19) The government compelled the defendant to admit that he had
      filed false tax returns by forcing him to give government agents
      his financial records, which were inconsistent with the infor-
      mation he had written on his returns.

We should recall that for most of this country's history, until 1976, it was thought that the Fifth Amendment applied to situations covered by (18) and (19).

I expect that not everyone will agree with these judgments. "Admit" is like any other concept in that it becomes fuzzy at the margins. Thus, one may argue in support of the current state of the law that producing the papers is tantamount to saying "see for yourself" and that this is not communicative enough or self-incriminating enough for an admission. To the extent that intuitions vary, the "admit" test will have produced focused disagreement about these cases.

The line that the Supreme Court has drawn in *Schmerber, Fisher,* and other cases reflects a distinction that is recognized in the theory of speech acts. John Searle, departing somewhat from Austin, distinguishes between two aspects of a speech act: its *illocutionary force* and its *propositional content.* The illocutionary force of a sentence refers to the kind of utterance that is intended, such as stating, questioning, commanding, promising, and the like, to use Searle's own examples.[56] The propositional content, on the other hand, is the statement or promise being made, the question being asked, the command being given, and so on. Thus, in (13), repeated below, the illocutionary force is an admission, and the propositional content is "Bill murdered John" (putting aside the necessity of first associating "Bill" and "he").

(13) Bill admitted that he murdered John by testifying that he committed the crime.

The remainder of the sentence, "by testifying that he committed the crime," describes how the illocutionary act, admitting, was performed.

In the cases described above, the Supreme Court seems to have taken the position that only admissions like the one in (13) are immune from government compulsion. That is, government may not compel an individual to make an utterance whose propositional content can properly be seen as an admission. In both *Schmerber* and *Fisher,* no utterance was compelled, and no Fifth Amendment violation was found. When the admission is inferred from the act being compelled, and not from the propositional content of compelled speech, the Court has been reluctant to prohibit government compulsion. The Court has been especially reluctant to find admissions in nonverbal acts, such as giving blood and producing papers.

This analysis can help us understand other Fifth Amendment decisions, such as *United States v. Wade,* the case holding that the government may compel a defendant to repeat the words that the perpetrator of a crime uttered.[57] There, the Court separated the content of an utterance (i.e., its propositional content) from the act of saying it (i.e., the illocutionary act of stating). That is, the Court has distinguished between compelling the act of speech and compelling someone to say something, the substance of which is relevant to the determination of a case. Under current Fifth Amendment doctrine, only the latter is protected. Since the propositional content of the voice exemplar was not being used to incriminate the defendant, the Court held that it was not unconstitutional for the government to force the defendant to produce the voice exemplar.

Can the police's compelling the production of a voice exemplar properly be seen as the compulsion of an admission? Again, our intuitions depend on how we characterize what is being compelled. Consider the following:

(20) The defendant admitted that he committed the crime by repeating the words that the actual perpetrator had spoken.

(21) The defendant admitted that he sounded very much like the perpetrator by repeating the words that the actual perpetrator had spoken.

Sentence (20) does not sound like much of an admission. While (21) may be a bit strained for some, it sounds more like one. Repeating some words may not amount to a confession of guilt, but the act of speaking may be seen as an admission of the quality of one's voice, just as the act of production may be seen as an admission of what documents one possesses.

Of course, one may still argue that someone's voice is not sufficiently private to qualify its exposure as an admission, even if one's papers are. After all, we all regularly make the quality of our voices public, and admitting implies the revelation of a secret. According to this view, (21) is better understood as a confirmation of public information than as an admission. But it is a mistake for the Court to hold that the act of speaking is not a communicative act just because the propositional content of the speech is ignored. The speech act itself may be communicative, just as the act of production or the act of standing up to identify oneself may be. The same holds true for other cases described earlier, such as those involving handwriting exemplars, fingerprinting, and wearing certain clothes. Again, the "admit" test helps us see the issues in these cases, but falls short of resolving them.

In contrast, I would be hard pressed to explain how submitting to a photograph is compelled communication. The experience of being photographed is entirely passive, and unlike giving blood, it does not require the individual to produce anything to the government. It is very difficult to say that someone made an admission by submitting to photography.

This leaves us with the act of production as the only instance in which the Supreme Court is regularly willing to draw the inference of an admission from a compelled act without reference to the propositional content of a compelled utterance. Consider (22):

(22) Frank admitted that he had illegal betting slips in his posses-
      sion by handing over a box of them to the United States
      Attorney.

I expect that most readers will find (22) relatively easy to accept. In fact, as noted above, the Supreme Court speaks of the act of production in terms of admissions.

Analytically, however, I find it very difficult to justify a doctrine that recognizes (22) as a communicative act, but does not recognize (18) (repeated below) as one.

(18) The defendant admitted that he had filed false tax returns by
      giving government agents his financial records, which were in-
      consistent with the information he had written on his returns.

In (22), the inference of an admission follows from the production itself and from an understanding of the content of the documents produced, i.e., illegal betting slips. In (18), on the other hand, the inferred admission comes only from the content of the documents produced. The distinction is real, but does not, as far as I can tell, justify the recognition of only (22) as an admission. While I would argue that the doctrine should be enlarged to recognize both acts as admissions protected from government compulsion by the Fifth Amendment, the greater likelihood, in my opinion, is the demise of the act of production doctrine with the result that only the propositional content of a compelled utterance will be examined in determining whether a Fifth Amendment violation has occurred.

In coming to grips with the meanings of words, then, the courts are faced with a difficult task: matching real life situations against a set of lexical features. In hard cases, the match is not a simple one, and the result depends on how one characterizes the events in the world. The decisions pass the limits of linguistics, and become personal, based on one's political persuasion, and other extralinguistic matters.

What Is a Search?

Let us return to the Fourth Amendment to the Constitution. It provides that

> The right of the people to be secure in their persons, houses, papers, and effects, against unreasonable searches and seizures, shall not be violated, and no Warrants shall issue, but upon probable cause, supported by Oath or affirmation, and particularly describing the place to be searched, and the person or things to be seized.

Over the past twenty-five years or so, the Supreme Court has ruled on many occasions whether a particular police activity constitutes an unreasonable search. Most, but not all, of these rulings come as the result of the growth of sophisticated technology that allows the government (and anyone else interested in doing so) to look into people's lives and belongings without breaking into their houses or businesses. These rulings have produced a body of law so dependent on the unique facts of each case that it takes enormous effort to sort it out.[58]

Recently, Professor Clark Cunningham has written an extremely insightful analysis of search and seizure law, organized around a linguistic analysis of the word "search."[59] Much of what I write below derives from Cunningham's careful parsing of the search and seizure cases. But for reasons that I will touch on, Cunningham's linguistic analysis falls short in ways that reduce somewhat the power of his argument. I therefore have adopted what seems to me to be a better linguistic analysis.

THE WORD "SEARCH"

In earlier chapters, we had occasion to look at some syntactic rules and some strategies for sentence processing. In this chapter, we have been looking at another aspect of linguistic knowledge: the lexicon. To see the issues that arise in construing the Fourth Amendment, we must first look a little more closely at our tacit knowledge, as speakers of English, of certain aspects of the lexicon.

One thing that all native speakers tacitly know about their native language is its phrasal structure. This includes the nature of the phrases required, permitted, and prohibited in the predicates of sentences containing the various verbs of the language. For example, "put" requires a direct object, which is the thing being moved (called the "theme"[60] by linguists), and it also requires a *location* phrase. Consider the examples in (23):

(23) He put the exhibits on the table.
      He put the exhibits.
      He put on the table.
      He put.

Only the first of these sentences is grammatical. We can represent as follows the lexical characteristics of the verb "put" that makes this so:[61]

agent PUT theme location

Let us look at "eat" as a second example:

(24) The defendant ate.
      The defendant ate the evidence.

Since "eat" is grammatical either with or without a theme, as in the sentences in (24), "eat" can be represented as follows:

agent EAT (theme)

The parentheses around "theme" indicate that it appears optionally with this verb.

Note that even when there is no direct object, we understand the verb to mean that the defendant ate something or other. That is, "eat" has an implied object, which is the thing eaten. There has been considerable discussion in the linguistic literature about the status of absent but implied arguments in our mental representations of sentences.[62]

Our understanding of the word "search" depends crucially on our recognizing that certain arguments are implied even if not verbally realized. The word "search" takes a number of arguments, all of which are optional. Consider the following:

(25) The police continued to search.
      The police searched the room.
      The police searched for marijuana.
      The police searched the room for marijuana.
      The police searched with dogs.
      The police searched the room with dogs.
      The police searched the room for marijuana with dogs.

From this array, we can derive a partial lexical representation for "search":

agent SEARCH (theme) (for goal) (with instrument)

In this case, we use the word "theme" to indicate the thing being searched. The goal is the thing that the searcher is trying to find, and the instrument is the means by which the search is conducted. Both require prepositions before them.[63] Again, when we use and hear the word "search," we make automatic use of these facts.

This last point, while perhaps obvious, is of great significance. For when we hear the word "search," just by virtue of our knowledge of English we know that there exists a theme (a place being searched) and a goal, implicit or explicit.[64] To see this, consider the following sentences, which contain prepositions that usually do not denote a goal. You will find yourself concocting peculiar scenarios in an effort to impose on these sentences the required agent-search-theme-for-goal structure.

(26) The police searched from the boots after the storm.
      They searched above the thought around the hill.

In the first of these, I understand "from the boots" to delineate the starting point of the search, which makes it part of the theme—the thing being searched. The goal is not mentioned, but must be inferred by the reader.

The second sentence requires more imagination, but I find myself attempting to construct a possible world in which there exists searchable psychic space, or something of the sort. The sentence is probably best seen as a potential line of a poem, in which the theme and goal are interpreted metaphorically.

As we will see below, debate about the Fourth Amendment generally amounts to argument about the range of "themes" that government should be permitted to search and the range of "goals" for which it should be permitted to search.

The Fourth Amendment and the Lexicon

Let us now apply the lexical analysis of "search" just developed to the language of the Fourth Amendment. The text speaks of "the right of the people to be secure in their persons, houses, papers, and effects, against unreasonable searches and seizures." It also requires search warrants to be specific and to be based on probable cause. On its face, the text deals with just one of the arguments of "search": the theme. But we can infer that the searching agent must be the government, since the Fourth Amendment is about limitations on government action. By filling in certain of the arguments from our lexical representation, we begin to see the sorts of searches that the Fourth Amendment regulates:

Fourth Amendment: first approximation:
government must not unreasonably SEARCH {persons, houses, papers, effects} (for goal) (with instrument)

But this initial effort tells only part of the story. As Cunningham points out, while the text does not specify the goal of the search or the searching agent, it is clear historically that the Fourth Amendment was adopted to protect people from government intrusion into their secrets. As a practical matter, secrets are exactly what the government is looking for when it conducts an investigation.

The Supreme Court has adopted this perspective. As noted above, most of the controversy in Fourth Amendment cases involves the interpretation of the text in light of ever increasing technological advances in police work. For example, in the seminal case of *Katz v. United States,*[65] the Court held in 1967 that it was unconstitutional under the Fourth Amendment for the police to have placed a listening device on the outside of a phone booth without having first obtained a search warrant based on probable cause. Justice

Harlan's concurrence explains that the Fourth Amendment protects people from searches of areas in which they have "a reasonable expectation of privacy,"[66] and that people entering a phone booth to make a call do indeed have a reasonable expectation that their conversations will be private.

In essence, Justice Harlan has defined a class of "themes" that are off limits to the police except under special circumstances. To make our lexical description of "search" capture Justice Harlan's conceptualization of what the Fourth Amendment prohibits, which has been very influential in Fourth Amendment analysis for more than twenty years, let us tentatively modify it as follows:

> *Justice Harlan's rule:*
> government must not unreasonably SEARCH area in which person
> has reasonable expectation of privacy (for goal) (by instrument)

Focusing on the fact that the government's intention in *Katz* was to record his secret conversation in order to gather evidence of a crime (illegal betting), Cunningham proposes an analysis based on Justice Harlan's statement of what the Fourth Amendment protects, but which includes acknowledgment of the areas specifically noted in the Constitution itself:

> [T]he approach that seems to offer the best articulation of *Katz*
> as well as a principled way of analyzing the decisions made in its
> wake . . . would indicate that a government action was a search
> *either* if agents conducted a search of houses, persons, papers, or
> effects *or* if they searched out objectively secret information.[67]

Since all of the arguments of "search" occur optionally, we can again modify our lexical description, this time incorporating the insights contained in Cunningham's analysis of what government activities are covered by the Fourth Amendment:

> *Modified version:*
> government must not unreasonably SEARCH {persons, houses,
> papers, effects} or for objectively secret information

In both the versions based on Justice Harlan's and Cunningham's analyses, the method of search, or instrument, is irrelevant, and is therefore omitted. For the most part the two analyses are equivalent, although Justice Harlan's has not taken into account the special status of persons, houses, papers, and effects. The modified version presented immediately above sets out a set of protected themes and a set of protected goals. Unreasonable governmental intrusion into any of these enclaves constitutes a Fourth Amendment violation.

As Cunningham aptly shows, most of the cases, which seemingly form an incoherent mess, can be recast in terms of the lexical properties of "search" (which Cunningham describes somewhat differently, see note 67) to form at the very least a coherent basis of discussion. Thus, cases deciding the legality of government agents flying at low altitude over a backyard to see marijuana growing;[68] agents tracking the location of a car by putting a beeper in it;[69] agents inserting a pen register into a person's telephone to see what numbers he is dialing;[70] agents taking high resolution areal photographs of a chemical plant to investigate violations of environmental laws;[71] agents placing a beeper inside a chemical drum and noting whose house it has entered to determine where a secret illegal drug laboratory was located;[72] and police looking at the serial number underneath a stereo while in someone's house for legitimate, but unrelated reasons[73] can all be looked at in terms of the nature of the direct object (i.e., theme) and in terms of whether the goal of the search is objectively secret information, where "objectively secret" means that a person would be reasonable in believing that it is secret.

Significantly, this linguistic analysis does little to reduce uncertainty in the outcomes of particular cases. That is, the justices on the Supreme Court can still disagree as to whether a backyard counts as a "house" or whether a backyard marijuana farmer reasonably could conclude that his crop was secret in today's world of casual airplane travel. As a general matter, the justices vote on such issues in keeping with their views on how expansive and intrusive the police power should be, and they write with the certainty that we have seen many times before. But the linguistic analysis does present a framework in which disagreements can be expressed coherently and in which the extent to which the language of the Fourth Amendment does determine its meaning becomes a little clearer. Put in terms of the lexical properties of "search," the Fourth Amendment specifies certain things that receive special protection: persons, houses, papers, effects. The analysis also includes the content of the goal: objectively secret information, which follows from Justice Harlan's opinion in *Katz*. This requirement can be inferred from the word "secure" in the Fourth Amendment. To be secure from unreasonable searches and seizures, one must have the status of being able to protect one's secrets from unreasonable government investigation.

Reliance on the "original intent" of the drafters is not very helpful here. In fact, a review of the opinions discussed above reveals very little mention of the drafters, by either the majorities or by dissenters. As the Court noted in 1980 in *Payton v. New York*,[74] it has been accepted for a century, based largely on the history of the adoption of the Constitution, that

> the principles reflected in the Amendment "reached farther than the concrete form" of the specific cases that gave it birth, and "apply to all invasions on the part of the government and its employees of the sanctity of a man's home and the privacies of life."

The primary evil concerning the framers was the issuance of general warrants by the British. But the pronouncement in *Payton* and the Court's history of recognizing the merit of this perspective make it clear that the notion "unreasonable searches and seizures" goes beyond any particular government invasion prevalent in the eighteenth century, while telling us nothing of how far beyond. To the extent that we can predict the reaction of the framers to the contemporary situations involving high technology, it is probably correct to assume that they would have regarded many of these as ugly science fiction.[75] Cunningham's having drawn the line at "objectively secret information" and Justice Harlan's having drawn it at places in which there is a "reasonable expectation of privacy" seem fair historically, if not sufficient to predict the outcome of difficult cases.

Examination of the lexical properties of the word "search," then, guides us to focused disagreement in hard cases and to resolution of straightforward ones. Most important, again to Cunningham's credit, the lexical analysis of "search" tells us neither that the law can be readily discovered from original sources, history, precedents, and the like, nor that the law is purely indeterminate and arbitrary. Rather, we are able to see exactly where the law becomes indeterminate—namely, where we have to decide what constitutes objectively secret information, or what we should consider the boundaries of a house. In fighting over such issues, judges will necessarily bring with them assumptions about how free from government observation we can and should reasonably expect to be, raising serious questions about the proper limits of police in our society. Here again, we see that knowledge of language severely restricts the range of possible interpretations, but certainly does not reduce the range to one.

What remains is the problem that Cardozo identified: the absence of a system sufficiently minute that it provides answers to questions that come before it, but flexible enough that an answer is available for each new question that arises for the first time.[76] In Fourth Amendment law, as elsewhere, judges sometimes succumb to the temptation of attempting to make this void itself seem invisible.

Some Easy Cases and Some Hard Ones

We are left with an interesting array of facts when we ask how a court attempts to derive the meanings of words in its interpretation of the Constitution. In many instances, the court will be faced with the temptation of making it appear that there exists a perfect match between events in the world and the lexical features of the words in the document. As we have seen, however, the match is not always straightforward, and how the judge characterizes the events in dispute will often govern. In these instances, the substantive debate is frequently hidden behind discussions of the words themselves.

Of course, each word in the Constitution does not present an identical interpretive problem. In some instances, the words in the Constitution so obviously underdetermine their applicability to particular situations that the justices do not even try to explain their decisions based on the plain meanings of the words. For example, the Fifth Amendment says in part that no person shall "be deprived of life, liberty, or property, without due process of law." While the Supreme Court has engaged in enormous debate about what constitutes "life, liberty, or property," focusing on the meanings of those words, it has for decades recognized that "the very nature of due process negates any concept of inflexible procedures universally applicable to every imaginable situation."[77] The result is a series of debates about what procedures an individual is entitled to in a host of situations, ranging from corporal punishment in the public schools[78] to the termination of social security benefits.[79] In this sense, "due process" is like "reasonable man," discussed in chapter 5.

In contrast, the Constitution contains many words that are referential in nature, and the source of little or no controversy at all. "The President," "the Vice-President," and "the Congress" are examples.

As we saw in chapter 4, philosophers have long recognized these difficulties and uncertainties associated with word meaning. Perhaps the clearest statements are those of Wittgenstein, who wrote:

> There are words with several clearly defined meanings. It is easy to tabulate these meanings. And there are words of which one might say: They are used in a thousand different ways which

gradually merge into one another. No wonder that we can't tab-
ulate strict rules for their use.[80]

Wittgenstein writes that "our craving for generality" inhibits us from recognizing the fact that we cannot account for language by positing strict rules.[81]
To the extent that by "language" Wittgenstein limits himself to aspects of
word meaning, the struggles over meaning described earlier in this chapter
appear to illustrate his point.

From this array we can draw a very general conclusion: When the linguistic argument is available to give the court the ability to write decisively
about a document, the court will frequently grab the opportunity, even
when the relationship between the words in the document and the events in
dispute are not as clear as the court would have us think. Where no such
analysis is available, courts may be forced to look more to the substance of
the issues being debated. Again, all of this does not happen because our
judges lack talent or integrity. Rather, it happens because judges are responsible for wielding enormous power, and are obliged to demonstrate the fit-
ness and firmness of the conclusions they reach.

7| Why It Hasn't Gotten Any Better

I ENDED CHAPTER 1 with the observation that Cardozo's commentary on the difficulties of judging are as relevant today as they were seventy years ago when he wrote his major work, *The Nature of the Judicial Process*. In a sense, this book illustrates the core problem that Cardozo described: how to make decisions that are at once uniquely responsive to the situation before the judge and loyal to the legal doctrines that have brought us up to the present. Throughout this book, I have attempted to show how judges and lawyers, writing about language, often attempt to bury the problems so well articulated by Cardozo, seeking to hide their existence from the parties to the dispute being decided, and from the entire community, in the case of published legal opinions. Most of the examples can be seen as exemplifying what happens when judges do not follow Cardozo's instructions to be candid, opting instead to create the impression of neutrality and scientific analysis. The result is that the system of justification collapses into incoherence, at the expense of the integrity of the entire system that the so-called scientific explanation was intended to protect.

As I noted in the introduction, the pressure to write decisively and to limit the range of argumentation to what is considered properly part of legitimate "legal doctrine" acts as a catalyst, leading the judge to publish as the basis of his decision reasons that at times do not fairly or accurately describe what really was in his mind when he made it. And this phenomenon is not reserved for judges who may not be quite up to par, but rather infects the opinions of the best and most highly respected judges as well. That is, we cannot seriously think that if only judges with a little more talent were appointed, none of this would happen.

But the staying power of Cardozo's observations also gives rise to another question—a question that probably has passed through the minds of many readers who have gotten this far: If we have known about these problems for so long, why haven't things gotten any better since Cardozo wrote about these matters in 1920? Even worse, since the law has survived the twentieth century, could it be wrongminded to be complaining so much about the status quo? Let us look once again at Mrs. Anderson's lawsuit against her insurance company in addressing these issues.

Anderson and the Status Quo

Recall from chapters 2 and 3 that Mrs. Anderson sued her insurance company, State Farm, in order to compel the insurer to pay the $13,000 that Mrs. Anderson owed Mr. Yocum after damaging his Cadillac.[1] Mrs. Anderson had been driving Mr. Yocum's car without his permission, apparently thinking that she was driving Mr. Larson's car. Applying a principle called the "last antecedent rule," the court held that Mrs. Anderson was covered by her insurance policy. The court ruled that the policy did not require permission of the owner when the car was driven by the "named insured."

I have presented the *Anderson* decision in many lectures, and I almost always hear laughter when I announce that Mrs. Anderson won the case on those linguistic grounds. In fact, I continue to marvel at Mrs. Anderson's lawyers' creativity in contriving the winning argument. The interpretation of the policy accepted by the court is so far-fetched that very few lawyers would have had the imagination (or audacity for that matter) to raise the point at all. I conjectured earlier that the court most likely had in mind that this outcome was the best way to make sure that Mr. Yocum, an innocent Californian, was compensated for the damage to his car.

Assume that I am right about the court's motives. If so, the *Anderson* court can be seen to have engaged in two acts: First, the court made a decision based on an entirely reasonable consideration—fairness to Mr. Yocum. There may have been other relevant factors worthy of consideration, and different judges may have weighed them differently. But these judges did what they thought was right for reasons that certainly are not outside the realm of what would concern any sensitive decision maker. Second, the court wrote an opinion that justified its decision based on what the system considers legitimate reasons, namely, problems with the way that the insurance policy was drafted. As we saw in chapter 3, the law has very little sympathy with insurance companies that try to avoid paying out benefits unless the insurance policy makes it very clear that the benefits should not be forthcoming. I began this book with the observation that judges do two things: they decide cases and they justify their decisions in opinions. An argument can be made that the *Anderson* court has only tried to do both of these tasks well. It rendered a decision that is at least defensible, and it justified its decision based on the kinds of considerations that courts generally take into account.

The differences between these two activities, decision making and justification, can be seen as part of the answer to the question of why the core problems of our system do not seem to go away. Under pressure to speak decisively and within the bounds of what is accepted as the legal doctrine of the day, judges will sometimes find it difficult to present acceptable justifications for their decisions, even when the judges are comfortable with the decisions themselves. Opinion writing has gotten no easier since the days of Cardozo. The laughter at my presentation of the *Anderson* decision may reflect exactly this difficulty. If the court had said instead that the insurance policy was written in such confusing language that the court simply had no basis for denying coverage, the reaction at lectures might have been diminished, although the decision would have been exactly the same.

In an extremely interesting essay on law and interpretation entitled "Dennis Martinez and the Uses of Theory,"[2] Stanley Fish exploits to the limit the differences between the judge's two tasks. Dennis Martinez is a baseball player, and Fish uses Martinez's greater ability to pitch than to discuss pitching theory as a metaphor for the difference between performing and theorizing generally. The judge, he rightly says, must do both. Referring to writings of Ronald Dworkin, Fish goes as far as he can in distinguishing between the judge's two obligations:

> It is time to acknowledge or reacknowledge the force of one of Dworkin's observations, that when judges themselves try to explain how it is that they work they present themselves as striving for just that articulate consistency that he sees as guiding the process of decision-making. And what is perhaps even more telling, judges engage in the same mode of self-presentation—a mode in which a present decision is explained or justified by an assertion of its fit with the principles underlying past decisions— when they hand down their decisions in the form of an opinion. How are we (that is, how am I) to account for this? Are judges concealing an unattractive truth? Or do they not know what they are doing? Not at all; they know perfectly well what they are doing. They are engaging in the practice of self-presentation, that is, the practice of offering a persuasive account of why they have done what they have done—decide the case this way rather than that—which is not the same thing (why on earth should it be?) as offering an account of how they actually did it.[3]

Fish's description, I believe, perfectly describes the activity of the *Anderson* court. The court has decided a case and has offered an account of what it has done—two different activities. In addition, I have no quarrel with Fish's conclusion that judges know what they are doing when they engage in writing opinions to justify decisions made for reasons other than those described in the opinions. Fish elaborates on the distinction:

> In short, "articulate consistency" is not the name of a theoretical perspective from which decisions issue, but of a pragmatic strategy by means of which decisions are successfully inserted into a field of practice that requires of its decisions that they be filled with certain forms of talk, in this case with theory-talk. Indeed, in this view, theory would be no more (or less) than a kind of talk; it would be precisely the kind of talk one was advised to engage in when presenting one's decisions to members of the present legal community. A judge would do theory-talk . . . not in order to provide an accurate description of the process by which they came upon their invention, but in order to better dress the product of that process in a garb appropriate to a situation in which their goal—and therefore the ground rules—had changed. Their goal is now persuasion, and they case around for appropriate means with which to effect it (this is, of course, the traditional Aristotelian definition of rhetoric) and find them, or at least a portion of them, in the rhetorical practice of talking theory.[4]

Judges should keep right on expounding the reasons for their decisions in legal terms, Fish argues, because as a rhetorical matter, it is the only way their decisions will be accepted:

> In that forum [the legal forum], to stop talking in philosophically conceptual terms would be to make a big political (i.e., rhetorical) mistake. It would not be a mistake because it would falsify our picture of what judicial decisionmaking is like—it has no relation to that picture—but because philosophically conceptual terms are what the legal community now expects to hear when it listens to a self-presentation.[5]

While I have been in agreement with Fish up to this point, I believe that the problems facing judges writing opinions extend well beyond problems of persuasive self-presentation. That is why I said earlier that the distinction between decision making and rhetoric provides only a partial answer to the question of why things do not change very much. The deeper difficulties stem from a question that Fish poses but does not address seriously: "Are judges concealing an unattractive truth?" Much of the time, I believe, that is exactly what judges are doing, and the linguistic examples presented throughout this book illustrate the activity. The unattractive truth that they are concealing is that they are unable to make decisions easily and based on the legitimate factors on which they are supposed to rely, a truth that plagues even the greatest judges.

It is no accident that discussion of legal theory is the rhetorical device that judges use successfully. In fact, the very reason that judges engage in "theory-talk" and not "personal anecdote-talk" or "hate-talk" or "socialism-talk" is because they want to convince the parties to the case being decided and the public as well that the theory is the actual reason for the decision. And they do this to keep up the impression that each decision is made on the basis of a discoverable rule of law that governs the situation, or at the very least, the impression that however it was made, the decision is the only one consistent with the theory. In essence, they view it as their task to pass as the reality Cardozo's admittedly false idealization of the legal system discussed in chapter 1, the idealization that the law is sufficiently minute to be predictable while at the same time sufficiently flexible to engulf new situations as they arise.

The notion that judges articulate one set of reasons for their decisions while actually deciding cases on other grounds is not a new one. The observation was a point of great discussion by the legal realists who wrote earlier in this century,[6] and has more recently become one of the focal points of the critical legal studies movement.[7] Mainstream legal scholars have made the same observation. In fact, there exists a literature addressing the issue of judicial candor.[8]

Cardozo himself claimed to have taken the notion of judicial precedent seriously. When Cardozo theorized, he meant it, or at least he thought he did.[9] Thus, Cardozo and Fish part company before the dialogue even begins. They part company because Fish fails to recognize that judges really do try to take advantage of those instances in which legal doctrine makes their job easy. While there may be disagreement about exactly when legal doctrine is informative, judges, it appears to me, regard the theory as more than a sideshow.

In simpler cases, judges and lawyers alike routinely do rely on what Fish calls theory-talk and what law professors call doctrine, and they use it substantively. For example, I recently advised a client that a promise that he had secured from another individual had to be reduced to writing, because that kind of promise falls within the ambit of the statute of frauds. If he failed to get a writing and the matter went to court, I am reasonably confident that the court would not enforce the promise. I am also reasonably confident that a court would not enforce the promise precisely because the doctrine (i.e., the theory) says that the promise should not be enforced if the promisor has not signed a paper acknowledging his promise. During this same period, I advised a different client that the statute of limitations had run on certain claims that he wanted to bring. If he tried to bring all of the claims in court, a judge would throw out those that had already lapsed because of the passage of time since the claims arose. Again, I have little doubt about the accuracy of this advice because I believe that a judge deciding the case would rely on exactly the same statute book that I relied on in formulating the advice. Judges must love it when they are able to rely without controversy on the statute of frauds or on a statute of limitations.[10]

The judge's problems arise when the doctrine says nothing about how a particular dispute should be resolved, or when what it says cannot be clearly applied to the facts in dispute, or when it says something that will lead the judge to commit what he considers an injustice. In this realm, Fish's description of the judge as a civil servant holding two jobs—decision maker and rhetorician—becomes much more accurate. This book has discussed many examples in which this appears to have been the case.

It is a temptation facing judges to make it appear that all cases are like the statute of limitations case that I just described.[11] When the doctrine fails to provide an answer to a dispute, judges are under pressure to make it appear as if the doctrine does provide an answer. The temptation was around seventy years ago, and it is still here. As long as it remains, the gap between decision making and rhetoric in hard cases will continue to exist, perhaps widening as the ever growing body of statutes and decisions makes it increasingly convenient to justify any decision reached. A judge wanting to permit the next Mr. Yocum to collect his $13,000 may again find some peculiar linguistic turn in the insurance policy.

In his extrajudicial writings, Cardozo admitted to only two choices for a judge facing a difficult decision: adherence to precedent or candid abandonment of precedent in favor of a new rule. But in his opinions, as we have seen, he occasionally sneaked in the third alternative: presenting the current theory as mandating a single result even where, as demonstrated by the dissent, it did not. In these cases, including *Palsgraf*,[12] Cardozo must have known just what the judges deciding *Anderson* must have known fifty years later: full candor can have the undesired, ironic effect of announcing that in hard cases there is no rule of law operating. Cardozo himself was not immune from the pressure to write decisively.

At least two problems arise as a result of judges succumbing to this temptation. First, when a judge gets caught at this game, the discovery converts a rhetorical coup into a devastating failure. Accepting the distinction between the judge's two tasks, the judge cannot possibly be a persuasive opinion writer when the reader knows that the opinion states reasons for the decision that are simply irrelevant to how the decision was made. Because court deliberations are secret, judges will ordinarily not get caught. But where, as in the examples presented earlier in this book, the body of cases creates an incoherent mass, readers have the right to draw the almost inescapable inference that the judges are not being candid in their opinions. And this lack of candor is sufficient to rob the opinions of their rhetorical force. What makes the matter worse is that when judges choose to rely on linguistic argumentation to justify their decisions, incoherence will quickly become the rule—not the exception—an observation to which I will return at the end of this chapter.

Second, succumbing to the temptation produces more than bad rhetoric. To the extent that we, as readers, perceive that an "unattractive truth" is being hidden from us, we take it that we are being lied to, and we react negatively to this on ethical grounds.[13] This, I believe, is one reason that we see so much passion in iconoclastic movements, such as legal realism and critical legal studies.

We are thus confronted with the intractable problem that I described in the introduction. A judge who justifies his decisions by issuing opinions based on linguistic sleight of hand risks getting caught in a lie, thereby damaging the credibility of the system that he was attempting to protect. But the judge who is candid can, in hard cases, do nothing other than announce that the system, at least in the case being decided, has no answer, and that the fate of the parties is in the hands of the judge himself, who will simply do the best he can. The result is the same—a reduction in confidence that a rule of law governs the exercise of power by government.

In light of this problem, let us look at the alternatives that faced the *Anderson* court, and ask whether the situation can be improved.

Expanding Legal Doctrine

If the *Anderson* decision provokes laughter, we should ask ourselves what options the court really had. As I see it, the court had two other choices.

First, the court could have decided the case as it did, but have justified its decision straightforwardly. For the sake of argument, assume that my characterization of the reasons behind the decision are accurate. The court could simply have said that the purpose of insurance is to make sure that innocent victims are compensated for accidents that they did not cause. Mr. Yocum was clearly such a victim, and he should be compensated. Under these circumstances, courts need not pay too much attention to what an insurance policy says. It is better for an insurance company to take a few lumps once in a while than to burden each Mr. Yocum with the onus of trying to collect his $13,000, which he may never succeed in doing.

The court might expand on this reasoning by arguing that the cost of this sort of decision will be shared by all insured individuals through only slightly higher premiums, and that the increase in premiums is more than justified by the increase in the number of injured individuals who will now be compensated. Assuming that something like the above more closely reflects the "real reasons" behind the *Anderson* decision, it is indeed possible to write an "honest" opinion in a case like *Anderson*.

Had the court made such a statement, it would have caused quite a stir among insurance companies. For it would have announced that insurers were left with no hope of staving off claims that they did not think that they had agreed to accept. That is, the court would have decreed that the rule of law concerning the liability of insurance companies is that there is no rule of law whenever a victim seems to a judge to be deserving enough of the money. Or, alternatively, there is a rule of law, but the rule is nothing more than the judge's perception of how deserving the victim is.

As a practical matter the *Anderson* case tells us that at least to some degree this is how things work right now. But the rule that there is no rule is certainly not consistent with current stated legal doctrine that bases the liability of insurance companies on what the parties bargained for in the insurance policies. And the rule itself announces its own unpredictability.

The expansion of legal doctrine to permit open debate about such issues as these is a major theme in current legal academics. In fact, the integration of what are considered nonlegal, political issues into legal discourse is a stated goal of the critical legal studies movement.[14] It would be a mistake, however, to conclude that tolerance of expanded legal doctrine would lead to the adoption of a particular political agenda. Just because a judge feels comfortable writing about political and social concerns does not make him a champion of the left. Cardozo's *Palsgraf* decision illustrates this fact. Cardozo's vision of the limits to which people owe each other a duty of care, as articulated in *Palsgraf,* is politically candid, but totally inconsistent with notions of community and shared loss that characterize the thinking of the left. To the extent that the critical legal studies movement and other movements place their hope for substantive changes in the law in broader judicial discourse, they cannot expect their agendas to be carried out by virtue of the candor itself. The candor must be accompanied by a will to use the expanded doctrine to change the law in a prescribed manner.

To illustrate this situation further, let us contrast two death penalty cases decided by the Supreme Court of the United States in the 1980s. *California v. Brown,*[15] discussed in chapters 2 and 3, involved an odd linguistic analysis of the following jury instruction, which admonished jurors that they: "must not be swayed by mere sentiment, conjecture, sympathy, passion, prejudice, public opinion or public feeling." The Court held that the instruction was constitutional since it prevents juries from relying on "mere" sympathy but does not prevent them from being swayed by ordinary sympathy.

In chapter 2, I argued that the linguistic analysis presented by the majority was faulty, and that it was most likely more than a coincidence that the justices on the Supreme Court appear to assign interpretations to adjectives in keeping with their voting records on capital punishment cases. While we can never, of course, accumulate absolute proof, the most reasonable inference is that the justices voted according to their views on capital punishment, and the linguistic analysis was nothing other than rhetoric (accepting Fish's term). But from this analysis, we cannot conclude that if this sort of linguistic argumentation were eliminated the members of the Court that support the death penalty would curb their enthusiasm for carrying out death sentences.

Such a conclusion, in fact, would be wrong, as demonstrated in *McCleskey v. Kemp,*[16] a death penalty case decided by the Supreme Court in 1987. In that case, Warren McCleskey had been sentenced to death in Georgia after having been convicted of murder and armed robbery. McCleskey was black and the murder victim was a white police officer. Eventually, McCleskey petitioned the federal courts, claiming that the death penalty in Georgia is imposed differentially depending on racial considerations, and is therefore unconstitutional. The trial court rejected McCleskey's arguments. On appeal, the United States Court of Appeals reversed, accepting McCleskey's position. The case then went to the Supreme Court, which again reversed in a 5–4 decision, reinstating the death penalty.

In support of his position, McCleskey presented a study conducted by Professor David Baldus and others, which examined over 2,000 murder cases in Georgia, and found a disparity in the imposition of the death penalty depending on the race of the murder victim and the defendant. In an opinion written by Justice Powell, the Supreme Court summarized the Baldus statistics:[17]

Race of Defendant and victim	Death penalty sought	Death penalty assessed
Black-white	70%	22%
White-white	32	8
White-black	19	3
Black-black	15	1

The Court accurately understood the case as a challenge to the most basic institutions in the criminal justice system. For if McCleskey's right to equal protection under the law or to be free from cruel or unusual punishment were held to have been violated here, there may be no basis in future cases for rejecting other statistical studies showing, for example, racial disparity in judge's issuance of prison sentences, conviction of noncapital offenses, and so on. Other biases in the criminal justice system, such as gender bias, may also later be ruled out. If this were to happen, the whole system would topple. The Court was very much aware of this possibility:

> Two additional concerns inform our decision in this case. First, McCleskey's claim, taken to its logical conclusion, throws into serious question the principles that underlie our entire criminal justice system. The Eighth Amendment is not limited in application to capital punishment, but applies to all penalties. . . . Thus, if we accepted McCleskey's claim that racial bias has impermissibly tainted the capital sentencing decision, we could soon be faced with similar claims as to other types of penalty. Moreover, the claim that his sentence rests on the irrelevant factor of race easily could be extended to apply to claims based on unexplained discrepancies that correlate to membership in other minority groups, and even to gender. Similarly, since McCleskey's claim relates to the race of his victim, other claims could apply with equally logical force to statistical disparities that correlate with the race or sex of other actors in the criminal justice system, such as defense attorneys, or judges.[18]

The Court further perceived in McCleskey's challenge a threat to the jury system. McCleskey was sentenced by a jury, and to deny the legitimacy of the

sentence based on the likelihood that the jury was swayed by racist considerations is to deny the impenetrability of the jury system as a whole.[19] Thus,
the Court held that the statistical data were not adequate to prove racism in
this particular case (although statistics are adequate elsewhere in the law),
and that the jury system, while not perfect, is good enough to meet constitutional standards.

What strikes me as especially significant about the *McCleskey* decision is
the Court's willingness to address difficult political issues, such as what
should happen when we learn, with reasonable certainty, that our criminal
justice system is influenced by illegitimate considerations, like race. An important lesson can be learned from the result of the Court's foray: faced with
even the remote threat of radical change caused by the Court's refusal to
tolerate a system in which government executes citizens based in part on
racial prejudice, the Court decided to support the status quo. Although the
opinion was as openly political as anyone could expect, the result was a victory for stability. But the vote was close, a fact which itself portrays the tension between stasis and change on which Cardozo focused much of his
attention in his writings.

The call for expanding legal doctrine, in fact, can be heard loudly from
divergent political camps. On the one hand, we hear the critical legal studies
movement asking that legal doctrine be enlarged to include political discourse, destabilizing current hierarchical relationships entrenched in our
current system.[20] On the other hand, we hear proponents of the law and
economics movement advocate, with considerable success, for the increased
use of market economic theory as the basis for judicial decisions.[21] While
both camps lament the shortcomings of current doctrine, neither would be
happy with the solution that the other proposes. The issue, then, is not the
expansion of doctrine for the sake of expansion, but the direction in which
the expansion moves. These difficulties do not, of course, present an argument against expansion of legal discourse in an effort to increase candor.
They rather highlight the risk for anyone hoping to take advantage of the
expansion for the sake of promoting a particular substantive program.

Getting Tough

The other possible course that the *Anderson* court could have taken was to
get tough and rule in State Farm's favor. Why play these language games at
all? Even if the judges would like to find a way to get Mr. Yocum his
$13,000, the system would be better off if the court were to adopt the more

natural interpretation of the insurance policy. Again, when I present the case at universities, at least a few students invariably argue that this should have happened, and I have a hunch that many more feel this way but are ashamed to admit it.

To pursue this point, let us imagine, contrary to fact, that the linguistic justification presented in the *Anderson* case was not available to the court. (Perhaps some expanded plain language law has made it illegal.) In this imaginary world, there is no guarantee that the court would rule as it did in the real *Anderson* case. Faced with the choice between letting the cat out of the bag about its notions of distributive justice and making life more difficult for Mr. Yocum, a judge may well choose to let Mr. Yocum find the $13,000 that he needs for a new Cadillac elsewhere. In fact, this would be a natural reaction of any judge who has a greater commitment to the stability of the system than to achieving a particular result in a given case.

But this "get tough" attitude is not always so easy to apply. In so many of the cases that I have discussed in this book the very essence of the dispute is what the language in a document means. These interpretive problems will not go away simply by our changing our attitudes toward language, however we alter our perspective. Often enough, it is not at all clear what it would mean to get tough even if we wanted to. Furthermore, as Cardozo so aptly pointed out, we may not always want to stiffen in our loyalty to the law as it stands now if adhering to the old rules would lead to results with which we would have trouble living:

> In these days, there is a good deal of discussion whether the rule of adherence to precedent ought to be abandoned altogether. I would not go so far myself. I think adherence to precedent should be the rule and not the exception. I have already had occasion to dwell upon some of the considerations that sustain it. To these I may add that the labor of judges would be increased almost to the breaking point if every past decision could be reopened in every case, and one could not lay one's own course of bricks on the secure foundation of the courses laid by others who had gone before him. . . .
>
> But I am ready to concede that the rule of adherence to precedent, though it ought not to be abandoned, ought to be in some degree relaxed. I think that when a rule, after it has been duly tested by experience, has been found to be inconsistent with the sense of justice or with the social welfare, there should be less hesitation in frank avowal and full abandonment.[22]

Cardozo thus encouraged the judge to go as far as he could in honestly dis-avowing legal rules that can lead only to a result that he deemed to be unfair. Fairness was to come from the judge's absorption of the normative values of the community.

The "get tough" perspective on judicial decision making is akin to the notion of "strict construction" as a system of constitutional thought. As Ronald Dworkin has put it, the strict constructionist "would enforce the law as it is, and not 'twist or bend' it to suit their own personal con-victions . . . "[23] The goal of strict construction is to interpret constitu-tional principles narrowly in deciding whether government action is per-mitted.

The problem with strict construction lies with the great variety of ways in which the Constitution says things. Some constitutional provisions list rights that people are guaranteed, others lay out acts that government must perform and still others are written as acts that government may not per-form. Thus, for example, if one construes the Fifth Amendment strictly, one will be committed to deeming unconstitutional fewer alleged acts of com-pelled self-incrimination or violations of due process. This, in essence, en-hances state power by permitting the executive branch of government, through the police, to interact more forcefully with the population.

But Article II, Section 1 of the Constitution says: "The executive Power shall be vested in a President of the United States of America." Section 2 enumerates various executive powers. Presumably, a true strict construc-tionist would be forced to interpret Article II strictly as well. Strict construc-tion of Article II, however, would serve to diminish the power of the executive. Since Article II grants government powers, rather than limiting them, construing Article II narrowly will reduce the powers that govern-ment is granted. Few people, if any, will be bent on enhancing police power through interpreting the Bill of Rights narrowly, but giving back that power by also interpreting Article II narrowly.[24]

An interpretive philosophy of strict construction will lead to problems very quickly unless all the documents being interpreted are written with the same syntactic and conceptual structure. If some sentences in the Con-stitution grant individual rights and others grant government powers, strict construction is a recipe for an incoherent set of interpretations. This sce-nario is typical of what happens when courts rely on interpretive principles as a matter of substantive law. Let us now look at the situation more gen-erally.

The Language of Judges

By now it should be no secret. Judges speak the same language that the rest of us speak. Their knowledge of language, which all of us acquired as young children as the consequence of a highly developed innate language faculty, makes interpreting language easy and automatic to a large extent, while leaving open a variety of possible interpretations in other instances. But the consequences of how the judge understands the open issues in the language that he hears and reads, and what he says about them are frequently more awesome than the consequences of how the rest of us construe sentences and express our understanding. We all may, in our darkest moments, wish that some evil-doer were dead. But judges are the ones who can properly use the expression, "I hereby sentence you to death," as a performative to sentence someone to death. Armed with this enormous power, and faced with the responsibility of exercising it on a daily basis, judges will, at times, grab at any argument that the system accepts as legitimate in order to convince the parties and the community at large that the court did what it was supposed to do. After close analysis, the court was left with only a single option, the judge tells us.

When a court resorts to interpretive principles to justify its decisions, analytical problems immediately ensue. As we have now seen many times, the principle that appeared to give the right result in one case all too often appears to give the wrong result in the next case. The judge, then, not only has to decide the second case fairly, but now has the additional burden of coping with the renegade interpretive principle that ruled the day in the first case. Without doubt, the lawyers for the litigant in the second case who would be helped by the application of this interpretive principle will have brought it to the court's attention, making the problem impossible to ignore.

At the root of this problem are some rather straightforward observations. First, the relationship between words and events in the world is largely underdetermined by our knowledge of the words. There is simply no theory of meaning that tells us whether a corporation should be considered a person for purposes of determining whether the corporation is entitled to constitutional rights. Nor is there a theory of meaning that forces us to reach a particular view of whether the Fifth Amendment's prohibition against compelled self-incrimination protects us against government forcing us to submit to blood tests against our will. In instances like these, a court's resort to the plain meaning of the document or of some interpretive principle will almost invariably come back to haunt it. For a precedent will have been created that will more likely than not stand as an obstacle to the adjudication of some later case.

This leads to the second point. Interpretive principles do not make good legal principles. Our knowledge of language renders much of interpretation automatic and beyond dispute, as Chomsky and others have shown us. That is, enormous amounts of interpretation occur without our ever noticing it. No one has ever argued that the Fifth Amendment really sets standards for the meat-packing industry, or that RICO is really about the financing of schools.

But the linguistic rules that we apply unconsciously do not limit to one the possible interpretations of every aspect of every utterance. The difficulties begin once courts impose rules for filling these interpretive gaps. There is no perfect match between an interpretive principle on the one hand and one's sense of justice on the other.[25] For each interpretive principle that becomes the rule of law, even in cases in which it is relatively easy to apply, there will always be instances in which judges will want to avoid applying it because its application would lead to what the judge perceives as an injustice. Thus, we saw that courts regularly attempt to see plain meaning where ambiguity exists and to find ambiguity where there is none in order to subvert principles like the rule of lenity, the rule that ambiguous insurance policies are interpreted against the insurer and the plain language rule.

I end this book with no prescription. Judges will always be confronted with the task of interpreting language. In fact, that is largely what they do for a living. In performing their jobs, they will necessarily be faced with the task of trying to justify what they consider the right result in such a way that they appear decisive and utilize only the sorts of arguments that our system considers proper. Much of the time, all of this can be accomplished. In more difficult cases, however, judges often have three choices: give a less than candid reason for the decision since the full reasons would be unacceptable; tell the whole truth anyway even if it leads to instability in the system; or get tough and be loyal to precedent even if it seems wrong.

I have focused on how judges frequently choose the first option when it comes to cases that require the interpretation of documents. It is an easy path, but not a very satisfying one. To venture out onto the second path requires a willingness to risk the stability of the system for its integrity without any guarantee of where this risk-taking will lead. The third path, available only some of the time, frequently leads to injustice, as Cardozo warned.

David Shapiro wrote of the need for "judicial candor":

> In a sense, candor is the sine qua non of all other restraints on abuse of judicial power, for the limitations imposed by constitutions, statutes, and precedents count for little if judges feel free to believe one thing about them and to say another. Moreover, lack of candor seldom goes undetected for long, and its detection only serves to increase the level of cynicism about the nature of judging and of judges.[26]

Shapiro's standards, despite the appearance of simple morality, are not easy to achieve. We can all prove this to ourselves by imagining what we would likely have said if it had been up to us to write the various opinions discussed in this book, some of which I criticized sharply.

Judges will continue to find themselves under pressure to write opinions based on interpretive principles, knowing that they could have, with equal force, justified the opposite decision using the same or other interpretive principles. Like the rest of us, judges differ in their degree of daring, and not every judge will accept every opportunity to avoid these interpretive difficulties. Nonetheless, if judges were to accept a few more of these opportunities, breaking away from this temptation, I believe along with many others that our judicial system would ultimately be well served. To the extent that judges are not able to do so, Cardozo's writings will last another seventy years.

Notes

Notes to Introduction

1. I thank John Conley for pointing this out.

2. This had been a focus of the legal realism movement and currently is a focus of the critical legal studies movement, to which I return briefly in chapter 7.

3. Compare, for example, R. Dworkin, *Law's Empire* 93 (1986), with S. Fish, *Doing What Comes Naturally* (1989), especially the essay entitled, "Force."

4. 91 N.J. 488, 453 A.2d 527 (1982).

5. 453 A.2d at 535.

6. What makes candor more risky in any particular case will be the subject of some speculation in chapter 7.

7. 73 N.J.331, 375 A.2d 259 (1977).

8. These include the Lincoln Tunnel, the Holland Tunnel, and the major airports in the New York metropolitan area.

9. 375 A.2d at 261.

10. *Id.* at 265.

11. The literature on language and law is growing. For example, there are a number of articles written by linguists about their experiences as experts in various legal cases. See, e.g., W. Labov, "The Judicial Testing of Linguistic Theory," in D. Tannen, ed., *Linguistics in Context: Connecting Observation and Understanding* 159 (1988). For an overview of this literature, see J. Levi, "The Study of Language in the Judicial Process," in J. Levi and A. Graffam Walker, eds., *Language in the Judicial Process* 3 (1990), and other papers in that volume. Two other collections on language and law are P. Pupier and J. Woehrling, eds., *Langue et droit—Language and Law* (1989) and R. Rieber and W. Stewart, eds., *The Language Scientist as Expert in the Legal Setting,* 606 *Annals of the New York Academy of Sciences* (1990).

12. The fact that applying principles of interpretation generally results in an incoherent legal doctrine has not escaped legal writers. For a classic discussion of the issue, see K. Llewellyn, "Remarks on the Theory of Appellate Decision and the Rules or Canons About How Statutes Are to Be Construed," 3 *Vanderbilt Law Review* 401 (1950). This and further remarks appear in K. Llewellyn, *The Common Law Tradition: Deciding Appeals* (1960).

13. The concept of "legitimacy" has been the subject of extensive discussion in

the legal literature. Ronald Dworkin poses the issue as follows: "A conception of law must explain how what it takes to be law provides a general justification for the exercise of coercive power by the state, a justification that holds except in special cases when some competing argument is specially powerful." R. Dworkin, *Law's Empire* 190 (1986). For a good overview of some of the problems in establishing legitimacy in the courts, see G. Calabresi, *A Common Law for the Age of Statutes* 91–119 (1982). For a discussion of legitimacy in the context of statutory interpretation, see W. Eskridge, "Dynamic Statutory Interpretation," 135 *U. Pa. L. Rev.* 1479 (1987).

Notes to Chapter 1

1. *Palsgraf v. Long Island R. Co.*, 248 N.Y. 339 (1928).
2. Many of these works are collected in M. E. Hall and E. W. Patterson, eds., *Selected Writings of Benjamin Nathan Cardozo* (1947).
3. Some of these foundations may not be worth saving, at least to some. To the extent that one takes this position, one would redefine the problem in terms of the law needing only flexibility. In some ways, the critical legal studies movement adopts this perspective. We will discuss this movement briefly in chapter 7.
4. See B. Cardozo, *The Paradoxes of Legal Science* (1928).
5. B. Cardozo, *The Nature of the Judicial Process* 143 (1921).
6. *Id.* at 161.
7. B. Cardozo, *The Growth of the Law* 68 (1924).
8. R. Pound, "Mechanical Jurisprudence," 8 *Columbia Law Review* 603 (1908).
9. See chapter 4 for some discussion of this maxim.
10. *The Nature of the Judicial Process*, note 5 above, pp. 167–68.
11. R. Dworkin, *Law's Empire* (1976).
12. See N. Chomsky, *Syntactic Structures* (1957), a short book which had a profound effect on the field of linguistics. Also see Chomsky's "Review of B. F. Skinner, *Verbal Behavior*," 35 *Language* 26 (1959), for an early important work that focused on the relationship between linguistic research and the mind, arguing against a behavioristic view of linguistic knowledge. For more recent works of Chomsky that are generally accessible to those without technical training in linguistics, see his *Knowledge of Language* (1986) and *Language and Problems of Knowledge: The Managua Lectures* (1988). The short overview of linguistics to follow in this chapter relies heavily on these works. For a historic perspective on the development of linguistic theory, see F. Newmeyer, *Linguistic Theory in America* (1980). In focusing on Chomsky's work, I do not wish to give the false impression to those unfamiliar with linguistic research that the field, now quite large and active, is limited to the work of one scholar. However, when it comes to stating and defining the goals of linguistic research (at least as I describe them here), I believe that it is fair to direct the reader's attention to Chomsky's writings.
13. N. Chomsky, *Reflections on Language* 36 (1975).
14. *Id.* at 10–11.
15. *Language and Problems of Knowledge: The Managua Lectures*, note 12 above, p. 34.
16. Chomsky writes extensively about what the word "know" means in this con-

text. See, e.g., his *Knowledge of Language,* note 12 above. This issue, as Chomsky points out, really should not be the source of significant debate. People demonstrate their knowledge of the system of English auxiliary verbs, for example, in the sense that they are able to use it routinely in the production and comprehension of sentences and they can identify instances in which the system is not used properly.

17. This notion, that grammatical operations are dependent on structure, rather than simply on the order of the elements in a string, has played a significant role in linguistic research. See the references cited earlier, among many others.

18. See, e.g., J.-Y. Pollock, "Verb Movement, Universal Grammar and the Structure of IP," 20 *Linguistic Inquiry* 365 (1989), for a recent analysis developing the current theory.

19. See my *Pronominal Reference: Child Language and the Theory of Grammar* (1983) for technical discussion, including a review of the literature.

20. For a more optimistic view on the matter, see J. Rawls, *A Theory of Justice* 47 (1971).

21. See note 6 above.

22. 248 N.Y. at 341. This is Cardozo's version of what happened. For a very interesting review of this case, including evidence that Cardozo's recitation of the facts may not be entirely accurate, see R. Posner, *Cardozo: A Study in Reputation* (1990).

23. 217 N.Y. 382 (1916).

24. *Id.* at 391.

25. *Id.* at 387.

26. 246 N.Y. 369 (1927).

27. *Id.* at 373.

28. Cardozo's argument was that the pledge stated that the sum donated ($5,000) should be known as the "Mary Yates Johnston memorial fund," and specified certain uses for the money. This required the college to refrain from putting the money to other uses, which Cardozo held was good enough to be deemed consideration.

29. *Id.* at 375.

30. For a fuller, and very interesting discussion of Cardozo's most famous opinions, I refer the reader to Judge Posner's recent book on Cardozo (see note 22).

31. See chapter 5 for additional discussion of the rules governing the interpretation of pronouns and reflexives as these issues have made their way into judicial writing.

Notes to Chapter 2

1. See, e.g., K. Llewellyn, "Remarks on Theory of Appellate Decision and Rules or Canons About How Statutes Are to be Construed," 3 *Vanderbilt L. Rev.* 401 (1950); reprinted with further remarks in K. Llewellyn, *The Common Law Tradition: Deciding Appeals* (1960).

2. 75 Cal. Rptr. 739, 741 (2d Dist. 1969).

3. *Id.*

4. See, e.g., S. Crain and J. D. Fodor, "How Can Grammars Help Parsers?" in D. Dowty, L. Karttunen, and A. Zwicky, eds., *Natural Language Parsing* 94 (1985).

5. See, e.g., L. Frazier, *On Comprehending Sentences: Syntactic Parsing Strategies,* unpublished doctoral dissertation, University of Connecticut (1978); L. Frazier, "Syntactic Complexity," in *Natural Language Parsing,* note 4 above, p. 129.

6. L. Frazier, "Syntactic Complexity," note 5 above, p. 136.

7. J. R. Ross, *Constraints on Variables in Syntax,* unpublished doctoral dissertation, MIT (1967).

8. Frazier and Fodor suggest that the processor applies the coordinate structure constraint through the first two conjuncts, but that once a third is added the processor runs out of memory space and regards the last conjunct as the phrase currently being processed for purposes of applying strategies such as late closure. L. Frazier and J. D. Fodor, "The Sausage Machine: a New Two-Stage Parsing Model," 6 *Cognition* 291 (1978).

9. 50 Cal. App. 3d 920, 123 Cal. Rptr. 830 (2d Dist. 1975).

10. 50 Cal. App. 3d at 926, 123 Cal. Rptr. at 834.

11. Cal. Educ. Code §13404.

12. *People v. Corey,* 21 Cal. 3d 738, 147 Cal. Rptr. 639 (1978).

13. 149 Cal. App. 3d 994, 997, 197 Cal. Rptr. 194, 196 (5th Dist. 1983).

14. Cal. Health and Safety Code §§11379, 11055(d).

15. See K. Llewellyn, note 1 above. Llewellyn lists the last antecedent rule as number 23 among his canons. While he does not discuss the across the board rule, Llewellyn does consider the proviso in the last antecedent rule that it not apply when context requires a different interpretation as providing courts with the opportunity to arrive at any result. For some discussion of the canons and their role, see R. Posner, "Statutory Interpretation—in the Classroom and in the Courtroom," 50 *Univ. Chi. L. Rev.* 800 (1983).

16. G. Miller, "Pragmatics and the Maxims of Interpretation," 1990 *Wis. L. Rev.* 1179 (1990).

17. See P. Grice, *Studies in the Way of Words* (1989).

18. W. Lehman, "Rules in Law," 72 *Georgetown L. J.* 1571 (1984).

19. R. Posner, *The Problems of Jurisprudence* 280 (1990).

20. 490 F. 2d 846 (5th Cir. 1974).

21. *Id.* at 849.

22. *Id.* at 853.

23. See chapter 6 for an extensive discussion of this principle and its difficulties.

24. 515 F. 2d 295 (9th Cir. 1975).

25. *Id.* at 297.

26. 491 F. 2d 481, 484 (3d Cir. 1974).

27. I.R.C. §2038.

28. 491 F. 2d at 483.

29. *Id.* at 484.

30. 648 F. 2d 1286 (10th Cir. 1981).

31. *Id.* at 1289–90.

32. *Id.* at 1288.

33. *McKinney's Cons. Laws of N.Y.,* Statutes §365.

34. *Id.*

35. See, e.g., *Sutherland on Statutory Interpretation;* D. Mellinkoff, *The Language of the Law* (1969); M. Bryant, *English in the Law Courts* (1930).

36. *New York Gen. Bus. Law* §350-d(3).

37. 120 Misc. 2d 848, 467 N.Y.S. 2d 471 (1st Dept. 1983).

38. 467 N.Y.S. 2d at 474.

39. This is an oversimplification, sufficient for purposes of this exposition, but inaccurate in some crucial respects. See M. Siegel, "Compositionality, Case and The Scope of Auxiliaries," 10 *Linguistics and Philosophy* 53 (1987) for discussion of details of this phenomenon.

40. 217 Cal. Rptr. 685 (1985).

41. Cal. Penal Code §25(b).

42. 205 Cal. Rptr. 119 (3rd Dist. 1984).

43. De Morgan's Rules are routinely discussed in texts on propositional logic. See, e.g., R. Purtill, *Logic for Philosophers* 25 (1971).

44. Other scope problems exist as well. See Charles B. Nutting, "The Difficult Choice Between 'And' and 'Or,'" 46 *A.B.A. Journal* 310 (1960).

45. 21 U.S.C. §881.

46. 21 U.S.C. §881(a)(7).

47. 710 F. Supp. 46 (E.D.N.Y. 1989). My thanks to John Kornfeld for bringing this case to my attention.

48. *Id.* at 50.

49. 739 F. Supp. 111 (E.D.N.Y., 1990).

50. Cal. Educ. Code §13404.

51. 911 F. 2d 870 (2nd Cir. 1990).

52. *Id.* at 878.

53. *Id.*

54. *Id.* at 879.

55. 6 N.Y. 2d 536, 190 N.Y.S 2d 683 (1959).

56. Domestic Relations Court Act of the City of New York §56-a.

57. 70 Misc. 2d 178, 333 N.Y.S. 2d 208 (Dist. Ct. Suf. Cy. 1972).

58. N.Y. Penal Code §240.25(5).

59. 333 N.Y.S. at 209.

60. Note, incidentally, that the statute contains a last antecedent rule problem, in that it is not clear whether the words "which alarm or seriously annoy such other person and which serve no legitimate purpose" modifies both of the conjuncts or only the second. This issue is not discussed by the court.

61. 479 U.S. 538 (1987). My gratitude to John Orenstein for bringing this case to my attention.

62. *Id.* at 540.

63. 40 Cal. 3d 512, 537 (1985).

64. 479 U.S. at 543.

65. *Id.* at 542.

66. *Id.* at 549.

67. *Id.* at 560.

68. See the discussion of late closure above in connection with the application of the last antecedent rule.

69. See B. Nakell and K. Hardy, *The Arbitrariness of the Death Penalty* 243 (1987).

70. 442 U.S. 95 (1979).

71. Justice Rehnquist, who sided with the minority in the 5–4 decision reversing the conviction, did not write an opinion.

72. See, e.g., Chief Justice Rehnquist's speech to the American Law Institute, May 15, 1990, reprinted in part in *The New York Times,* May 16, 1990, page A1.

73. G. Calabresi, *A Common Law for the Age of Statutes* 6–7 (1982).

74. Llewellyn makes this point as well: "[A]gain and again, in order to avoid misinterpretation, I have had to insist that the range of techniques correctly available in dealing with statutes is roughly equivalent to the range correctly available in dealing with case law materials." K. Llewellyn, note 1 above, *The Common Law Tradition* 371.

Notes to Chapter 3

1. N. Chomsky, *Aspects of the Theory of Syntax* 21(1965).

2. The reader will recall that the last antecedent rule requires that a clause be interpreted as modifying the last possible antecedent rather than a more remote one, unless such a reading does not make sense.

3. See, e.g., W. Eskridge, "Public Values in Statutory Interpretation," 137 *U. Pa. L. Rev.* 1007, 1011 (1989).

4. For discussion of these, see Eskridge, note 3 above; C. Sunstein, *After the Rights Revolution* (1990).

5. See Sunstein, note 4 above. For some doubts, see W. Eskridge, note 3 above; and R. Posner, *The Problems of Jurisprudence* 292–93 (1990).

6. Sunstein, note 4 above, p. 183.

7. See *United States v. Bass,* 404 U.S. 336, 347–49 (1971), quoted in *Moskal v. United States,* 111 S. Ct. 461, 477 (Scalia, J. dissenting).

8. See *Dowling v. United States,* 105 S. Ct. 3127, 3131 (1985).

9. *Id.*

10. This issue has arisen in the context of interpreting the federal Racketeer Influenced and Corrupt Organizations Act (RICO), discussed later in this chapter and in chapter 4. See R. Blakey, "The RICO Civil Fraud Action in Context: Reflections on *Bennett v. Berg,*" 58 *Notre Dame L. Rev.* 237, 245–47 (1982) for discussion.

11. 18 U.S.C. §1001.

12. 468 U.S. 63 (1984).

13. *Id.* at 66.

14. *Id.* at 67.

15. *Id.* at 77–78.

16. This example is taken from W. LaFave and A. Scott, *Criminal Law* §27 (1972) (quoted in *Liparota v. United States,* discussed below).

17. See R. Jackendoff, *Semantic Interpretation in Generative Grammar* (1972).

18. See Chomsky, *Lectures on Government and Binding* (1981) for more detailed and technical discussion of these sorts of facts and their implications.

19. More recently, a United States Court of Appeals disagreed with the dissent's reading of the majority opinion in *Yermian.* In *United States v. Bakhtiari,* 913 F. 2d

1053 (2nd Cir. 1990), the court found that the majority in *Yermian* had approved the hybrid *mens rea* requirement, but had not insisted on it. Consequently, the *Bakhtiari* court affirmed a conviction based on a jury instruction that contained no element of *mens rea* with respect to the jurisdictional portion of the statute.

20. *Liparota v. United States,* 471 U.S. 419 (1985).

21. 7 U.S.C. §2024(b).

22. 471 U.S. at 422.

23. *Id.*

24. *Id.* at 424–25.

25. 468 U.S. at 78–79. More recently, Justice Scalia made the same argument, dissenting in *Moskal v. United States,* note 7 above, 111 S. Ct. at 477. That case involved the meaning of the expression "falsely made." Is a document containing false information falsely made, or does the expression refer to a forged or altered document? In the former interpretation, "falsely" applies to the result of the making, while in the latter it applies to the process itself. In *Moskal,* the defendant was prosecuted for transporting documents that were not counterfeit, but which did contain false information, under a statute that prohibits the transfer of certain falsely made documents. The majority held that the expression is clearly enough susceptible to the first meaning to render the rule of lenity inapplicable. Scalia's dissent pointed out that there is considerable likelihood that the statute in question (18 U.S.C. §2314) was intended to refer only to forged documents, and at best the expression is sufficiently unclear to trigger the rule of lenity.

26. *People v. Hardin,* 149 Cal. App. 3d 994, 997, 197 Cal. Rptr. 194, 196 (5th Dist. 1983).

27. 18 U.S.C. §§1961–1968.

28. Congressional Statement of Findings and Purpose.

29. See A. Milner, "A Civil RICO Bibliography," 21 *Case Western L. Rev..* 409 (1985).

30. 18 U.S.C. §1962(c).

31. 18 U.S.C. §1963.

32. 18 U.S.C. §1961.

33. 18 U.S.C. §1961(1).

34. 18 U.S.C. §1961(5).

35. 452 U.S. 576 (1981).

36. 18 U.S.C. §1961(4).

37. 452 U.S. at 587.

38. *Id.* at 580–81.

39. *United States v. Turkette,* 632 F. 2d 896, 898–900 (1st Cir. 1980).

40. Since *Turkette,* courts have been faced with many other issues concerning the meaning of "enterprise." For example, courts have held that the RICO enterprise must be something other than a defendant in the action. Thus a corporation engaged in mail fraud cannot be both the enterprise and the defendant.

41. 632 F. 2d at 899.

42. 464 U.S. 16 (1983).

43. 18 U.S.C. §1963(a).

44. The *Russello* opinion contains a statement of the status of this issue. 464 U.S. at 19–20.

45. See 18 U.S.C. §§1962(a), 1963(a)(2), 1964(a).

46. The rule that a statute should be interpreted to give meaning to all of its words is one of the canons of construction. See discussion in chapter 2 of G. Miller, "Pragmatics and the Maxims of Interpretation," 1990 *Wis. L. Rev.* 1179 (1990).

47. 464 U.S. at 29.

48. 18 U.S.C. §1962.

49. 452 U.S. at 587.

50. 464 U.S. at 27.

51. 473 U.S. 479 (1985).

52. *Id.* at 491.

53. *State Farm Mutual Automobile Insurance Co. v. Jacober,* 10 Cal. 3d 193, 110 Cal. Rptr. 1 (1973).

54. 110 Cal. Rptr. at 12.

55. *Id.* at 7.

56. *Id.* at 13.

57. See S. Kuno, *Functional Syntax* (1986).

58. 130 Cal. Rptr. 520 (1976).

59. 10 Cal. 3d 94, 98, 109 Cal. Rptr. 811, 813–14 (1973).

60. 109 Cal. Rptr. at 818.

61. *Id.* at 821.

62. 27 Cal. 2d 305, 163 P. 2d 689 (1945).

63. Courts recognize this relationship. See, for example, *Ponder v. Blue Cross of Southern California,* 145 Cal. App. 3d 709, 193 Cal. Rptr. 632 (2nd Dist. 1983).

64. 162 Cal. App. 3d 618, 208 Cal. Rptr. 676 (4th Dist. 1984).

65. 208 Cal. Rptr. at 679.

66. Cal. Civ. Code §3333.2(c).

67. 208 Cal. Rptr. at 681.

68. 4 Cal. 3d 11, 92 Cal. Rptr. 704 (1971).

69. 92 Cal. Rptr. at 711.

70. 597 F. 2d 146 (9th Cir. 1979).

71. Actually, a company called Antex was the named party in the letter of credit. Antex, the seller of the goods, assigned the letter (or the proceeds from the letter) to Arrays, a supplier.

72. As Judge Posner points out, cases involving the parol evidence rule generally focus on the issue of whether a party should be permitted to present to the jury facts relating to the making of a contract, or whether a judge may decide the issue. See *Agfa-Gevaert, A.G. v. A.B. Dick Co.,* 879 F. 2d 1518 (7th Cir. 1989) (Posner, J.).

73. 597 F. 2d at 149.

74. *Rainier Credit Co. v. Western Alliance Corp.,* 171 Cal. App. 3d 255, 217 Cal. Rptr. 291, 295 (1st Dist. 1985).

75. See Sunstein, note 4 above.

Notes to Chapter 4

1. E. H. Levi, *An Introduction to Legal Reasoning* 6 (1949).

2. Our knowledge of the English auxiliary system, described in part in chapter 1, provides another classic example of this type of knowledge.

3. See, e.g., C. Sunstein, *After the Rights Revolution* 113–14 (1990).

4. Compare, for example, R. Posner, *The Problems of Jurisprudence* (1990) (especially chapter 9), and S. Fish, *Doing What Comes Naturally* (1989).

5. *United States v. Yermian,* 468 U.S. 63 (1984); *Liparota v. United States,* 471 U.S. 419 (1985).

6. *California v. Brown,* 479 U.S. 538 (1987).

7. *Logical form* is a term of art in linguistic theory, defining a level of mental representation in which certain logical relationships become overt.

8. See R. May, *Logical Form* (1987) for discussion of many related linguistic phenomena.

9. L. Wittgenstein, *Philosophical Investigations* 31–32 (1953).

10. W. V. O. Quine, *Word and Object* 126 (1960).

11. See H. Putnam, *Meaning and the Moral Sciences* 71–72 (1978).

12. See, H. L. A. Hart, *The Concept of Law* 125–26 (1961); C. Sunstein, note 3 above, p. 118.

13. R. Jackendoff, *Semantics and Cognition* (1983).

14. *Id.* at 117.

15. *Id.* at 103. Jackendoff summarizes and argues with some of the linguistic and philosophical literature that takes a contrary position. For the most part, I will not engage in the debate here, and refer the reader to Jackendoff's book and the references that he cites. For additional discussion of categorization, see G. A. Miller, *The Science of Words* (1991).

16. The glass snake is such an animal. See A. Romer, *The Vertebrate Story* 163 (4th ed. 1959).

17. For discussion of various approaches to biological taxonomy, see E. Sober, *Reconstructing the Past: Parsimony, Evolution, and Inference* (1988). I am grateful to Victor Rush for bringing the examples and literature to my attention.

18. For discussion of the problems with relying on experts to provide us with complete word meanings, see Jackendoff's discussion of Hilary Putnam in *Semantics and Cognition,* pp. 117–19. I note that judges quoting from dictionaries, apparently in an effort to derive meaning from some source more authoritative than the judge's own knowledge of language, similarly fails to add clarity to the limits of the concepts in dispute.

19. Ronald Dworkin correctly takes this position. See R. Dworkin, *Law's Empire* (1986). I will return to Dworkin's perspective on statutory language later in this chapter.

20. It is on this problem that legal writers frequently focus in criticizing the plain language rule. See, e.g., R. Posner, *The Problems of Jurisprudence* 263–64 (1990). The seminal linguistic work on the subject of discourse is P. Grice, *Studies in the Way of Words* (1989). For an excellent discussion of issues in pragmatics, see D. Sperber

ing.

and D. Wilson, *Relevance* (1986). For an analysis of various canons of construction in terms of Grice's principles, see G. Miller, "Pragmatics and the Maxims of Interpretation," 1990 *Wis. L. Rev.* 1179 (1990) (discussed briefly above in chapter 2). For an application of discourse analysis to a particular legal case, see R. Shuy, "Evidence of Cooperation in Conversation: Topic-Type in a Solicitation to Murder Case," in R. Rieber and W. Stewart, eds., *The Language Scientist as Expert in the Legal Setting,* 606 Annals of the New York Academy of Sciences (1990). And for a general discussion of discourse analysis in legal theory, see P. Goodrich, *Legal Discourse: Studies in Linguistics, Rhetoric and Legal Analysis* (1987).

21. This issue does arise in legal cases. See, e.g., *Taylor v. United States,* 110 S. Ct. 2143 (1990), in which the Supreme Court had to decide which of many technical definitions of "burglary" should be used in construing a federal statute that calls for enhanced sentencing of defendants who had earlier been convicted of committing other crimes, including burglary.

22. 473 U.S. 479 (1985).

23. 18 U.S.C. §1964(c).

24. See 18 U.S.C. §§1961–62.

25. 473 U.S. at 506 (Marshall, J., dissenting), referring to ABA task force report. As an aside, civil RICO is one area of substantive law that lawyers regularly discuss among themselves as a serious problem in the legal community. Many lawyers representing plaintiffs are unhappy with the prospect of suing a defendant for RICO, thereby calling the defendant a "racketeer" and claiming damages of three times the loss plus attorney's fees. But these doubts conflict with ethical mandates that a lawyer represent his or her client vigorously within the bounds of the law. When the law allows such a windfall, angry litigants will often be reluctant to pass up a chance to grab it, and lawyers certainly cannot hide the existence of RICO remedies from their clients. Defendants sued under RICO, of course, are terrified, since the stakes are enormous.

26. Justice Powell's dissent, 473 U.S. at 527, does acknowledge some ambiguity, but does not analyze it as such.

27. 473 U.S. at 495.

28. *Id.*

29. E. Selkirk, "Some Remarks on Noun Phrase Structure," in P. Culicover, T. Wasow, and A. Akmajian, eds., *Formal Syntax* 285 (1977). I would like to thank Barbara Hall Partee for her ideas concerning this section.

30. I ignore the problem that *activity* is singular here, which tends to make the nondistributive reading the more likely one.

31. 473 U.S. at 509–10.

32. 109 S. Ct. 2893 (1989).

33. 18 U.S.C. §1961(5).

34. 109 S. Ct. at 2900.

35. *Id.* at 2901.

36. *Id.* at 2900.

37. *Id.* at 2902.

38. See Jackendoff, note 13 above, for discussion of the problems with lexical

decomposition. For a classic work on the issue, see J. A. Fodor, "Three Reasons for Not Deriving 'Kill' from 'Cause to Die,'" 1 *Linguistic Inquiry* 429 (1970).

39. 109 S. Ct. at 2909.

40. 452 U.S. 576 (1981).

41. 18 U.S.C. §1961(4).

42. 452 U.S. at 580.

43. *Russello v. United States,* 464 U.S. 16 (1983).

44. A. Murphy, "Old Maxims Never Die: The Plain Meaning Rule and Statutory Interpretation in the Modern Federal Courts," 75 *Columbia L. Rev.* 1299 (1975).

45. See, e.g., R. Posner, "Statutory Interpretation—in the Classroom and in the Courtroom," 50 *U. Chi. L. Rev.* 800, 817 (1983) (discussing also what role, if any, the canons of construction should play in judicial interpretation); F. Easterbrook, "Statutes' Domains," 50 *U. Chi. L. Rev.* 533 (1983).

46. The most noteworthy proponent of the plain language rule today is Justice Antonin Scalia, about whose views I comment later in this chapter.

47. O. W. Holmes, "The Theory of Legal Interpretation," 12 *Harv. L. Rev.* 417, 419 (1899).

48. See, e.g., G. Calabresi, *A Common Law for the Age of Statutes* (1982); R. Dworkin, *Law's Empire,* note 19 above; R. Posner, *The Problems of Jurisprudence* (1990); A. Aleinikoff, "Updating Statutory Interpretation," 87 *Mich. L. Rev.* 20 (1988); W. Eskridge, "Dynamic Statutory Interpretation," 135 *U. Pa. L. Rev.* 1479 (1987). I do not mean to suggest that these writers all agree with one another. Nonetheless, taken together, this body of work suggests an approach to statutory interpretation that is more fluid than either the plain language rule or the quest for legislative intent.

49. 426 U.S. 1 (1976).

50. 33 U.S.C. §1362(6).

51. 42 U.S.C. §2201(b).

52. 426 U.S. at 10.

53. 437 U.S. 153 (1978).

54. 16 U.S.C. §1533.

55. 437 U.S. at 172.

56. *Id.* at 173.

57. *Id.* at 184.

58. *Id.* at 189–91. The Court cites *Committee for Nuclear Responsibility v. Seaborg,* 463 F. 2d 783 (D.C. Cir. 1971). This is a "substantive canon" of the sort discussed in chapter 3. For discussion, see Sunstein, note 3 above, p. 169.

59. In fact, Jackendoff considers *actions* to be among a small set of primitive categories, such as *things* and *events,* not subject to further analysis.

60. Rehnquist also questioned the clarity of the language. However, his analysis did not depend on linguistic considerations.

61. R. Dworkin, note 19 above, pp. 338, 350–54.

62. *Id.,* p. 352.

63. *Id.,* p. 337.

64. See, e.g., *Watt v. Alaska,* 451 U.S. 259 (1981).

65. See, e.g., *Rubin v. United States,* 449 U.S. 424 (1981); *Burlington Northern Railroad Co. v. Oklahoma Tax Comm'n,* 481 U.S. 454 (1987).

66. See, e.g., W. Eskridge, "The New Textualism," 37 *U.C.L.A. L. Rev.* 621 (1990); N. Zeppos, "Justice Scalia's Textualism: The 'New' New Legal Process," 12 *Cardozo L. Rev.* 1597 (1991).

67. There are many such cases. See, e.g., *Taylor v. United States,* 110 S. Ct. 2143, 2160 (1990) (Scalia, J. concurring) ("I can discern no reason for devoting ten pages of today's opinion to legislative history except to show that we have given this case careful consideration. We must find some better way of demonstrating our conscientiousness.") *Id.* at 2161; *United States v. Stuart,* 109 S. Ct. 1183, 1193 (1989) (Scalia, J. concurring in the judgment); *United States v. Taylor,* 108 S. Ct. 2413, 2423 (1988) (Scalia, J. concurring in part).

68. See, e.g., *Pauley v. Bethenergy Mines, Inc.,* 111 S. Ct. 2524, 2539 (1991) (Scalia, J. dissenting), a case interpreting regulations concerning miners' rights to benefits under the Black Lung Benefits Act. Scalia, who was the lone dissenter, argued that the language of the regulations in question was plain, and that therefore the interpretation by government agencies should not be given deference by the Court, under the doctrine of *Chevron, U.S.A., Inc. v. NRDC,* 467 U.S. 837 (1984), which holds that an agency's interpretation of an ambiguous statute should be accepted by the courts. On this topic, see also, A. Scalia, "Judicial Deference to Administrative Interpretations of Law," 1989 *Duke L. J.* 511 (1989).

69. 111 S. Ct. 1138 (1991).

70. 42 U.S.C. §1988.

71. 111 S. Ct. at 1147. Elsewhere, Scalia has expressed concern about the ability of legislators to manipulate the legislative history to insure certain results in court down the road: "It should not be possible, or at least should not be easy, to be sure of obtaining a particular result in this Court without making that result apparent on the face of the bill which both Houses consider and vote upon, which the President approves, and which, if it becomes law, the people must obey." *United States v. Taylor,* note 67 above, 108 S. Ct. at 2424 (Scalia, J. concurring in part).

72. 111 S.Ct. at 1147–48. The argument that Justice Scalia rejected resembles Judge Posner's method of "imaginative reconstruction." "The judge should try to think his way as best he can into the minds of the enacting legislators and imagine how they would have wanted the statute applied to the case at bar." R. Posner, note 45 above, 50 *U. Chi. L. Rev.* at 817.

73. *Id.* at 1150–51. See *Missouri v. Jenkins,* 491 U.S. 274 (1989).

74. *Id.* at 1151, relying on *Friedrich v. Chicago,* 888 F. 2d 511, 514 (7th Cir. 1989) (Posner, J.).

75. 111 S. Ct. at 1153–55. Justice Stevens continues by quoting a similar philosophy from the writings of Learned Hand. For discussion of cases in which the Court attempted literal interpretation despite very good reason to look past the language of the statute, see R. Posner, "Legal Formalism, Legal Realism, and the Interpretation of Statutes and the Constitution," 37 *Case Western Res. L. Rev.* 179 (1986).

76. 111 S.Ct. at 1154.

77. See subsequent modifications to 16 U.S.C. §1536.

78. This point is discussed in the linguistic literature. See, e.g., E. Williams, "The NP Cycle," 13 *Linguistic Inquiry* 277, 283 (1982).

79. The statute's lack of clarity does not, however, resolve the case in favor of the dissenting position. Scalia's principal argument was the fit between his interpretation of the statute and the Court's similar interpretation of other statutes. My point relates specifically to the plain language rule and the propriety of using it to cut off inquiry into the legislative history.

80. See *United States v. Locke,* 105 S. Ct. 1785 (1985), in which the Court construed the term "prior to December 31" to bar an individual from asserting his rights on December 31, rejecting his argument that Congress probably meant "on or before December 31." This case is discussed by Posner, note 75 above. See also, Sunstein, note 3 above, pp. 116–21, for discussion of interpretive problems such as indeterminacy and vagueness, underinclusiveness and overinclusiveness.

81. The plain language rule does have a safety valve in the absurd result rule, which the Supreme Court noted in *Turkette.* Justice Scalia, in fact, has relied on this canon, which says that plain language should be ignored when it leads to absurd results. See *Green v. Bock Laundry Machine Co.,* 109 S. Ct. 1981, 1994 (1989) (Scalia, J. concurring in the judgment).

82. See note 48 above. See also the discussion in chapter 2 of the canons of construction as initial strategies for making sense of difficult communicative problems.

83. 426 U.S. at 10.

84. Eskridge, in particular, seems to set priorities as I envision them here, looking first to the text, and subsequently to both the history and evolution of the statute and its application. Eskridge, note 48 above, 135 *U. Pa. L. Rev.,* p. 1483. However, nothing that I have said is inconsistent with either Dworkin's or Posner's perspective on statutory interpretation.

Notes to Chapter 5

1. *Anderson v. State Farm Mutual Automobile Ins. Co.,* 75 Cal. Rptr. 739 (2d Dist. 1969). See chapters 2 and 3.

2. D. Mellinkoff, *The Language of the Law* (1963).

3. *Id.* at 293.

4. *Id.* at 293–95, quoting Morton, "Challenge Made to Beardsley's Plan for Plain and Simple Legal Syntax," 16 *J.S.B. Calif.* 103 (1941). In the text, Mellinkoff quotes Morton at much greater length.

5. *Id.* at 301–04.

6. W. Prosser, *Handbook of the Law of Torts* 151 (4th Ed. 1971). The "reasonable person" standard has been written about in many contexts in the literature, including a psycholinguistic perspective. See M. Johnson, "Language and Cognition in Products Liability," in J. Levi and A. Graffam Walker, eds., *Language in the Judicial Process* 291, 301–04 (1990).

7. Such theories are entertained, for example, in G. Gopen, "The State of Legal Writing: *Res Ipsa Loquitur,*" 86 *Mich. L. Rev.* 333 (1987). I will discuss this perspective later in this chapter.

8. For a thoughtful article on the subject of legal language, see R. W. Benson,

"The End of Legalese: The Game Is Over," 13 *N.Y.U. Rev. L. & Soc. Change* 519 (1985). We return to Benson's article below.

9. We return to this issue in chapter 6.

10. For recent case law on double jeopardy, see *Grady v. Corbin,* 110 S. Ct. 2084 (1990).

11. See *Baltimore City Dep't of Social Services v. Bouknight,* 110 S. Ct. 900 (1990). This case is discussed in a different context in chapter 6.

12. *Id.*

13. The relationship between the two is assumed in those cases in which the issue is mentioned at all. See chapter 6 for further discussion of this issue.

14. For a fairly nontechnical discussion of these and other issues, see N. Chomsky, *Language and Problems of Knowledge: The Managua Lectures* (1988), discussed in chapter 1. For a far more technical discussion, see N. Chomsky, *Lectures on Government and Binding* (1981), and much other recent work, some of which Chomsky refers to in the works cited here.

15. These, and similar issues in connection with our understanding of pronouns are discussed in my book *Pronominal Reference: Child Language and the Theory of Grammar* (1983).

16. In a different context, Chomsky has proposed an "avoid pronouns" principle of language processing. See N. Chomsky, note 14 above, *Lectures on Government and Binding.*

17. *Gray v. Handy,* 349 Mass. 438, 439, 208 N.E. 2d 829 (1965).

18. *Socony Mobil v. Cottle,* 336 Mass. 192, 194, 143 N.E. 2d 265 (1957).

19. *Cook v. Adams,* 89 So. 2d 6 (Fla. 1956).

20. *Stanfield v. Brewton,* 228 Ga. 92 (1971).

21. See G. Evans, "Pronouns," 11 *Linguistic Inquiry* 337 (1980).

22. *Gilligan, Will & Co. v. SEC,* 267 F. 2d 461, 467, (2d Cir. 1959).

23. *Blair v. Comm'r,* 300 U.S. 5, 12 (1937).

24. There exists a philosophical literature on naming and reference. See, e.g., S. Kripke, *Naming and Necessity* (1980); W. V. O. Quine, *Word and Object* (1960).

25. See Mellinkoff, note 2 above, p. 318.

26. *Id.* at 306 (footnotes omitted).

27. *Dodge v. Ford Motor Co.,* 204 Mich. 459 (1919).

28. *Faird-es-Sultaneh v. Comm'r,* 160 F. 2d 812, 813 (2d Cir. 1947).

29. *Commerce Union Bank v. Kinkade,* 540 S.W. 2d 861, 862 (Ky., 1976).

30. D. Runes, "Our Obsolete Legal English," 42 *Dickinson, L. Rev.,* 143, 144 (1938).

31. See "The Elusive Definition of a 'Security'—1990 Update," vol. 24, no. 2 *Review of Securities & Commodities Regulation* (Standard & Poors) (January 23, 1991) for a summary of recent cases on this matter.

32. There exists a large body of case law discussing what it means to act with scienter. For a plentiful crop, see cases deciding what an individual must do to violate section 10(b) of the federal Securities Exchange Act of 1934.

33. See Mellinkoff, note 2 above, pp. 346–62.

34. *Allegheny College v. National Chautauqua County Bank of Jamestown,* 246 N.Y. 369 (1927).

35. The introduction of technical legal vocabulary introduces a philosophical problem not related to the problem of precision. As pointed out by writers in the critical legal studies movement, the repeated use of technical words tends to reify concepts that have developed as a matter of historical struggle, thus increasing the resistance to change. The example of "consideration," presented in the text, is a case in point. The very existence of the word as part of the legal vocabulary of the law of contracts makes it more difficult to revamp thinking entirely with respect to which obligations our society should consider worth enforcing. See M. Kelman, *A Guide to Critical Legal Studies* 269–75 (1987).

36. Gopen, note 7 above, 86 *Mich. L. Rev.,* pp. 344–45.

37. Of course, lawyers can be both dishonest and greedy, and lawyers regularly behave differently when they believe that their clients are watching. For example, it is not uncommon to see a lawyer taking unreasonable positions at the deposition of his client, in order to look tough, while that same lawyer will generally adopt responsible positions when he is not being watched so carefully. Ironically, this posturing, so pleasing to the client, ordinarily serves to increase the cost of legal services, by introducing time-consuming distractions over which to argue, and in some instances, litigate. Lawyers know this, but many do it anyway.

38. Benson, note 8 above.

39. 13 *N.Y.U. Rev. L. & Soc. Change* at 540–45.

40. R. Charrow and V. Charrow, "Making Legal Language Understandable: A Psycholinguistic Study of Jury Instructions," 79 *Columbia L. Rev.* 1306 (1979). For a brief summary of several studies on the comprehensibility of jury instructions, see J. Levi, "The Study of Language in the Judicial Process," in J. Levi and A. Walker, eds., *Language in the Judicial Process* 3, 20–24 (1990).

41. Charrow and Charrow also performed more specific linguistic analysis. For example, rewriting nominalization constructions increased comprehension from 31 percent to 45 percent. The percentage of increase is large, but actual comprehension is still extremely low, given the enormous consequences of a juror's vote.

42. Other work on the comprehensibility of jury instructions has concluded that presenting the instructions to jurors in writing increases comprehension dramatically over verbal presentation. See A. Elwork, B. Sales and J. Alfini, *Making Jury Instructions Understandable* (1983). This work is discussed by Benson, pp. 546–47, and by Levi, note 40 above.

43. New York General Obligations Law §5–702(a).

44. See New York General Obligations Law §5–702(a), R. Givens, Practice Commentaries (McKinney's).

45. This example is presented in B. Goldstein, "Plain Language—Ten Years After: Some Reflections on its Basic Assumptions," *N. Y. St. Bar J.* (May 1989). Other examples, such as "quiet enjoyment," are discussed in B. Goldstein, "Code Words Contained in Leases," *N. Y. L. J.,* June 12, 1991, p. 35.

46. See the discussion of Ray Jackendoff's work in chapter 4.

Notes to Chapter 6

1. 18 U.S.C. §1961.

2. See M. Horwitz, "Santa Clara Revisited: The Development of Corporate The-

ory," 88 *W. Va. L. Rev.* 173 (1985); *The Transformation of American Law* (1977). Horwitz's work, in turn, has been evaluated in linguistic terms by Sanford Schane, in his article "The Corporation is a Person: The Language of a Legal Fiction," 61 *Tulane L. Rev.* 563 (1987).

3. 9 U.S. (5 Cranch) 61 (1809).

4. *Id.* at 88.

5. 43 U.S. 497 (2 How.) (1844).

6. 28 U.S.C. §1332(c).

7. For case references, see, e.g., *Paul v. Virginia,* 75 U.S. (8 Wall.) 168 (1868) (Article IV); *Pembina Consolidated Silver Mining Co. v. Pennsylvania,* 125 U.S. 181 (1888) (Fourteenth Amendment); *Santa Clara County v. Southern Pacific R.R. Co.,* 118 U.S. 394 (1886) (Fourteenth Amendment); *Southern Railway Co. v. Greene,* 216 U.S. 400 (1910) (Fourteenth Amendment). Horwitz argues from the historical development of corporate theory that the movement to the "person" conceptualization of the corporation corresponds to expansion of the corporation as a political and economic force in the United States.

8. For example, we saw in chapter 2 that courts apply the last antecedent rule differently in different cases without any theory of when it should be applied one way and when it should be applied another way. In chapter 3, we saw this problem again in the Supreme Court's interpretation of adverbs in *Yermian* and *Liporata,* cases involving the rule of lenity.

9. 201 U.S. 43 (1906).

10. *Id.* at 74.

11. *Id.* at 74–75.

12. *Id.* at 76.

13. See *United States v. Barth,* 745 F. 2d. 184 (2nd Cir. 1984), *cert. denied,* 470 U.S. 1004 (1984).

14. Quoting *Providence Bank v. Billings,* 29 U.S. (4 Pet.) 514, 562 (1830).

15. See Schane, note 2, above.

16. I am grateful to Mark Baltin for his contributions to this point.

17. There does exist one set of circumstances in which people are not even considered "persons" under the law. Aliens who have entered the United States illegally are at times subjected to indefinite periods of detention without due process. See "The Right to Recognition as a Person before the Law: The Case for Abolishing the Immigration Law Entry Doctrine," Association of the Bar of the City of New York, Committee on Civil Rights, 1991 *The Record* 304. This state of affairs is obviously at odds with the natural rights approach articulated in *Hale v. Henkel.*

18. 221 U.S. 361 (1911).

19. *United States v. White,* 322 U.S. 694 (1944).

20. 417 U.S. 85 (1974).

21. *Id.* at 103.

22. Earlier, I did not discuss Mr. Hale's refusal to testify here, since it was not relevant to the issues at hand. But he did indeed refuse to testify.

23. 116 U.S. 616, 630 (1886).

24. 417 U.S. at 87–88.

25. 425 U.S. 391 (1976).

26. 384 U.S. 757 (1966).

27. *Id.* at 761.

28. *Holt v. United States,* 218 U.S. 245 (1910).

29. *Gilbert v. California,* 388 U.S. 263 (1967).

30. *United States v. Wade,* 388 U.S. 218 (1967).

31. In 1988, the Court added to this list in *Doe v. United States,* 108 S.Ct. 2341 (1988). In *Doe* (which we will call *Doe₂*, since an earlier case with virtually the same name will be discussed below), the Court held that the Fifth Amendment does not protect an individual from being compelled to sign authorization forms requesting that a foreign bank produce records of accounts for which the defendant has signatory authority.

32. 425 U.S. at 409.

33. *Id.* at 410 n. 11.

34. *Id.* at 421 n. 6.

35. *Id.* at 418, citing L. Levi, *Origins of the Fifth Amendment* 390 (1968).

36. Relying on the original intent of the framers has its difficulties. Frequently enough it is clear that the drafters had no thoughts about the matter at all, since the facts of a particular case were not foreseeable. For discussion of problems with original intent, see, e.g., R. Dworkin, *Law's Empire* 359–69 (1986); P. Brest, "The Misconceived Quest for Original Understanding," 60 *B.U. L. Rev.* 204 (1980). For earlier observation of the difficulties, see, e.g., B. Cardozo, *The Nature of the Judicial Process* (1921) (discussed in chapter 1); E. H. Levi, *An Introduction to Legal Reasoning* (1949) (discussed in chapter 4). For discussion of why the framers' intent should be of interest to those attempting to interpret statutes and the Constitution, see R. Posner, *Law and Literature* 240–47 (1987).

37. 465 U.S. 605 (1984).

38. *Id.* at 618.

39. I should not exaggerate the hopelessness of Justice Marshall's dissenting position. It has been adopted by a United States District Court in *In Re Grand Jury Subpoena Duces Tecum Dated May 9, 1990,* 741 F. Supp. 1059 (S.D.N.Y. 1990).

40. 108 S.Ct. 2284 (1988).

41. The Court explicitly left open the Fifth Amendment ramifications of a case in which the corporation is so small that the only reasonable inference is that a particular individual produced the documents.

42. 108 S.Ct. at 2300.

43. The act of production doctrine was tested to its limits in 1990. In *Baltimore City Dept. of Social Services v. Bouknight,* 110 S.Ct. 900 (1990), a social services agency ordered that a mother produce her child, who had allegedly been abused. The mother refused, asserting her rights under the act of production doctrine, claiming that her ability or inability to produce the child might incriminate her. Put bluntly, if she was asked to turn her child over to authorities, but could not, the child's absence might be seen in a later homicide trial as evidence that she had killed him. The Court avoided the issue by holding that the social services agency was not part of the criminal justice system at all, and that, therefore, the Fifth Amendment, which applies in criminal cases, was not implicated.

44. J. L. Austin, *How to Do Things with Words* (2d ed. 1972).

45. S. Schane, "A Speech Act Analysis of Consideration in Contract Law," in P. Pupier and J. Woehrling, eds., *Langue et Droit—Language and Law* (Wilson and Lafleur Itee, 1989).

46. B. Danet, "Language in the Legal Process," 14 *L. & Soc. Rev.* 445, 457–61 (1980).

47. P. M. Tiersma, "The Language of Defamation," 66 *Tex. L. Rev.* 303 (1987). See also P. M. Tiersma, "The Language of Offer and Acceptance: Speech Acts and the Question of Intent," 74 *Cal. L. Rev.* 189 (1986); M. Hancher, "Speech Acts and the Law," in R. Shuy and A. Shnukal, eds., *Language Use and the Uses of Language* 245 (1980).

48. J. Searle, *Expression and Meaning* 6–7 (1979).

49. 465 U.S. at 613 n.11.

50. 108 S.Ct. at 2288. At this point, I should make my own admission. While "admit" fits the Fifth Amendment well, it may not be a perfect fit, and it may not be the only glove. One may ask why not consider other performatives, such as "concede," "confess," or "testify." Any of these are possible substitutes, but none of them is as close to the essence of the Fifth Amendment as is "admit," in my opinion. "Confess," for example, is too strong. One can be forced to be a witness against oneself by being forced to admit to some of the elements of a crime without having confessed to having committed the crime itself. "Testify," on the other hand, is too weak. One can be forced to testify without being forced to be a witness against oneself. In fact, when a subpoena is issued, that is exactly what happens, generally independent of any Fifth Amendment ramifications. "Concede" means more or less the same as "admit." In short, my choosing "admit" as the verb that comes closest to meaning "be a witness against oneself" is triggered by properties of "admit": It principally but not exclusively describes a verbal act, which is communicative and implies self-damage. It is not necessary that there be no other English word that incorporates these characteristics. It is only necessary that "admit" be useful as an analytical tool.

51. Austin, in his *How to Do Things with Words,* describes the "by" test as one for determining whether a speech act is *perlocutionary* in nature; that is, whether the act has affected others. I use the test somewhat differently here.

52. Note 26 above, 384 U.S. 757 (1966).

53. That is not to say that (15) could not in principle involve an attempt at communication. Assume that Frank did want someone to find out his blood alcohol level, which he knew to be too high, but could not speak, for example. Sentence (15) may be an appropriate way of communicating. Acting out a mime may be another.

54. 425 U.S. 391 (1976).

55. 465 U.S. 605 (1984).

56. See J. Searle, *Speech Acts* 23–24 (1973).

57. 388 U.S. 218 (1967).

58. See W. LaFave, *Search and Seizure: A Treatise on the Fourth Amendment* (2d ed. 1987) for an encyclopedic view.

59. C. Cunningham, "A Linguistic Analysis of the Meanings of 'Search' in the Fourth Amendment: A Search for Common Sense," 73 *Iowa L. Rev.* 541 (1988).

60. The notion "theme" as part of the semantic structure of sentences was first developed by Ray Jackendoff, *Semantic Interpretation in Generative Grammar*

(1972). The term was introduced by Jeffrey Gruber in his 1967 doctoral dissertation, reprinted in J. Gruber, *Lexical Structures in Syntax and Semantics* (1976).

61. This analysis and formalism follows from N. Chomsky, *Lectures on Government and Binding* (1981) and B. Levin and M. Rappaport, "The Formation of Adjectival Passives," 17 *Linguistic Inquiry* 623 (1986). However, certain details, not relevant to the discussion here, have been omitted.

62. See, e.g., R. Jackendoff, note 60 above; T. Roeper, "Implicit Arguments and the Head-Complement Relation," 18 *Linguistic Inquiry* 267 (1987).

63. The theme may also optionally be mediated by a preposition, as in "the police searched through the papers," or "they searched along the river."

64. It may well be that the concept "search" is innate, and English happens to have a word to describe it. See J. Fodor, *The Language of Thought* (1975).

65. 389 U.S. 347 (1967).

66. *Id.* at 360.

67. Cunningham, note 59 above, 73 *Iowa L. Rev.* at 607. Throughout his paper, Cunningham distinguishes between several senses of "search": "search of," "search for," and "search out." The first two correspond to the theme and goal arguments that I have described. "Search out," on the other hand, is what Cunningham argues is the appropriate sense of "search" for purposes of Fourth Amendment analysis. I disagree with Cunningham on this point for several reasons. First, "search out" is an odd expression in English, and neither the Constitution nor any of the cases ever uses it. This makes an analysis dependent on "search out" as the core meaning of "search" suspect. If "search out" is what is meant, why is it never used? Second, "search out" is perfective, that is, it implies successful completion of the search, which to me seems beside the point. Third, reliance on "search out" requires the same substantive restrictions on arguments as does reliance on "search of" and "search for" in combination. Thus, from a linguistic perspective, nothing is gained.

68. *California v. Ciraolo,* 476 U.S. 207 (1986) (Court held no search).

69. *United States v. Knotts,* 460 U.S. 276 (1983) (Court held no search).

70. *Smith v. Maryland,* 442 U.S. 735 (1979) (Court held no search).

71. *Dow Chemical Co. v. United States,* 476 U.S. 227 (1986) (Court held no search).

72. *United States v. Karo,* 468 U.S. 705 (1984) (Court held there to have been a search covered by the Fourth Amendment).

73. *Arizona v. Hicks,* 480 U.S. 321 (1987) (Court held that a search had occurred).

74. 445 U.S. 573, 585 (1980), citing *Boyd v. United States,* 116 U.S. 616, 630 (1886). As discussed earlier in this chapter, *Boyd* has been essentially overruled with respect to its holdings under the Fifth Amendment, but its recitation of the history of the Fourth Amendment is still accepted.

75. See note 36 above for some references on arguments based on the original intent of the framers.

76. B. Cardozo, *The Nature of the Judicial Process* (1921). See chapter 1 for extensive discussion.

77. *Cafeteria and Restaurant Workers Union Local 473 v. McElroy,* 367 U.S. 886, 895 (1961).

78. See *Ingraham v. Wright,* 430 U.S. 651 (1977).

79. See *Mathews v. Eldridge,* 424 U.S. 319 (1976).

80. L. Wittgenstein, *The Blue and Brown Books* 28 (1960).

81. *Id.* at 17. It is interesting to note an analogous statement by Holmes about the law: "General propositions do not decide concrete cases." *Lochner v. New York,* 198 U.S. 45, 76 (1905) (Holmes, J. dissenting). See also W. Lehman, "Rules in Law," 72 *Georgetown L. J.* 1571, 1576 (1984). See also the discussion of Jackendoff in chapter 4.

Notes to Chapter 7

1. *Anderson v. State Farm Mutual Automobile Insurance Co.,* 75 Cal.Rptr. 739, 741 (2d Dist. 1969).

2. In S. Fish, *Doing What Comes Naturally: Change, Rhetoric, and the Practice of Theory in Literary and Legal Studies* 372 (1989).

3. *Id.* at 388–89.

4. *Id.* at 389–90.

5. *Id.* at 391.

6. See, e.g., J. Frank, *Courts on Trial* (1949)(Atheneum edition 1971); F. Cohen, "Transcendental Nonsense and the Functional Approach," 35 *Columbia L. Rev.* 809 (1935). See also, K. Llewellyn, *The Common Law Tradition: Deciding Appeals* (1960), discussed in chapter 2.

7. See, e.g., M. Kelman, *A Guide to Critical Legal Studies* (1987); D. Kennedy, "Form and Substance in Private Law Adjudication," 89 *Harv. L. Rev.* 1685 (1976).

8. See, e.g., D. Shapiro, "In Defense of Judicial Candor," 100 *Harv. L. Rev.* 731 (1987); R. Leflar, "Honest Judicial Opinions," 74 *Northwestern L. Rev.* 721 (1979); G. Calabresi, *A Common Law for the Age of Statutes* 178–81 (1982).

9. Cardozo has been criticized for exaggerating the extent to which he actually relied on judicial precedent to make decisions. See J. Frank, note 6 above, p. 56. See also R. Posner, *Cardozo: A Study in Reputation* (1990), discussed in chapter 1.

10. This distinction—between easy cases and hard cases—is used regularly by legal philosophers writing in the positivist tradition. For discussion, see R. Dworkin, "Hard Cases," in R. Dworkin, *Taking Rights Seriously* 81 (1978). The issue that Dworkin raises is how judges decide hard cases. The issue that I raise is a different one: how judges attempt to mask the fact that a case is hard in the first place. The critical legal studies movement rejects the entire distinction, arguing that once certain hidden assumptions are revealed, all cases are hard. (See references in note 7 above.)

11. Of course, I do not mean to say that every judicial opinion in a complicated case is directed to the goal of hiding the real reasons for the decision. For one thing, judges may not be completely aware of all the factors that go into their decisions. Fish no doubt had this in mind when he used his baseball metaphor to draw so sharply the distinction between deciding and presenting. One can be a good decision maker without having a level of self-awareness that makes articulating the reasons for the decision possible, even if one wanted to articulate them with great

accuracy. Moreover, many opinions do appear to articulate the real reasons behind the decisions, a fact to which we return a bit later.

12. *Palsgraf v. Long Island R. Co.*, 248 N.Y. 339 (1928).

13. This point is also made by David Shapiro, note 8 above, 100 *Harv. L. Rev.* at 737.

14. See R. Unger, *The Critical Legal Studies Movement* (1986); M. Kelman, note 7 above. There is also a vast law review literature from within this movement, much of which is cited in Kelman's book.

15. 479 U.S. 538, 542 (1987).

16. 481 U.S. 279 (1987).

17. *Id.* at 286–87.

18. *Id.* at 314–17.

19. The Supreme Court has ruled that it is unconstitutional for a prosecutor intentionally to reject potential jurors based on race. See *Batson v. Kentucky*, 476 U.S. 79 (1986).

20. See, e.g., R. Unger, note 14, above.

21. See R. Posner, *Economic Analysis of Law* (3d ed. 1986). More and more courts are integrating this kind of analysis into their opinions. For a discussion of whether this is always the right thing to do, see *Saint Barnabas Medical Center v. County of Essex*, 111 N.J. 67, 85 (1988) (Pollock, J., concurring).

22. B. Cardozo, *The Nature of the Judicial Process* 149–50 (1921). For discussion that relates this aspect of Cardozo's judicial philosophy to Wittgenstein's thinking, see D. Stroup, "Law and Language: Cardozo's Jurisprudence and Wittgenstein's Philosophy," 18 *Valparaiso Univ. L. Rev.* 331 (1984).

23. R. Dworkin, *Taking Rights Seriously* 130 (1978).

24. A hybrid rule, calling for strict construction only when fundamental rights are guaranteed by the document may be closer to what some "strict constructionists" actually espouse. But this is no longer a general principle of interpretation.

25. An apparent exception to this statement is the set of substantive interpretive rules discussed in chapter 3. These are designed to carry out principles of justice through interpretations favoring one cause over another. The interpretive rules, however, do not themselves constitute a theory of interpretation. Rather, they form an ad hoc set of decisions about who should be favored under particular circumstances, and are frequently in conflict with one another. See C. Sunstein, *After the Rights Revolution* (1990), discussed in chapter 3.

26. 100 *Harv. L. Rev.* at 737.

Table of Cases

Agfa-Gevaert, A. G. v. A. B. Dick Co., 196n.72

Allegheny College v. National Chautauqua County Bank of Jamestown, 25, 132, 191n.28

Anderson v. State Farm Mutual Automobile Ins. Co., 29–35, 61–63, 66, 87, 118, 173–75, 177–79, 182–83

Arizona v. Hicks, 168, 207n.73

Baker v. Sadick, 88–89, 92

Baltimore City Dep't of Social Services v. Bouknight, 202n.11, 205n. 43

Bank of the United States v. Deveaux, 141–42

Batson v. Kentucky, 209n.19

Bellis v. United States, 147–49, 153

Beslity v. Manhattan Honda, 46–48

Blair v. Comm'r, 128, 202n.23

Board of Trade of San Francisco v. Swiss Credit Bank, 90–92

Board of Trustees of the Santa Maria Joint Union High School District v. Judge, 34–36, 61–63

Boyd v. United States, 149–52, 160, 207n.74

Braswell v. United States, 152–53, 158

Brooks v. Metropolitan Life Insurance Co., 87

Burlington Northern Railroad Co. v. Oklahoma Tax Comm'n, 200n.65

Cafeteria and Restaurant Workers Union Local 473 v. McElroy, 207n.77

California v. Brown, 49, 55–61, 95, 180

California v. Ciraolo, 168, 207n.68

California State Automobile Ass'n Inter-Insurance Bureau v. Warwick, 85

Chevron, U.S.A., Inc. v. NRDC, 200n.68

Commerce Union Bank v. Kinkade, 129, 202n.29

Committee for Nuclear Responsibility v. Seaborg, 199n.58

Cook v. Adams, 127, 202n.19

Department of Welfare of City of New York v. Siebel, 53–54

Dodge v. Ford Motor Co., 129, 202n.27

211

Doe v. United States (Doe₂), 205n.31

Dow Chemical Co. v. United States, 168, 207n.71

Dowling v. United States, 194n.8

Eddings v. Oklahoma, 60

Faird-es-Sultaneh v. Comm'r, 129, 202n.28

First National Bank of Denver v. United States, 44, 63

Fisher v. United States, 149–52, 160–61

Friedrich v. Chicago, 200n.74

Gilbert v. California, 150, 205n.29

Gilligan, Will & Co. v. SEC, 128, 202n.22

Grady v. Corbin, 202n.10

Gray v. Handy, 126, 202n.17

Green v. Bock Laundry Machine Co., 201n.81

Green v. Georgia, 60

Hale v. Henkel, 143–50, 153, 204n.17

H. J. Inc. v. Northwestern Bell Telephone Co., 104–06, 108

Holt v. United States, 150, 205n.28

Ingraham v. Wright, 170, 208n.78

In Re Grand Jury Subpoena Duces Tecum Dated May 9, 1990, 205n.39

Katz v. United States, 167–68

Liparota v. United States, 72–75, 95, 204n.8

Lochner v. New York, 208n.81

Louisville, Cincinnati & Charleston Railroad Co. v. Letson, 141–42

Mahoney v. Mahoney, 3–4

Mathews v. Eldridge, 170, 208n.79

Mathey v. United States, 42–44, 63

McCleskey v. Kemp, 180–82

McPherson v. Buick Motor Co., 24–25

Missouri v. Jenkins, 200n.73

Moskal v. United States, 194n.7, 195n.25

Palsgraf v. Long Island R. Co., 12, 23–25, 177–79, 191n.22

Paul v. Virginia, 204n.7

Pauley v. Bethenergy Mines, Inc., 200n.68

Payton v. New York, 169

Pembina Consolidated Silver Mining Co. v. Pennsylvania, 204n.7

People v. Caine, 54–55

People v. Corey, 36, 192n.12

People v. Hardin, 36–37, 61–63, 76

People v. Horn, 49

People v. Skinner, 40, 48–49, 63

Ponder v. Blue Cross of Southern California, 196n.63

Providence Bank v. Billings, 204n.14

Rainier Credit Co. v. Western Alliance Corp., 91–92

Rubin v. United States, 200n.65

Russello v. United States, 79–81, 107–08

Saint Barnabas Medical Center v. County of Essex, 209n.21

Santa Clara County v. Southern Pacific R.R. Co., 204n.7

Schmerber v. California, 149–51, 158–61

Sedima, S.P.R.L. v. Imrex Co., Inc., 81, 99–104, 108

Smith v. Maryland, 168, 207n.70

Socony Mobil v. Cottle, 126, 202n.18

Southern Railway Co. v. Greene, 204n.7

Stanfield v. Brewton, 127, 202n.20

State v. Cohen, 4–7,. 74

State Farm Mutual Automobile Insurance Co. v. Jacober, 81–85, 87

State Farm Mutual Automobile Insurance Co. v. Partridge, 85–87

Tahoe National Bank v. Phillips, 89–92

Taylor v. United States, 198n.21, 200n.67

Tennessee Valley Authority v. Hill, 109–13

Train v. Colorado Public Interest Research Group, Inc., 109, 112

United States v. Bakhtiari, 194–95n.19

United States v. Barth, 204n.13

United States v. Bass, 40–41, 48, 63

United States v. Certain Real Property and Premises Known as 171–02 Liberty Avenue, 50–53

United States v. Certain Real Property and Premises Known as 890 Noyac Road, 51–53

United States v. Doe (Doe₁), 151–52, 157, 160

United States v. Karo, 168, 207n.72

United States v. Knotts, 168, 207n.69

United States v. Locke, 201n.80

United States v. 141st Street Corp., 52–53

United States v. Sourapas, 41–42, 63

United States v. Stuart, 200n.67

United States v. Taylor, 200nn.67,71

United States v. Turkette, 78–79, 81, 106–08, 195n.40, 201n.81

United States v. Wade, 150, 161–62, 205n.30

United States v. White, 147, 204n.19

United States v. Yermian, 67–75, 95, 204n.8

Watt v. Alaska, 199n.64

West Virginia University Hospitals, Inc. v. Casey, 113–16

Wilson v. United States, 147

Index

absurd result rule, 51, 107, 201n.81
across the board rule. *See* last antecedent
  rule
adjectives, 56–61, 95
admissions, 155–63. *See also* Constitution
  (Fifth Amendment)
adverbs, 21, 67–75, 95
Aleinikoff, A., 199n.48
Alfini, J., 203n.42
and/or rule, 45–55, 62, 72, 74, 76
Andrews, Justice W., 23–24
Austin, J. L., 154, 205n.44, 206n.51
auxiliary verbs, 18–19

Baldus, D., 180–81
Benson, R., 134–35, 201–02n.8, 203n.42
Blackmun, Justice H., 61
Blakey, R., 194n.10
Brennan, Justice W., 57–61, 73, 104–05,
  149–51, 160
Brest, P., 205n.36
Burger, Chief Justice W., 74, 110, 113

Calabresi, G., 63, 190n.13, 194n.73,
  199n.48, 208n.8
canons of construction, 37–38, 65, 111,
  196n.46, 199n.45; substantive canons,
  65, 199n.58. *See also* last antecedent
  rule; and/or rule
capital punishment, 55–62, 180–82
Cardozo, B., 4, 8, 11–15, 17, 22–27, 63,
  72, 132, 142, 169, 172–74, 176–78,
  182–84, 186–87, 190nn.2,4,7,
  191nn.22,28, 205n.36, 207n.76,
  208n.9, 209n.22

categorization, 96–99
Charrow, R., 135, 203nn.40,41
Charrow, V., 135, 203nn.40,41
Chomsky, N., 8, 11, 15–22, 26, 118,
  186–87, 190nn.12,13,15,16,
  194nn.1,18, 202nn.14,16, 207n.61
clear language rule. *See* plain language rule
Cohen, F., 208n.6
consideration, 25, 132, 203n.35
Constitution: admissions test, 157–63;
  Eighth Amendment, 55–56, Fifth
  Amendment, 42, 205n.31; Fourth
  Amendment, 5, 12; meaning of person
  in, 41–42, 143–48; meaning of search
  in, 12, 20–21, 163–70; production of
  papers within protection of, 149–53,
  157, 162–63, 205n.43; pronouns and,
  122–25; speech act theory and, 154–
  63; status of corporations under, 144–
  48
contracts, resolving ambiguities in, 87–92,
  137
coordinate structure constraint, 33–34
corporations, 140–148; Fifth Amendment
  protection of, 143–48; Fourth Amendment protection of, 144–48
Crain, S., 191n.4
critical legal studies movement, 27, 176,
  179–80, 182, 189n.2, 190n.3, 203n.35,
  208n.10
Cunningham, C., 163–64, 166–69,
  206n.59, 207n.67

Danet, B., 155, 206n.46
death penalty. *See* capital punishment
De Morgan's Law. *See* De Morgan's Rules

De Morgan's Rules, 49, 51–52, 58, 193n.43
Douglas, Justice W. O., 148
Dowty, D., 191n.4
Dworkin, R., 15, 112–13, 116–17, 174, 184, 189n.3, 189–90n.13, 197n.19, 199nn.48,61, 201n.84, 205n.36, 208n.10, 209n.23

Easterbrook, Judge F., 199n.45
Elwork, A., 203n.42
empathy, 84–85
Eskridge, W., 117, 189–90n.13, 194nn.3–5, 199n.48, 200n.66, 201n.84
Evans, G., 202n.21

Fish, S., 174–77, 180, 189n.3, 197n.4, 208nn.2,11
Fodor, J. A., 207n.64
Fodor, J. D., 191n.4, 192n.8
forfeiture statute, 49–53
Frank, Judge J., 208nn.6,9
Frazier, L., 31, 192nn.5,6,8
fuzziness of concepts, 97–98, 105, 107, 112, 160

generative grammar, 13, 15–16, 20–22. See also knowledge of language
Goldstein, B., 203n.45
Goodrich, P., 198n.20
Gopen, G., 133–34, 201n.7
Grice, P., 38, 192n.17, 197n.20
Gruber, J., 207n.60

Hall, M. E., 190n.2
Hancher, M., 206n.47
Hand, Judge L., 200n.75
Hardy, K., 194n.69
Harlan, Justice J., 167–69
Hart, H. L. A., 96, 98, 197n.12
Holmes, Justice O. W., 109, 199n.47, 208n.81
Horwitz, M., 141, 203–4n.2, 204n.7

insanity defense, 40–41, 48–49
insurance policies, construing ambiguities of, 81–87

Jackendoff, R., 96–98, 194n.17, 197nn.13,15,18, 198n.30, 199n.59, 206n.60, 207nn.62,81

Johnson, M., 201n.6
judicial candor, 7, 14, 176–80, 182, 186–87
jury instructions, comprehensibility of, 135

Karttunen, L., 191n.4
Kelman, M., 203n.35, 208n.7, 209n.14
Kennedy, D., 208n.7
Kennedy, Justice A., 153
knowledge of language, 10–11, 15–22, 26, 64, 94–95, 121, 124, 139, 185–86
Kripke, S., 202n.24
Kuno, S., 84, 196n.57

Labov, W., 189n.11
LaFave, W., 194n.16, 206n.58
language acquisition, 16
last antecedent rule, 29–38, 55, 59, 61–64, 64–65, 74, 76, 173, 192n.15, 193nn.60,68, 194n.2, 204n.8; across the board rule, 34–37, 61, 192n.15; processing strategies, 31–34, 38
late closure strategy, 31–34, 59, 193n.68
law and economics movement, 27, 182, 209n.21
Leflar, R., 208n.8
legal canons. See canons of construction
legal doctrine, 176–82
legalese. See legal language
legal language, 118–38
legal realism, 176
legislative intent, 103, 108–10
legitimacy, 7, 14, 15, 27, 189n.13
Lehman, W., 38, 192n.18, 208n.81
lenity. See rule of lenity
Levi, E. H., 93, 197n.1, 205n.36
Levi, J., 189n.11, 201n.6, 203nn.40,42
Levi, L., 205n.35
Levin, B., 207n.61
lexical decomposition, 105
lexicon, 140, 164–66
linguistics. See generative grammar; knowledge of language
Llewellyn, K., 37, 189n.12, 191n.1, 192n.15, 194n.74, 208n.6
logical form, 95–96, 197n.7

Marshall, Chief Justice J., 141, 146
Marshall, Justice T., 60–61, 100, 109, 117, 152, 198n.25, 205n.39

May, R., 197n.8
may, scope of, 47–48
Mellinkoff, D., 119–21, 128, 132, 134, 201nn.2,4
mens rea, 67–68, 71–72, 195n.19
Miller, Geoffrey., 38, 192n.16, 196n.46, 198n.20
Miller, George., 197n.15
Milner, A., 195n.29
Murphy, A., 199n.44

Nakell, B., 194n.69
Newmeyer, F., 190n.12
Nutting, C., 193n.44

O'Connor, Justice S. D., 58, 60, 152
original intent, 151, 169, 205n.36

parol evidence rule, 89–92, 196n.72
party of the first part, 125–27
Pashman, Justice M., 3
Patterson, W., 190n.2
performatives, 154–56. *See also* speech acts
plain English laws, 119, 133–37
plain language laws. *See* plain English laws
plain language rule, 63, 93–117, 201n.81; RICO, 99–108
Pollock, Justice S., 1, 209n.21
Pollock, J.-Y., 191n.18
Posner, Judge R., 116–17, 191nn.22,30, 192nn.15,19, 194n.5, 196n.72, 197nn.4,20, 199nn.45,48, 200nn.72,74,75, 201nn.80,84, 205n.36, 208n.9, 209n.21
Pound, R., 14, 190n.8
Powell, Justice L., 69, 72, 111–12, 181–82, 198n.26
precision in legal language, 119–33
pronouns, 38–45, 55; ambiguity of reference, 19–20, 121–22, 125–30; Fifth Amendment, 122–25; in legal language, 121–30; number and gender agreement, 39–45, 62; replacing with names, 127–28. *See also* reflexive pronouns
Prosser, W., 120, 201n.6
Pupier, P., 189n.11, 206n.45
Purtill, R., 193n.43
Putnam, H., 96, 197nn.11,18

Quine, W. V. O., 96, 197n.10, 202n.24

Racketeer Influenced and Corrupt Organization Act. *See* RICO
Rappaport, M., 207n.61
Rawls, J., 191n.20
reflexive pronouns, 124–25, 127
Rehnquist, Chief Justice W., 70, 75–76, 112, 153, 194nn.71,72, 199n.60; and capital punishment, 56, 60–61
RICO: enterprise, 78–79, 106–07, 195n.40; injury, 100–04; interest, 79–80, 107–08; pattern, 104–06; rule of lenity and, 77–81, 106. *See also* plain language rule (RICO)
Rieber, R., 189n.11, 198n.20
Roeper, T., 207n.62
Romer, A., 197n.16
Ross, J., 33, 192n.7
rule of lenity, 66–81, 93, 186, 204n.8; and RICO, 77–81, 106
Runes, D., 202n.30

said, 128–29
Sales, B., 203n.42
same, 128–29
Scalia, Justice A., 106, 113–17, 195n.25, 199n.46, 200nn.67,68,71,72, 201nn.79,81
Schane, S., 141, 146, 155, 204nn.2,15, 206n.45
scienter, 131–32, 202n.32
Scott, A., 194n.16
Searle, J., 160, 206n.56
Selkirk, E., 102, 198n.29
Shapiro, D., 186–87, 208n.8
Shnukal, A., 206n.47
Shuy, R., 198n.20, 206n.47
Siegel, M., 193n.39
snail darter case, 109–13, 115–16
Sober, E., 197n.17
Solan, L., 191n.19, 202n.15
speech acts, 154–63; illocutionary force, 160; propositional content, 160–61
Sperber, D., 197n.20
Stevens, Justice J., 60–61, 113–15, 117, 200n.75
Stewart, Justice P., 79
Stewart, W., 189n.11, 198n.20
strict construction, 184, 209n.24
Stroup, D., 209n.22
Sullivan, Justice R., 83–84

Sunstein, C., 65–66, 92, 194nn.4–6,
    196n.75, 197nn.3,12, 199n.58,
    201n.80, 209n.25

technical vocabulary, 130–33
theme, 164–67, 206n.60
Tiersma, P., 155, 206n.47

Unger, R., 209nn.14,20

Walker, A., 189n.11, 201n.6, 203n.40

White, Justice B., 60, 74–75, 100, 150–
    51
Williams, E., 201n.78
Wilson, D., 198n.20
Wittgenstein, L., 96–97, 138, 170–71,
    197n.9, 208n.80
Woehrling, J., 189n.11, 206n.45

Zeppos, N., 200n.66
Zwicky, A., 191n.4